DAKOTA

DAKOTA

The Story of the Northern Plains

NORMAN K. RISJORD

UNIVERSITY OF NEBRASKA PRESS   LINCOLN & LONDON

Library of Congress Cataloging-in-Publication Data
Risjord, Norman K.
Dakota: the story of the northern plains /
Norman K. Risjord.
p. cm.
Includes bibliographical references and index.
ISBN 978-0-8032-6929-3 (paper: alk. paper)
1. North Dakota—History. 2. South Dakota—History.
I. Title.
F636.R57 2012
978.3—dc23   2012026937

Set in Swift EF.

For Connie
With thanks for the memories

CONTENTS

ILLUSTRATIONS

MAPS

PREFACE

Ventures into local history, together with some volunteer teaching, have been my hobby in retirement. After I published popular histories of Wisconsin, Minnesota, and Lake Superior, a move into the Dakotas seemed a logical step. Where Wisconsin and Minnesota were familiar territory, however, I had to start afresh in exploring the culture and landscape of the northern plains, but it was a very rewarding and enjoyable experience. My wife, Connie, and I traveled extensively through the Dakotas and were stunned by the grandeur of the Badlands, awed by the "Needles" of the Black Hills, and inspired by the mystic beauty of Spirit Lake. We walked the streets and visited the museums of such cultural gems as Yankton, Deadwood, Spearfish, Medora, Fort Totten, and Pembina.

Since this is a book of synthesis directed at a general audience, my research leaned heavily on the work of the many fine scholars in the universities and historical societies of the northern plains. My debt to some of these—though by no means all—is acknowledged in the Selected Reading section at the end of the book. I also owe a hearty thanks to Connie, my traveling companion, adroit editor, and fearless critic.

DAKOTA

CHAPTER ONE

A Sea of Wind-Blown Grass

Drawing his coat close around him and clutching his hat, the visitor asked the North Dakota ranch hand, "Does the wind blow this way here all the time?"

"No, Mister," answered the cowboy. "It'll maybe blow this way for a week or ten days, and then it'll take a change and blow like hell for a while."

Wind. It built the Great Plains. And then it scoured and shaped the land it had wrought. Wind and water. A hundred million years ago the granite-like craton that was to become North America was divided by an arm of the sea. The oceans had risen worldwide due to underwater mountain building. On the eastern (Illinois, Iowa, Kansas, Oklahoma) and western (Montana, Wyoming, Colorado) shores of this midcontinent sea were subtropical forests where dinosaurs roamed. The rotting detritus of these forests laid down beds of coal, oil, and natural gas. On the seabed that would become the plains, layer upon layer of sand and silt accumulated, brought by the westerly winds from a rising mountain chain on the western edge of the North American craton (the Sierra Nevada range today). Over millions of years the sea-bottom sand and mud would harden into sandstone and shale.

Beginning about 70 million years ago, a collision of tectonic plates on the western edge of North America started a new era of mountain building—the Rocky Mountain ranges of Idaho, Wyoming, and Colorado. Wind-driven sand, dust, and volcanic ash from this upheaval settled in the midcontinent seabed, covering the earlier sandstone and limestone. Tectonic shudders from this process created lesser ranges to the east—the Big Horn Mountains and the Black Hills. In the Black Hills the granite-like bedrock thrust up through beds of limestone, pushing the sedimentary rock aside and opening crevices. Over the millions of years since that time acidic groundwater seeped into the cracks and crevices, dissolved the limestone, and formed the gigantic caves that grace the Black Hills today.

Just as this era of mountain building came to an end, about 40 million years ago, worldwide sea levels began to fall, the plains emerged from the water, and North America approached the configuration (except for late-forming Florida and the Gulf Coast) that we know today.

Wind and water nevertheless continued their artwork. Heavy rains eroded the newborn Rockies, and rivers—the Missouri, Yellowstone, Grand, Cheyenne, and White in the Dakotas—carried new sediments onto the plains. The westerly winds added finer particles of dust and sand, but they also eroded what was already there. Wind erosion produced the drop-off that runs through the middle of the Dakotas, separating the eastern prairie plains from the high plains. In parts of the high plains the winds selectively eroded the fine silt and soft sandstone from earlier rock formations, whittling the spectacular multicolored pinnacles that make up the Badlands today.

1. "The Needles" in the Black Hills. Photo by author.

In the past 2 million years four, or perhaps five, glaciers descended from the Arctic to cover part of the Northern Hemisphere. The last of these—often called the Wisconsin Glacier because of its dramatic impact on the Badger State—crept onto the plains about twenty-five thousand years ago. While scientists are unsure of the cause of the Ice Age, they do know that glaciers fed on themselves. The ice reflected the sun's rays back into space, further cooling the earth and bringing on longer winters. As the snow and ice piled up, reaching more than a mile in thickness at their origin around Hudson Bay, the pressure melted the ice at the bottom, and the mass oozed southward. By the time it reached the present-day Great Lakes, the wall of ice was creeping forward at the rate of several hundred feet a year.

A western branch of the ice sheet (the Red River–Des Moines lobe) pushed into the Dakotas before coming to a halt some fourteen thousand years ago. Its terminal moraine closely tracks the Missouri River today. The Missouri, which originally followed the James River Valley through the Dakotas, carved a new bed for itself along the outer edge of the moraine. The earth, for reasons still unclear, began warming about that time, and the ice went into retreat. By twelve thousand years ago it had left the Dakotas, and within another thousand years the melting ice had created a gigantic freshwater lake in Canada (Lake Agassiz to geologists), the remnants of which today are the Lake of the Woods and Lake Winnipeg. An arm of Lake Agassiz occupied the valley of the Red River, and for several centuries it emptied southward along the Minnesota River to the Mississippi. After Lake Superior became free of ice, about five thousand years ago, Lake Agassiz began draining eastward, and a glacial moraine separated the northward-flowing Red River from the Minnesota River.

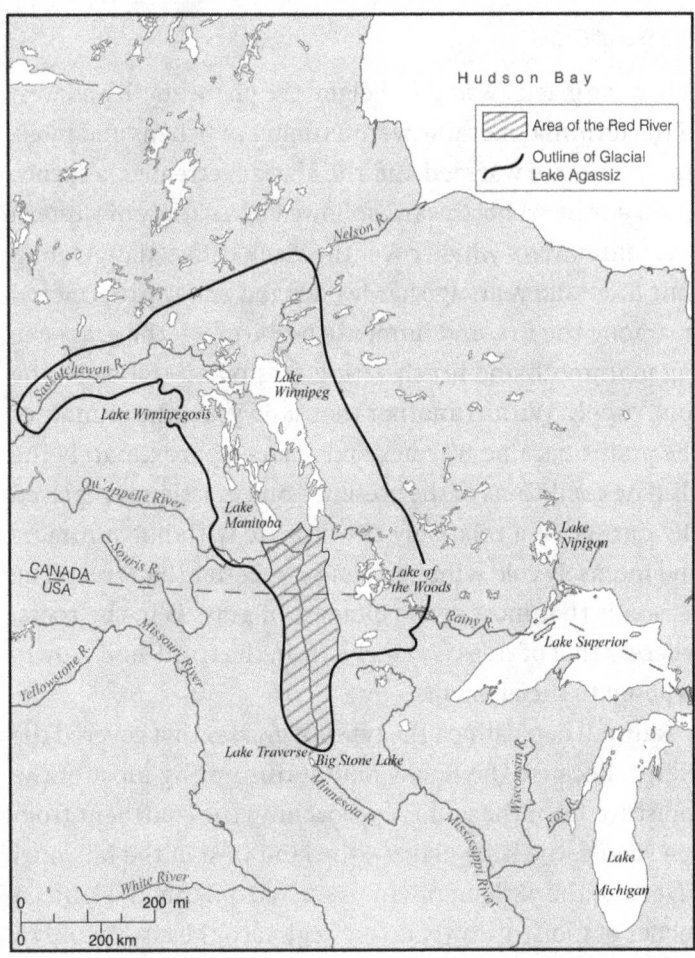

Map 1. Glacial Lake Agassiz.

The Sea of Grass

When the glacier was at its height, the plains south and west of the terminal moraine were a tundra of lichens and moss. As the climate warmed and the glacier retreated, a spruce forest advanced northward, followed by a variety of western firs, remnants of which cover the Black Hills today. Around nine thousand years ago hardwoods and grassy parks moved in among the firs, and immense herbivores—the grass-eating mammoth and brush-eating mastodon—followed the food supply. Within another thousand years the climate of the plains became warmer and drier—approximately the climate conditions of the present—and grasslands replaced the forests. In a relatively dry climate with hot summers and intensely cold winters grass fares better than trees. The reason is that most of the biomass of grass is in the roots, whereas that of trees is principally in the trunk and crown, exposed to the elements.

Rainfall determined the types of grasses that covered the plains. Because the Rocky Mountains wrung most of the moisture from the winds approaching the continent from the Pacific, the high plains—the land west of the Missouri River and the 98th meridian—received only about eighteen inches of moisture a year. This region could sustain only a few species of short grasses, commonly known as buffalo grass because it supported immense herds of buffalo when the first white explorers reached the plains. In the prairie plains, stretching south and east from the Red and Big Sioux Rivers to the Mississippi and beyond, annual rainfall averaged about thirty inches because of wet, cyclonic winds from the Gulf of Mexico. This region sustained a big bluestem, or tall-grass, prairie. The transition region between the two climatic zones—roughly the James River Valley in

2. The James River Valley, a mixture of grasses and trees.
Photo by author.

the Dakotas—contained a mixture of grasses, with groves
of cottonwood and elm near the streambeds. The prairie
plains also supported a wider variety of wildlife than the
high plains: white-tailed deer, elk, bear, and antelope in addition to the buffalo.

Also prowling the prairies and hardwood parks were various meat-eating animals—wolves, bears, and cats, large and
small. Some had originated in North America. Others had
migrated from Asia and Africa when the continents were
all joined together several hundred million years ago. The
short-faced bear, which evolved in North America, dwarfed
the modern grizzly and was the largest meat-eating animal
ever to have trod the earth. Equally fearsome was an American lion, twice the size and weight of the modern African
lion. The saber-toothed cat, which used its extended canines
to disembowel its prey, owed its ancestry to Africa or Asia

and was an American relic, its ancestors in the Old World having become extinct several thousand years earlier.

Many of these huge animals became extinct in North and South America within a few thousand years after the arrival of human hunters. Skilled hunters may have contributed to the die-off, but it seems unlikely that humans alone were responsible. On foot and armed only with stone-tipped spears, groups of them might have been able to overcome a large animal mired in a swamp, but large-scale kills seem improbable. And many of the species that disappeared from the earth—the short-faced bear, the saber-toothed cat, or the giant sloth—would have been either too dangerous to hunt or virtually inedible. Since the extinction was worldwide, human predation could not have been more than a minor factor. Another possibility was the dramatic climate change that made possible the movement of humans from Siberia to North America.

The First Humans

The earliest reliable evidence of humans in North America was first uncovered at a site near the village of Clovis, New Mexico, dated at about 12,000 BC. Their hunting instrument was a spear tipped with a point finely chiseled out of flint or chert. It was leaf-shaped, with a shallow groove or "flute" on each side, so that it could be firmly affixed to a wooden shaft. At Clovis, New Mexico, these points were found alongside the bones of mammoth, camel, and horse, all of which would later become extinct in North America (the camel ancestor survived in the form of the llama in South America, and the horse was reintroduced by Spanish ranchers in the Southwest).

The glaciers at their height had tied up so much of the world's water that sea levels dropped by as much as three hundred feet. The drop in sea level opened a thousand-mile-wide land bridge between Siberia and Alaska. Giant herbivores that were abundant in Asia—such as mammoths and mastodons—were probably the first to cross. The frozen tundra of Siberia discouraged Asian peoples from moving north of the 54th parallel until the climate began to warm about eighteen thousand years ago. Although Clovis spear points have been found in many kill sites (or hunting camps) in North America, no Clovis points have been found in Siberia. The Clovis spearhead seems to have been an early New World invention by the people whom archaeologists call Paleo-Indians.

One of the oldest kill sites in the plains, dated to about 9000 BC, is located in the Badlands of South Dakota. In addition to Clovis points archaeologists have found the partial skeleton of a butchered mammoth. Pollen and snail shells at the site indicate that the mammoth was killed in a swamp, either driven there by hunters or trapped while browsing on the lush vegetation.

Another type of spear point, called Plano, dated to about 8000 BC, has been found at various sites in western North America. Plano spearheads are long, leaf-shaped, and unfluted. The mammoth and mastodon had virtually disappeared by that time, and the modern bison, or buffalo, seems to have been the main target of hunters. Kill sites containing large numbers of buffalo bones indicate that Plano people hunted in groups and drove the animals over cliffs or into box canyons. A Plano site on the Missouri River, opposite the mouth of the Grand River, was apparently occupied off and on from 8000 BC until around the time of Christ. In addition to spear points, excavators found stone knives, scrapers, and perforators, indicating that the Paleo-Indians were using buffalo hides for clothing and perhaps housing.

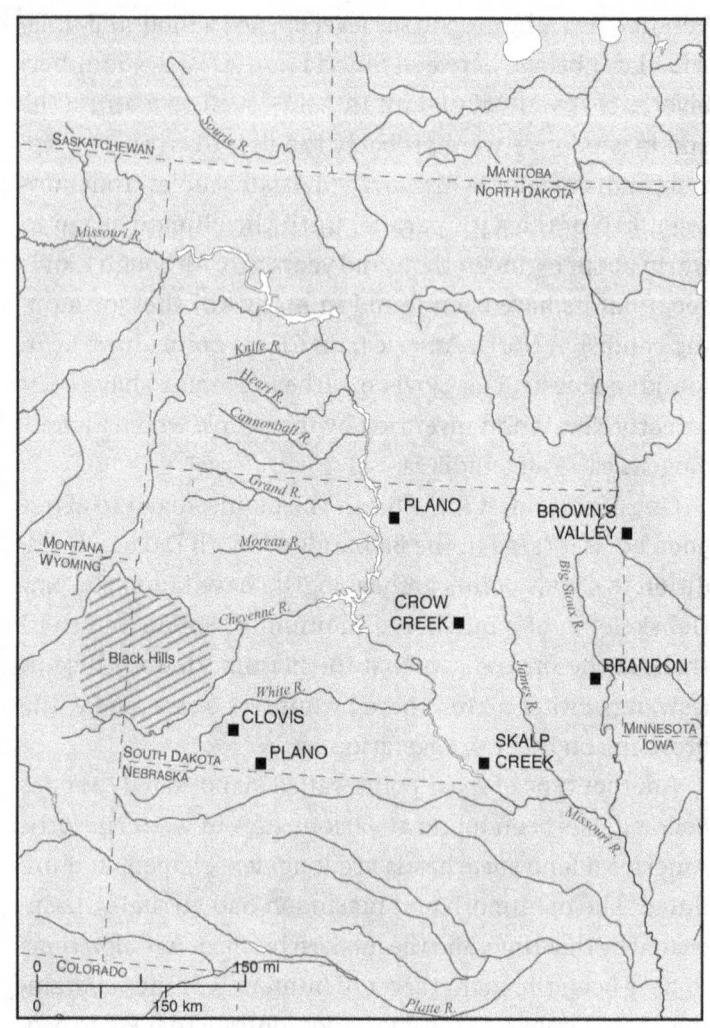

Map 2. Paleo-Indian sites, 9000 BC–AD 1500.

Like the later Plains Indians, the Plano folk wandered with the buffalo herds, and most of their sites have meager remains that suggest only temporary occupancy. A site near Hot Springs, on the edge of the South Dakota Badlands, dated to about 7000 BC, yielded grinding stones in addition to the usual slaughtering tools, suggesting that the Plano people may have found some sort of edible grass seed. We know nothing about the physical characteristics of the Plano people. The oldest human remains in the region, the skull of a young adult male and tentatively dated at 6500 BC, was uncovered at Browns Valley, Minnesota, near the headwaters of the Minnesota River.

By the time of the birth of Christ, the Paleo-Indians of the plains had greatly improved their hunting tactics and their weapons. Their prime quarry was still the buffalo and the antelope. However, instead of trying to stampede a herd over a cliff, they now preplanned the kill site and constructed a log corral at the foot of a drop-off or steep hill. The terrain was chosen so as to hide the corral from the animals until it was too late to escape the trap. Groups of hunters using brush as camouflage fanned out from the top of the hill, forming a large funnel that channeled the animals into the corral, where they were clubbed or speared. Hunters had also improved the range of a thrown spear with the addition of an atlatl, a rod attached to the end of the spear with a thong that gave added leverage (similar to the human elbow) to the throw. At some point during this period, perhaps earlier, the Paleo-Indians domesticated wolves or coyotes for use as pack animals. As late as the eighteenth century white fur traders observed that Indian dogs were semiwild and, instead of barking, howled like coyotes.

Another development during this time was the appearance of pottery. Earlier peoples had used animal skins for carrying water and cooking. They heated water by dumping fiery hot stones into the skins. Sometime around 800 BC, people learned to mix clay with grit (fine sand or ground-up clam shells) to make it workable. They then shaped it into a hollow cone using the heels of their hands or a wooden paddle and fired it in a charcoal oven. Because the earliest pots were cone-shaped at the bottom, they were probably placed in holes in the ground before being filled with water or berries. Decorations were quite primitive, usually markings about the mouth of the piece made with a stick or piece of bone.

The Woodland Tradition

From the time of Christ to about AD 1200, a succession of cultures, apparently borrowing pottery and housing styles from Eastern Woodland peoples, occupied the Missouri Valley of the Dakotas. From about 100 BC to AD 900 a rather sophisticated culture, known as Hopewell, thrived in the Ohio River Valley. The Hopewell people lived in semipermanent villages, grew corn and squash in cultivated fields, and obtained food from the rivers as often as from the forest. The Hopewells had trading relationships with people from the Great Lakes to the Gulf of Mexico, and they established important colonial settlements at Cahokia on the Mississippi River and at the big bend (present-day Kansas City) of the Missouri River. The Hopewell people developed a well-crafted and finely decorated pottery, and they buried their dead in ceremonial mounds.

The Woodland Culture of "Kansas City Hopewell" followed the Missouri River into the northern plains while Europe was undergoing the early Middle Ages, where bows and arrows had been in use for several centuries. In America the bow and arrow replaced the atlatl spear around AD 500.

Since this was far too late in time for communication across the Alaskan land bridge, they must have been independently invented in the Old and New Worlds. The people became more sedentary, with villages typically sited on the edge of rivers.

A site at Scalp Creek in the Missouri River floodplain (near the South Dakota–Nebraska border) was occupied off and on between AD 200 and 800. Although there is no evidence of corn-growing at the site, the people gathered wild plants and milled grass seeds. They hunted deer, elk, and rabbits, in addition to the buffalo, and they stored food in underground pits. Their pottery was globular, rather than conical, and decorated with rope impressions, similar to those of the Hopewell Culture. Near the village, archaeologists found a burial mound containing six skeletons in a flexed position, with knees drawn up to the chest, a position often used in burials in the Eastern Woodland tradition. Burial offerings—suggesting a belief in an afterlife—included knives, scrapers, bone perforators, and a stone hammer painted with red ochre.

From about AD 800 to 1250 North America and Europe experienced a relatively benign climate—warmer and wetter than it had been in the previous millennia. The people of the middle Missouri Valley began to grow corn, squash, and beans, and farm crops became as important in their diet as wild fruit and game. They settled in semipermanent villages along the beds of the Big Sioux, James, and Missouri Rivers. A better diet and less severe winters allowed a dramatic increase in population. More than thirty middle Missouri village sites, containing from twenty to ninety houses, have been uncovered in South Dakota alone.

An example of a middle Missouri village is the Brandon Site, which is situated on a flat-topped ridge some eighty-five feet above the Big Sioux River, just north of the modern city of Sioux Falls. The village contained about thirty rectangular houses, each about thirty-five by twenty feet in size—enough to accommodate an extended family. The houses were dug into the ground three or four feet, with the tramped bottom of the pit serving as floor. The superstructure of the lodge was a framework of heavy poles bound together by ropes made of roots or stringy bark. The walls consisted of small poles covered with either bark (where wood was plentiful) or buffalo hides. The bluff protected the village from attack on the river side, and a shallow ditch served as defense works on the exposed side. The casual nature of the defense works suggests the times were generally peaceful around AD 1000.

Lodges in most middle Missouri villages were arranged side by side in more or less regular rows. At intermittent locations in the village were sizable pits for storing corn and other vegetables during the winter. When emptied, the pits became middens for garbage and other refuse, such as bones and clam shells. Some of the villages had a central plaza, which may have been used for religious ceremonies. As we shall see in the next chapter, the development of shamanistic rituals, associated with the planting time or harvest, was one of the customs that helped define the emergence of modern Indian tribes in the plains.

In Europe in the late Middle Ages the relatively mild climate and flourishing agriculture provided the wealth and leisure time for the construction of the great Gothic cathedrals, and in the North Atlantic it allowed the Norsemen to colonize Greenland and even establish a momentary foothold on Newfoundland. But in the heartland of North America beneficent weather had its down side, at least for the Paleo-Indian population of the middle Missouri. To the south and east of their villages (i.e., in southern Wisconsin, Minnesota, and Iowa) lay the Oneota Culture, a Woodland people whose community structure and pottery were derived from the earlier Hopewell Culture. They produced abundant crops on fertile prairie lands, and their population exploded around AD 1100. We can trace their movements northward along the Missouri and Big Sioux rivers by their use of red pipestone quarried in southwestern Minnesota. An indication that the Oneota expansion was generally aggressive is the appearance (ca. AD 1200) of more elaborate defense works in the villages of the middle Missouri people: deeper ditches and log palisades. In addition, there is evidence of a retreat of middle Missouri people northward into present-day North Dakota.

Adding to the stress was another long-term climate change, beginning about AD 1250, of colder and drier conditions (lasting until about 1850; climatologists have titled it the "Little Ice Age"). In the North Atlantic the inclement weather forced the Norsemen to abandon their settlements in Greenland, and in the northern plains poor harvests led to malnutrition and conflict over scarce resources and arable land. A massacre at Crow Creek in the James River Valley some time around 1300 affords particularly gruesome evidence of conflict. When first occupied by a middle Missouri people, the village was unfortified. Aware of impending danger, they began building a fortification ditch 1,250 feet long. They were attacked, perhaps before the defensive fortification was completed, and more than five hundred people were killed. The assailants scalped the victims and mutilated them by cutting off hands, feet, and other body parts. At some later time the remains were gathered up, either by the victors or by survivors of the massacre, and dumped into one end of the fortification ditch, where they were covered with clay brought up from the creek bed. Archaeological excavation of the bones revealed much about the living conditions of the time. The skeletons showed evidence of nutritional deficiency, especially of protein and iron. They also revealed that conflict had been ongoing for some time. Some of the bones contained imbedded arrow points that had been grown over. Most of the lodges had been burned, which suggests a violent raid rather than aggressive colonization.

The fighting seems to have subsided by about 1500. Villages on the upper Missouri and Red River (present-day North Dakota) had only casual fortifications or none at all. There is also evidence of an annual trading mart about this time on the James River, where obsidian from the Rocky Mountains and ornamental shells from the Great Lakes were found. When the first Europeans arrived, they saw the trade mart being carried on by the Dakota Indians. By that time—the early eighteenth century—modern Indian tribes had evolved from a blend of the Oneota Culture and the Middle Missouri Tradition, with some accretion from the Eastern Woodlands.

CHAPTER TWO

Lords of the Northern Plains

When European explorers and traders ventured onto the northern plains in the eighteenth century, they encountered five Indian tribes who had been settled long enough to regard the region as their homeland. The oldest of the tribes, in terms of length of residence on the plains, were the Mandans and Hidatsas, who lived in well-established villages along the Missouri River. According to their oral traditions (i.e., collective memories handed down by tribal elders), supplemented by archaeological excavations of their villages, they had been on the river since about the thirteenth century. Of the Siouan language group, they were probably remnants of the Middle Missouri Tradition and the Oneota Culture of the upper Mississippi Valley.[1] A third tribe living in villages along the Missouri River, the Arikaras, who had broken off from the Pawnee tribe of the central plains and moved northward, had arrived a century or more later.

The arrival on the plains of a fourth tribe, the Cheyennes, cannot be dated with any precision. Members of the

Algonquian language group, they had originated in the north-eastern woodlands, but at the time the Europeans encountered them they were living a nomadic life in the valleys of the Red and James Rivers, following the buffalo herds. By the early eighteenth century they were drifting westward into the river valley (a tributary of the Missouri River in present-day South Dakota) that bears their name. Although their oral traditions place them on the plains from time immemorial (one scholar has them on the plains as early as the time of Christ), this cannot be confirmed by archaeology because of the scant remains in their short-lived campsites.

A fifth tribe, the Dakotas, were new arrivals in the early eighteenth century. Siouan-speaking, they were quite probably a branch of the Oneota Culture who had lived for several centuries in the woodlands of the upper Mississippi and St. Croix river valleys. Conflict with the European-armed and westward-advancing Ojibwas in the late seventeenth century had induced a branch of the Dakotas—the Teton Sioux—to seek the peace and safety of the Minnesota River Valley. From there they had drifted westward into the valleys of the Sioux and James Rivers, where Europeans first encountered them in the early eighteenth century. The continued westward movement of the Teton Sioux in the course of the century brought on almost continuous warfare with the feisty Arikaras.

On the northern edge of this Missouri River–Red River complex European explorers would encounter roving bands of Cree and Assiniboine hunters, whose home villages lay in present-day Canada. To the west were the buffalo-hunting Crows, whose homes were in the valleys of the Powder and Big Horn Rivers of present-day Wyoming. And to the south lay the numerous and powerful Pawnee and Kiowa tribes of present-day Nebraska and Kansas.

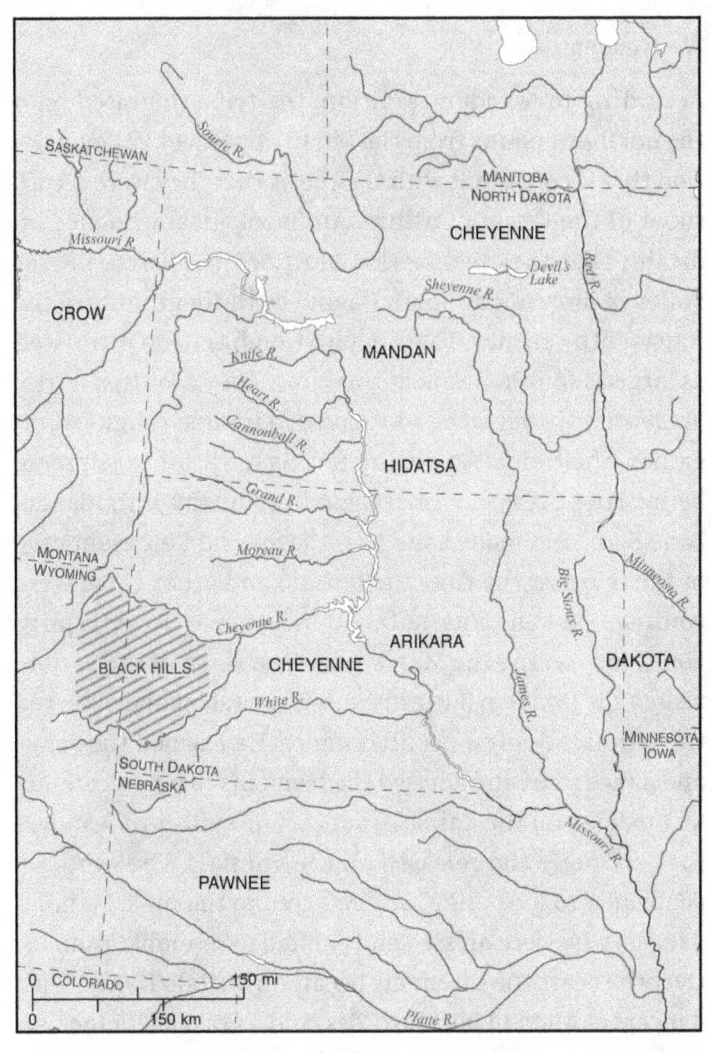

Map 3. Location of Indian tribes of the northern plains, ca. 1750.

The Mandans

According to Mandan tradition, the tribe migrated onto
the northern plains from the Mississippi River Valley, a notion that is consistent with the thesis that they were an off-
shoot of the Oneota Culture. Archaeological evidence in-
dicates that they had settled most of the Missouri River
Valley in present-day South Dakota by the beginning of the
fourteenth century. Their population has been estimated
as large as ten thousand at this time. They acquired a tribal identity through the adoption of a unique religious ceremony, the Okipa. According to this tradition, a supreme
being, First Creator, visited them in company with his son,
Lone Man, and made Lone Man the Special Representative
of the tribe. At the time the buffalo and other game were
confined on a mountain, Dog Den Butte, by an evil spirit.
Lone Man, seeing the Mandans on the verge of starvation,
visited the Dog Den Butte disguised as a rabbit and observed
the animals doing a peculiar dance. He learned the songs
and dance steps and advised the Mandans to hold a ceremony modeled on the animals' dance. The evil spirit watched
the ceremony and released all the animals. The word *okipa* meant "to look alike" and referred to the male Mandan
dancers who were dressed and painted to resemble animals.
Over the years the ceremony became a Buffalo Dance, with
dancers clothed in buffalo hides, and a Corn Medicine Ceremony celebrating the maturing of the first green corn in
midsummer. The Mandans performed the Okipa ceremony
annually until it was prohibited by federal Indian agents
when the tribe was herded onto a reservation in the late
nineteenth century.

The Mandans' acceptance of this theology by the fourteenth century is evident from the configuration of their

villages. In the center of each village was a plaza. Facing the plaza was a large rectangular lodge representing the Dog Den Butte. The lodge was built around six central posts that were buried in the ground. In front of the lodge was a circular fence of cottonwood logs representing the other great deed of Lone Man, who had erected a fence to save the Mandan villages from a great flood. Inside this structure was a red-painted cedar post that represented Lone Man and His charges, the Mandan people. The houses of each settlement huddled closely around the ceremonial lodge. They were laid out roughly in rows with walkways in between. The houses, about twenty by thirty feet in size, were built around upright posts, with slender poles serving as walls. We do not know whether the walls were finished with mud and moss or with buffalo hides. Most villages were surrounded by a shallow ditch and a log palisade for defense. By the end of the fifteenth century the Mandans had abandoned their villages in present-day South Dakota and had settled on a fifty-mile stretch of the Missouri River in present-day North Dakota. They were probably forced out by the bellicose Arikaras, who were advancing northward from the central plains.

The center of a new collection of more compact villages was at the junction of the Heart River with the Missouri. Although the Mandan population seems to have remained about the same, archaeologists have identified only ten village sites dating from the mid-1500s, all within twenty miles of the mouth of the Heart River. Houses in the new communities were circular rather than rectangular, a construction form probably borrowed from the Mandans' neighbors to the south, the Hidatsas and Arikaras. Each house was about forty feet in diameter, and in the center was a fire pit. Four large vertical posts formed a square around the fire pit and

3. A Mandan-Hidatsa house. Replica by the National Park Service. Photo by author.

bore most of the weight of the roof. The roof was formed by crossbeams between the posts and rafters extending from the inner square to the outer perimeter, like spokes on a wheel. The rafters sloped down to short vertical posts linked by crossbeams. Short leaners reached from the outer cross beams to the ground, creating the framework for a dome. Willow branches filled the space between the posts, and the whole structure was covered with several inches of packed earth and grass for insulation. Although each house had the outward appearance of an earthen mound, it was actually a wood structure composed of perhaps 150 trees of various sizes.

Although their housing design was probably borrowed from neighbors, the Mandans of the sixteenth century achieved a distinct artistic advance in their pottery, especially in vessels that were designed primarily to carry water.

A typical Mandan vessel of this sort was large and globular with elaborate decorations. The upper half of the vessel was S-shaped, curving gracefully inward at the neck, slightly outward above the neck, and inward again at the vessel mouth, making it easy to carry and pour. The curvature was decorated with patterns made by cord impressed into the clay.

Although each Mandan village on the upper Missouri was surrounded by a defensive fortification, suggesting a continued apprehension of danger, the living arrangements of the tribes, including their diet of buffalo meat, berries, beans, and corn, remained fairly stable from 1600 until the arrival of the first Europeans a little more than a century later.

The Hidatsas

Federal Indian agents in the nineteenth century conferred the comical French name Gros Ventres (Big Bellies) on the Hidatsas, and it is by that appellation they have gone into most history books. Explorers of the nineteenth century and the scientists who accompanied them inflicted, albeit unintentionally, a further indignity upon the Hidatsas by lumping them with the Mandans. They noted that the Hidatsas had housing similar to the Mandans and observed a Buffalo Dance similar to the Okipa ceremony, but they made little effort to determine whether these cultural features were borrowed or had some historical basis.

By Hidatsa oral tradition the tribe originated in the woodlands of the upper Mississippi Valley. Since the tribe, like the Mandans, was Siouan-speaking, it was probably a northern branch of the Oneota Culture. Archaeologists have identified village sites, dating from about 1500, on Devil's Lake, in the valley of the Sheyenne River, and on the banks of the Red River as proto-Hidatsa. The tribe may have moved out of the woodlands and onto the grasslands in search of game.

4. Interior of a Mandan-Hidatsa dwelling, showing construction and furnishings. Licensed under the Creative Commons Attribution-Share Alike 3.0 Unported (http://creativecommons.org/licenses/by-sa/3.0/deed.en) license.

Climatologists have noted that north-central America was just beginning to recover from a prolonged drought at that time. The tribe's oral tradition also remembered a time of periodic warfare, probably in the mid-seventeenth century. This probably referred to conflict with the Cheyennes, who had moved out of the eastern woodlands by 1600 and settled in the valley of the Red River and its lengthy tributary, the Sheyenne.

By the end of the seventeenth century this conflict had affected the Hidatsas in two ways. One group of Hidatsas—perhaps half of the tribe—pushed on farther west to hunt buffalo in the previously unoccupied Powder River and Big Horn Valleys (present-day Wyoming). When the first white explorers appeared in the area, this assortment of Siouan-speakers would be given the name Crow Indians. For much of the nineteenth century explorers and travelers would rank the Crow with the Mandans as the most sociable of all western Indian tribes. The remainder of the Hidatsa tribe settled on the Missouri River to the south of the Mandan villages, adopting the Mandan economy of mixed hunting and gardening.

The Cheyennes

The Cheyennes, whose oral tradition contained remembrances of a land of lakes and woods and a diet that featured maple sugar, probably originated in the northeastern woodlands. Linguistically they were members of the Algonquian language group. They may have drifted south and westward under pressure of the abnormally cold and dry climatic conditions of the fifteenth century. The oral traditions of both the Cheyennes and the Dakotas place them in the valley of the Minnesota River by about 1500. The tribe called itself the Tsistsistas, meaning "people" or "ourselves." The name "Cheyenne" is derived from a Siouan term, *sha hi ye na*, meaning "red talkers" or "people whose language is unintelligible." The fact that the Dakotas did not confer a pejorative name on the newcomers, as they did with their enemies, the Ojibwas, suggests fairly peaceful relations between the two. The oral traditions of both the Cheyennes and the Dakotas support this thesis; there is no recollection of warfare between the two tribes. The Cheyennes continued to drift westward, and by 1600 they were occupying the valley of the Sheyenne River, especially Devil's Lake, according to both oral tradition and archaeological evidence.

Like the Mandans, the Cheyennes achieved tribal self-identity through a religious ceremony, the Massaum. A form of animal worship, the Massaum probably originated in their woodland phase, for according to their oral tradition, the sacred animals initially were wolves and kit foxes. By the time they reached the plains the belief had become a form of buffalo worship. The ceremony was unique in the sense that it combined religious ritual with the hunt. The Cheyennes hunted buffalo in the same way that denizens of the plains had for a thousand years—by driving them into a funnel of logs and brush that led to a hidden corral, where the animals were slaughtered with spears or arrows. In the Cheyenne method the key figure was a medicine man versed in the Massaum mystique who had a routine that guided the animals rather than drove them. When the animals had been butchered for all edible parts, the Cheyennes' dogs were released to clean up the bones and the corral.

At that point—that is, the end of the summer hunt—the religious ceremony began. The bones were gathered into bundles and deposited in a shallow pit created by the removal of the heavy prairie sod. The cleaned bones of any human who had died in the course of the past year were placed among the buffalo remains, and the whole was sprinkled with red ochre, an earthen tincture sacred among many of the Eastern Woodland tribes.[2] After the sachems conducted a religious ceremony that freed the dead to join the spirit world, the pit was covered with a heavy layer of dirt and topped off with the original prairie sod. The spot thus became virtually invisible in the rolling grassland, and the lack of smell ensured that it would never be disturbed by scavengers.

The use of dogs as part of the ritual suggests their importance in Cheyenne life. All the Plains Indians had dogs, but their use among the Cheyennes is better documented than most. Their dogs were probably domesticated wolf pups, for as adults, they had the size and appearance of wolves, and according to travelers, they howled rather than barked. Each Indian family had at least a half dozen dogs, which it used as pack animals. They were equipped with either small pack-saddles or fitted with a travois. The dog travois, which had been in use on the plains for more than a thousand years, consisted of two slender poles that crossed at the dog's front shoulders and dragged behind. The load, whether firewood, tepee, or child, sat on crosspieces attached to the poles. Pack dogs gave the Cheyennes great mobility as they moved their villages to follow the movement of the buffalo herds.

In the last quarter of the seventeenth century most of the tribe moved southwest to the valleys of the Cheyenne and White Rivers (present-day South Dakota), which is where the first white explorers found them. Although Lewis and Clark in 1805 encountered a Cheyenne village at the junction of the White River with the Missouri, bands were by that date already roaming the Black Hills and the upper Platte River.

The Arikaras

The Arikaras—"Rees" to white fur traders—were the most feared tribe on the middle Missouri River. In the early nineteenth century their fierce resistance to traffic on the river forced fur traders to bypass the Missouri and follow the Platte River into the western mountains, thus opening a trading path that would become the pioneers' Oregon Trail. Despite their notoriety—or perhaps because of it—the Arikaras and their origin story were not recorded in detail by nineteenth-century investigators. By their own oral tradition, supported by linguistic evidence, they split off from the Caddoan-speaking Pawnees of the central plains and drifted northward. The Omaha Indians remembered encountering the Arikaras near the Missouri River in northeast Nebraska around 1500, a date that has been substantiated by

5. Buffalo on the high plains (Custer State Park today), a favorite prey of the Missouri Valley tribes. Photo by author.

archaeological excavations. The Omahas credited the Arikaras with teaching them to build earth lodges and cultivate corn.

Over the following century the Arikaras were either pushed or moved voluntarily northward up the Missouri River. This move coincided with the Mandans' abandonment of their villages in present-day South Dakota and their retreat northward to the Heart River region. The Arikaras occupied the Mandan sites and built new ones. Their houses were wood and earth domes of the sort later built by the Mandans and Hidatsas. The Arikaras obviously flourished in the new environment, for white traders who encountered them in the eighteenth century were told they had four thousand warriors, a figure that would have meant a total population of about twenty thousand. Their villages at this time extended along the river for about fifty miles from a point just below the mouth of the Cheyenne River to Crow Creek at the horseshoe bend of the Missouri (Lake Sharp today). The ruins of these fortress-cities can be seen today. A good example is a ruin about seven miles south of the city of Pierre on the east bank of the river. Situated on a high plateau and protected by steep ravines, it was made still stronger by a great earth wall with many bastions for archers. The village covered more than 130 acres, suggesting a population greater than any Hidatsa or Mandan village to the north. This chain of fortified Arikara villages thus constituted a human barrier to the westward moving Dakotas, and the clash between the two tribes brought decades of warfare to the middle Missouri Valley.

The Dakotas

The Dakotas (the name meant "friends") was a collection of clans—the Seven Council Fires—who lived, at the time white traders first encountered them, in the woodlands of the upper Mississippi and St. Croix Rivers. French traders called them "Sioux," which was an abridgement of the Ojibwa pejorative *nadouessioux,* or "poisonous snake." Dakota tradition claimed an origin in the Ohio Valley, but this is difficult to substantiate archaeologically. It is clear that they were long a part of the Oneota Culture, whose language has been labeled Siouan by entomologists. At the time they encountered the first French explorers in the mid-seventeenth century, the Dakotas had long been at war with the Crees, an Algonquian-speaking tribe that resided in the lake-dotted woodlands west of Lake Superior. The conflict probably involved beaver pelts, which were a favored item of Indian exchange even before the French arrived. In the last quarter of the seventeenth century, the Crees obtained firearms from British trading posts on Hudson Bay, and they were joined in the war against the Dakotas by their distant cousins, the Ojibwas, who had obtained firearms from the French at Sault Ste. Marie. The Dakotas, armed only with bows and arrows, suffered a series of deadly losses. Gradually over the next half century, they retired from the piney woodlands of the upper Mississippi and joined the southern Council Fires in the prairie grasslands of the Minnesota River Valley. The arrival of the newcomers, now identified as Yankton Sioux, tended to push the southern group, or Teton Sioux, farther westward. The Tetons moved northwest to the headwaters of the Minnesota River. A French trader who had a stockade in the region around 1700 labeled an advance village of the Tetons "a People Scattered into Many Bands." The Dakotas abbreviated the French phrase to "Oglala." That branch of the tribe would continue to lead the westward movement.

By the middle of the eighteenth century the Oglalas and another sub-branch of the Tetons, the Brules—a French name referring to burn scars on some of the tribal members (received, according to tradition, in a prairie fire)—were roaming the prairies as far west as the James River in search of game. They brought their pelts and buffalo hides to an annual trading fair at the headwaters of the Minnesota River. French traders who attended the fair came from trading posts as distant as the river's junction with the Mississippi at the Falls of St. Anthony. By that date also the Oglalas and Brules had begun a trade with the Arikaras, whose own hunters ranged as far west as the Black Hills. The relationship was at first friendly but soon turned deadly as a result of dramatic changes in the lives of the Plains Indians. The disruption was a by-product of Spanish settlement of the Gulf Coast and Mexico, a cultural intrusion that brought two new elements to life on the plains—the horse and a deadly small pox contagion.

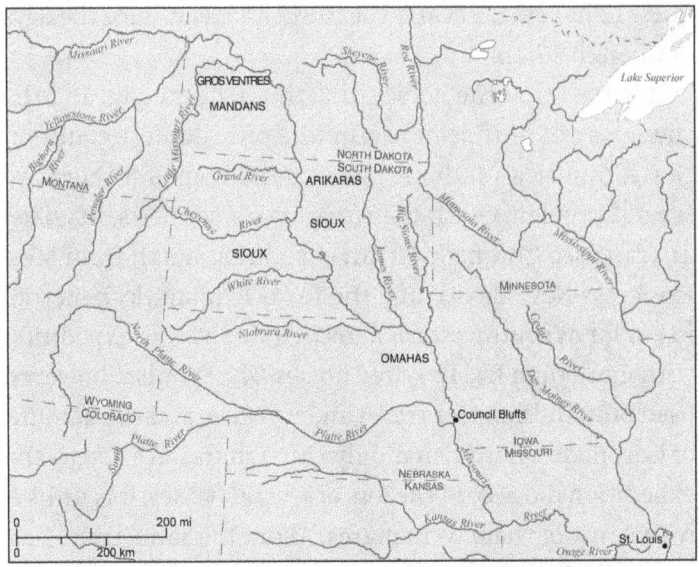

Map 4. Location of Indian tribes of the northern plains, ca. 1800.

The Indian and the Horse

One of the most durable myths of American culture is that the horse, so long associated with the Plains Indians, arrived in North America with the Spanish expeditions of Hernando De Soto and Francisco Coronado (1539–42). According to this story, horses that strayed from the Spanish expeditions multiplied in the plains environment and were captured and tamed by the Indians. In 1973 a network television show was built entirely on the story line of a lone Indian finding a stray Spanish horse lost on the plains. The Indian saw the horse, still equipped with saddle and bridle, its head drooping forlornly. The Indian approached the docile animal, climbed onto the saddle, and became the first of the mounted Indians, who in time became some of the finest light-armed cavalry the world had seen since the days of Ghengis Khan.

It is true that the horse—like the goat, the pig, and the cow—was of European origin (the only domestic animal North American Indians had was the dog). But there are several problems with the runaway horse thesis. In 1540–41 Francisco Coronado led an expedition north from Mexico across New Mexico and the Texas Panhandle, penetrating as far as southwestern Kansas. It was a large expedition with more than five hundred horses. The Spanish, however, used only stallions for travel and warfare, and the account of Coronado's herd listed only three mares. Although the expedition did record the loss of several horses, it is unlikely that any of them were mares. About the same time, Hernando De Soto, who had landed in Florida, led an expedition across the southeastern quarter of the continent and discovered the Mississippi River. At that point, in 1541, De Soto died of a fever on the west bank of the river. His men released several hundred pigs that they had shepherded across the continent (which became, according to legend, the Arkansas razorback hogs of today) and journeyed south to the Gulf and Spanish settlements in Mexico. They did attempt to take their horses, loading them on a raft roped to their own canoes, but they recorded that Indians cut the raft loose and slaughtered the horses. Even assuming that an animal of each sex escaped from the Spanish expeditions, there is a problem of distance. One historian has suggested that if God had placed Adam in Asia and Eve in Africa, they would have had a better chance of finding one another and mating than a mare in Arkansas and a stallion in New Mexico.

There is also a problem of timing. For more than a hundred years after the De Soto–Coronado expeditions no explorer, trader, or missionary reported seeing wild horses on the southern plains or a horse in the possession of an Indian. A final problem is that an Indian on foot had little or no chance of capturing and domesticating a wild horse, nor would he have known what to do with the animal once he had tamed it. Even when they eventually acquired horses, the Indians tended to regard them as pack animals. In almost every tribe the word for "horse" incorporated the word for "dog." The Hidatsas called them "red dogs"; the Cree term was "big dogs"; and the Dakotas honored them with "medicine dogs."

An explanation for the introduction of the horse that resolves all these issues is Spanish cattle ranching. By the end of the sixteenth century the Spanish had consolidated their hold on Mexico and had taken up ranching in addition to their quest for gold and silver. By the early seventeenth century their frontier—a mixture of cattle ranches and Catholic missions—extended to the valley of the Rio Grande. The Spanish founded Santa Fe in 1609 and took control of the Pueblo village of Taos seven years later. Missionaries sought to convert the Pueblo Indians; ranchers drafted young Indian men to work the cattle. In this way Indians learned about saddles and bridles and how to work a horse.

After a few years an Indian dissatisfied with his treatment might decide to flee, taking his equipment and perhaps an especially gentle horse or two. Unable to remain among his own people, he would ride across the Cimarron Desert to the Apache villages on the Arkansas River. The Apaches, who had become acquainted with horses through trade with the Taos Pueblos, would welcome the newcomer and his skills. Sometimes several cowhands would escape at once. Spanish records mention rather sizable breakouts in 1639 and again in 1642. In 1680 the Taos Pueblos, who had been virtually enslaved by both churchmen and ranchers, rose up in bloody rebellion and made off with several thousand horses. Not all were traded to the Apaches. For some years Spanish horses had been sent across Texas to the Comanches, who in turn had become accomplished horsemen and traders. Because a well-fed mare can have a colt every other year, a village might have a surplus to sell after fifteen or twenty years. As an example of the speed by which the horse culture spread, in 1682 Henri Tonti, companion of the French explorer Robert de La Salle (who reached the mouth of the Mississippi and claimed the entire valley for France), recorded the purchase of horses from the Natchez Indians. Because horses, according to Tonti, were "very common" in the tribe, the Frenchman was able to purchase four for the price of "seven hatchets and a string of large glass beads."

Perhaps not surprisingly the use of horses spread more rapidly in the high plains than in the Mississippi Valley. Buffalo hunting became a task for individuals rather than the cooperative effort of an entire village. A single rider on a reliable horse—most tribes initially preferred mares to stallions—could, by using care in the approach, be reasonably sure of culling and killing at least one buffalo in a grazing herd. It has been estimated that a single horse might double the daily amount of meat available for an entire village.

The value of the horse to the Indian was such that within sixty years all of the plains tribes owned them. The Wichitas, who lived along the Great Bend of the Arkansas River, secured their first horses about 1680; the Kansa tribe, who lived on the Kaw River, secured horses in 1724, a transaction recorded by a French trader; the Pawnees, who lived in the valley of the Platte River, obtained horses about the same time. The Arikaras, according to their own tradition, obtained horses from the Crow Indians around 1740. At that time the Dakotas did not have horses, and the Arikaras viewed their footsore, beggarly neighbors with some distain. Within a decade, however, the Oglalas and Brules were mounted, and their lightning raids on Arikara villages, often involving the theft of horses, became more and more troublesome. From midcentury onward the Missouri River tribes built corrals and log sheds to protect their equine stock from winter storms and year-round raids. Although the westward-advancing Dakotas were a rising threat, the Arikaras—so they informed Lewis and Clark in 1805—were able to hold them at bay until the sedentary Missouri River tribes were decimated by small pox and rendered almost helpless.

The Dread Small Pox

Like the horse, smallpox on the plains originated in the Spanish settlements. It began in San Antonio, where it was picked up by Comanches who visited the post to trade. It spread rapidly northward, reaching the villages on the Missouri River in the spring of 1781. The epidemic was particularly deadly among the close living quarters of the Missouri Indians. Native medicine aggravated the problem. Indians treated a fever with a steam bath (each village had a permanent sweat lodge) and a plunge into a nearby stream. This was exactly the wrong thing to do with a body weakened by small pox, and it usually brought a quick death to the stricken patient. The Mandans, Hidatsas, and Arikaras lost an estimated two-thirds of their population in the epidemic. Under pressure from the Dakotas, the Arikaras abandoned their fortified cities and gathered in huddled settlements next to the Mandans and Hidatsas.

Fatalities among the Dakotas, on the other hand, were less severe. The Brules and Oglalas were still living and hunting in small bands of kinsmen that ranged far across the plains. Relative isolation saved many of them, and their fatalities have been estimated at only a few thousand. When the epidemic receded in 1782, the Dakotas, with an estimated population of twenty-five thousand, made up perhaps one-third of all the Plains Indians. They and their horses would dominate life on the northern plains for the next century.

CHAPTER THREE

Explorers and Fur Traders, 1730–1800

The Virginians were just beginning to settle the Shenandoah Valley, and no Europeans had yet crossed the Appalachians to visit Kentucky or Tennessee when the first Frenchman, Pierre Gaultier de Varennes, the sieur de la Vérendrye, ventured onto the northern plains. Born in Three Rivers, a fur trade entrepot on the St. Lawrence River, Vérendrye had served in the French army—both in Canada and in France—during the conflict with England known in the American colonies as Queen Anne's War (1701–13). After the war he became a successful fur merchant, and the combination of military experience and fur trade connections brought him to the attention of the governor of New France. In 1727 the governor named Vérendrye commander of the French outpost on Lake Nipigon, a large body of water that drains into Lake Superior.

The fort on Lake Nipigon had once been a vital link in the fur trade because the lake and the rivers flowing into it were part of a canoe route connecting Lake Superior with Hudson Bay. Shipping furs through posts on Hudson Bay was faster and cheaper than sending them all the way to Montreal. The strategic value of Nipigon evaporated, however, when the Peace of Utrecht (1713) ended Queen Anne's War and gave Britain exclusive control of Hudson Bay. The French were left with only the Great Lakes and the St. Lawrence for their fur exports; for their supply of furs, they had to turn to the Indians who resided in the woodlands west of Lake Superior. A further complication was that west of the Laurentian Divide, which lay only a few miles inland from Lake Superior, the waters flowed west and north to Lake Winnipeg and from there, by way of the Nelson River, to Hudson Bay. This meant that in addition to winning the friendship of the Indians west of Lake Superior, the French had to persuade them to send their furs east to Montreal rather than north to the British.

Although it would seem that the twin goals of befriending the Indians and securing their custom in furs ought to have been a primary objective of French policy, neither the governor in Quebec nor the minister of marine in Paris was disposed to provide financial assistance to any western ventures that Vérendrye might undertake. (It was precisely this sort of myopia that contributed to the loss of the French empire in North America thirty years later.) Vérendrye, to be sure, expected to profit personally by the expansion of his fur business west of Nipigon, and in all of his explorations he obtained his own supplies on credit, expecting to repay his debts from fur trade proceeds. As so often happens with venture capital, short-term expenses obscured the promise of long-term gains, and difficulties with his creditors delayed his ventures and abbreviated his travels. The French government became impatient with him and never fully exploited militarily or diplomatically his immense contributions to European knowledge of the North American heartland.

As soon as he arrived at his post on Lake Nipigon, Vérendrye began to debrief the resident Cree Indians concerning their knowledge of the western waters. Incredibly he located a Cree chief who had actually traveled as far as a great freshwater "sea" (later named Lake Winnipeg) a great many days' journey to the west. The Indian spoke of a great arm of Lake Superior, Thunder Bay, just to the west of Nipigon, into which flowed the Kaministiquia River. Following this stream through a series of strenuous portages, a voyager could cross over the divide and onto westward-flowing waters that led into long, narrow Rainy Lake. From this body of water the Rainy River flowed northwest to another great lake with many bays and islands, the Lake of the Woods. From the north shore of this lake the Winnipeg River ran a course (145 miles) over rapids that caused the canoeist to make some thirty portages before dropping into the great inland sea, Lake Winnipeg. The Cree chief knew little of what lay beyond this body of water except that a stream entering from the south (the Red River) turned the waters of the lake "red like vermillion" (in Vérendrye's phrase), and at the northern end of the lake the Saskatchewan River entered from the west and the Nelson River flowed out to the northeast.

Armed with this intelligence, Vérendrye in 1729 moved to a fur trade post at the mouth of the Kaministiquia River. The governor, who was excited by Vérendrye's report on the gateway to the West but not enough to finance an expedition, agreed to his move and ordered a replacement at Nipigon. At his new post Vérendrye continued his interrogations and this time chanced upon a captive slave belonging to an aged Cree chief. The captive, probably a Mandan or Hidatsa who had been captured by the Assiniboines and sold to the Crees, came from a country far to the south of Lake Winnipeg. He told Vérendrye that his people lived on a great river in permanent villages of earth houses. They had fields of grain and hunted plentiful game with bows and arrows. Because there was little wood in that country, his people used buffalo dung for fuel and made boats of buffalo hides stretched over wooden frames (called "bullboats" in the later fur trade).

Because the captive made no mention of furs, Vérendrye could envision no benefit to himself from this tale, but he was intrigued by the mention of a "great river" (evidently the Missouri). Ever since Marquette and Joliet had discovered the Mississippi in 1673, the French had pictured the continent as drained by great river systems—the Great Lakes/St. Lawrence flowing to the east, the Mississippi to the south, and (it stood to reason) a "River of the West" that emptied into the "Western Sea."[1]

Anticipating that the governor would be equally excited and authorize an expedition into the Southwest (though he was not so sanguine as to expect financing), Vérendrye made further inquiries as to the best canoe route out of Lake Superior. He learned that the Indians preferred a departure from the mouth of the Pigeon River (the present boundary between the United States and Canada). Because the river made a precipitous drop through a series of waterfalls into Lake Superior, the route required an initial carry of ten miles (later known as the Grand Portage) to the height of land and westward-flowing waters. The route thereafter was much easier and shorter to Rainy Lake than the Kaministiquia pathway.

By early 1731 Vérendrye had concocted a plan to build a post on Lake Winnipeg, make a dash from there for the River of the West, and ride it down to the Western Sea. Both the governor and the minister of marine agreed to the plan, in part because Vérendrye claimed (in a monumental misinterpretation of the Indians' estimate of distances) that he could reach the Western Sea in only ten days from Fort Winnipeg. This disastrous misestimate would be a major source of the French government's later impatience with him. The governor authorized the expedition and even, with unaccustomed generosity, supplied him with presents to the value of 2,000 livres to smooth Indian relations.[2]

Vérendrye returned to Montreal to organize the expedition and found the city abuzz with excitement over the prospect of a chain of posts in the far Northwest and then a route to the Western Sea. Montreal fur merchants invested funds, and Vérendrye had no difficulty recruiting fifty voyageurs (French fur traders) to paddle his canoes and man his outposts. Vérendrye also enlisted his three oldest sons—Jean-Baptiste, Pierre, and François—each destined to become a pioneering explorer in his own right. They embarked on June 8, 1731, in four Montreal canoes, vessels specially built for travel on the Great Lakes—each thirty-five feet long, four feet abeam, and capable of carrying four tons of passengers and cargo. Consisting of a skeleton of pine and cedar and covered with strips of birch bark sewn together and made watertight with pitch, each was worked by eight men: six paddlers, a bowman, and a steersman in the stern. The route was one already familiar to fur traffickers—up the Ottawa River to its source, a portage to waters flowing into Georgian Bay (an arm of Lake Huron), a right turn from the straits between Huron and Michigan into the St. Mary's River, a portage around the falls, and a three-hundred-mile paddle along the shore of awesome and capricious Lake Superior.

The party reached the Grand Portage at the Pigeon River on August 26. At that point the voyageurs rebelled and refused to go farther. Employed by Montreal merchants to collect furs, they had no stomach for spending a winter in the wilderness living off the land like Indians.[3] Vérendrye managed to persuade a few of the mutineers to proceed on to Rainy Lake under the command of his twenty-three-year-old nephew Christophe de la Jemeraye. For inland travel this party would use smaller, twenty-foot canoes purchased from the Indians. Vérendrye and the remainder of the expedition retired to Kaministiquia for the winter.

In the spring Jemeraye built a fort at the point where Rainy Lake emptied into the Rainy River and named it after his uncle, Fort Pierre. In June Vérendrye sent one of his sons, Jean-Baptiste, to Michillimackinac (the fur trade entrepot in the straits between Lakes Huron and Michigan) for supplies while he, his other two sons, and about twenty grumpy voyageurs proceeded on to Rainy Lake. Before departing, the expedition was augmented by fifty canoes of Crees—entire villages with women, children, and dogs—apparently to welcome the prospect of fur trade posts in their midst. Vérendrye was delighted, for the Crees could act as guides to the Lake of the Woods and ambassadors to any local residents.

Arriving at the Lake of the Woods in midsummer, Vérendrye built a fort, intended to be his base of operations, on a peninsula on the west side of the lake.[4] Named Fort St. Charles in honor of the minister of marine (Charles, the comte de Maurepas), it was a log palisade laid out on a rectangle one hundred feet on each side and sixty on each end. Inside was a house and church for the missionary, a house for the commander, four bunkhouses for voyageurs, and a warehouse for furs.

The fort was completed by the end of the summer, and although Jean-Baptiste had not yet arrived with supplies, the garrison weathered the winter on an ample supply of venison and wild rice. At that point Vérendrye's luck, never very good, all but left him. Instead of continuing his explorations, he had to spend the spring and summer of 1733 trying to prevent an Indian war. The Crees and Assiniboines, emboldened apparently by their ties with the French, planned to attack the Dakotas, who lived on the prairies to the south. An Indian war would have been a disaster for Vérendrye's plans, for an expedition to locate the River of the West would have to cross vast grasslands where the Dakotas roamed. If they perceived the French as enemies, as they surely would in the event of war with the Crees, any exploring party would be doomed. Vérendrye's diplomacy was generally successful; although there were a few isolated incidents, he managed to prevent a serious clash.

Just as that crisis ebbed, a new one arose. Montreal merchants, dissatisfied with the paltry amount of furs he had sent east, denied him further credit or trade goods. Vérendrye dashed back to the French commercial capital in 1734; it would be four years before he could resume his explorations. His troubles stemmed from a combination of factors, not least of which were the tight-fistedness of Montreal merchants and the growing hostility of the governor in Quebec and the minister of marine in Paris. In addition, he suffered unexpected disaster in the West. In 1735 a party of voyageurs, on Vérendrye's orders, built a trading post and fort on a bit of high ground in the delta of the Red River, three miles from the point where the river entered Lake Winnipeg. Vérendrye named it Maurepas in hopeful honor of the minister of marine and placed Jemeraye in command. In the spring of 1736 Jemeraye was taken seriously ill, and Vérendrye's sons decided to carry him to Fort St. Charles on the Lake of the Woods, where he might receive better care. Instead of returning by way of the Winnipeg River, the party, at the suggestion of friendly Indians, blazed a new route. They ascended the Red River for about fifty miles and then turned east, paddling up a small stream, the Roseau River, which arose a short portage from the southwest shore of the Lake of the Woods. Because the shortcut saved several days of paddling and at least thirty portages, Vérendrye would use it thereafter in his westward explorations. In the short run, however, it did not benefit Jemeraye, who died on the journey. Compounding Vérendrye's sorrows, his eldest son, Jean-Baptiste, was killed in a Dakota ambush of a Montreal-bound fur convoy later that summer. The emotional distress, the financial loss, and the reluctance of voyageurs to enlist for a venture into the unknown delayed further exploration for another two years.

Vérendrye among the Mandans

Knowing it might prove to be his last chance, Vérendrye redoubled his efforts to put together an expedition in the spring of 1738. News from the West was ironically "good"—an Assiniboine design to attack the Dakotas with a force of eight hundred warriors had been canceled due to an outbreak of small pox. He was also able to contract—for the most part with a merchant-nephew—for almost 10,000 livres in trade goods. He enlisted reluctant voyageurs by telling them he planned nothing more than to occupy a trading post far out in Assiniboine country. At this point the post existed only in Vérendrye's imagination, but building it and using it as a jumping-off point for exploration was part of the grand plan.

Vérendrye departed Montreal on June 18, 1738, with about twenty men under contract (*engagés*) and his sons, Pierre, François, and Louis-Joseph. It was a leisurely trip, with stops to inspect each post along the way. He reached the farthest outpost, Fort Maurepas, on September 22 and found it garrisoned by fourteen men. From Maurepas he paddled up the Red River to the mouth of the Assiniboine and then turned west to follow that meandering stream onto the plains. About fifty miles up this shallow stream he encountered a party of Assiniboines who told him that he could not proceed farther on the river without damaging his canoes. Learning that the spot was also the beginning of a portage trail to Lake Manitoba by which the Assiniboines sent their furs to the English on Hudson Bay, Vérendrye decided to pause and build another fort (thereby also keeping a promise made to his *engagés*).

While the post was being constructed, Vérendrye was joined by a party led by Charles Nolan Lamarque, a Montreal fur merchant who shared Vérendrye's appetite for combining commerce with adventure. The two commanders selected from their combined force twenty men who seemed most able and willing to make a rugged overland journey. To this group they added about twenty-five Crees to act as guides, interpreters, and, if necessary, added military support. The expedition, including Vérendrye's sons François and Louis-Joseph, totaled fifty-two. In addition to powder, ball, and tobacco, Vérendrye issued to each Frenchman a pair of *souliers*, leather boots that he had apparently brought from Montreal. While paddling canoes, French traders had adopted the soft deerskin moccasins worn by the Indians of the Great Lakes because anything more sturdy was apt to punch a hole in a fragile birchbark canoe. In bringing a supply of boots, Vérendrye had clearly anticipated a long overland excursion.

The expedition departed Fort La Reine (Queen's Fort) on October 18 and began a trek southwestward across a never-ending sea of grass. Unfamiliar with the landscape, all but one of the Crees returned home. The frustration of the

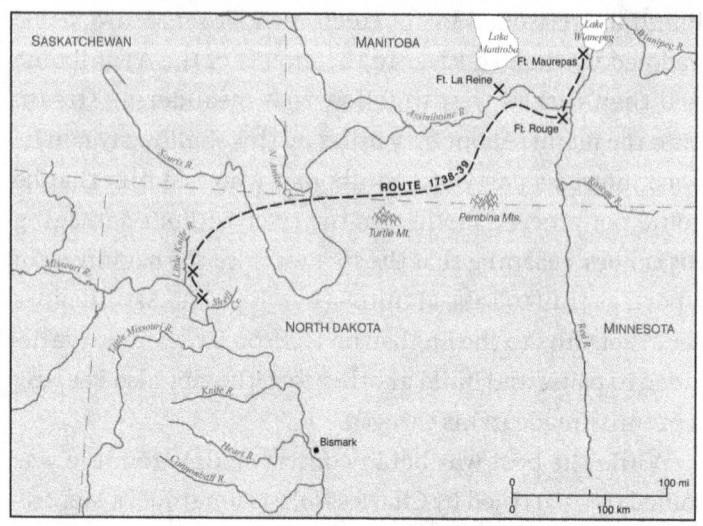

Map 5. Pierre de la Vérendrye's route to the Mandans, 1738–39.

Frenchmen mounted when they began to realize that their Cree guide had no sense of purpose or concern for the approach of winter. He strayed miles off a compass course in order to visit Assiniboine villages where the French were expected to spend a day listening to speeches of welcome and passing out presents. Vérendrye's goal was the Mandan villages on the River of the West, which he expected to use as a base for a dash to the sea before winter set in. With all the meandering, it took forty-six days to reach the first Mandan village (Vérendrye would make future trips in half the time), and the season was too far advanced for further exploration.

The Mandans Vérendrye encountered were a total surprise. For a decade, since interviewing a Mandan captive at Fort Kaministiquia, Vérendrye had been quarrying information on the Missouri River tribe. All informants had agreed that the tribe's villages were constructed on the riverbank.

In addition, the Assiniboines, who had extensive trade with the Mandans, claimed that the Missouri River tribe was much like the French themselves—of light skin, some with reddish hair, and given to farming. According to the Assiniboines, the Mandans grew such quantities of corn, beans, peas, and oats (wild rice?) that they used the vegetables in trade. Given this intelligence, Vérendrye expected a ceremonious reception from a proud and wealthy chieftain when he entered the first Mandan village. He accordingly placed his men in marching column, with his sons in the front carrying a flag painted with the arms of France and Vérendrye himself born on the shoulders of several Assiniboine men. Entering the village in late afternoon on December 3, 1738, with drums beating and flags flying, Vérendrye raised his hand, and from his column a salute of three volleys rang out across the prairie.

Although the Mandans greeted him with a welcoming delegation, the encounter was a disappointment. Far from being a great trade entrepot, the tiny village lay on a prairie mound miles from any river. "I admit I was surprised," Vérendrye wrote (probably in a letter to the governor), "having expected to see a people different from other Indians, especially in view of the account we had been given. They are not at all different from the Assiniboines; they go naked, covered only with a buffalo robe carelessly worn without a breachcloth. I knew by this time that we would have to discount everything we had been told about them." The village chief greeted them cordially through their Assiniboine interpreter and explained that his was but an outpost, that the main villages of the Mandans lay on the river several miles to the southwest.

On closer inspection Vérendrye's estimate of the Mandans brightened. His men counted 130 earthen houses surrounded by a wood palisade. Outside the palisade was a ditch fifteen feet deep and fifteen to eighteen feet wide. "All the streets," he wrote, "open places, and dwellings are similar, and some of our Frenchmen often lost their way among them. The streets and open places are kept very clean, and the ramparts are smooth and broad.... If all their forts are similar to this one, they may be called impregnable against Indians. Their fortification is not at all Indian-like." Vérendrye also found some basis for the rumors that the Mandans were a cross between Indians and Europeans:

> The women are fairly good-looking, especially the light-complexioned ones; many of them have blonde or fair hair. They are a very industrious people, both men and women. Their dwellings are large and spacious, and are divided into apartments by broad planks. Nothing is left lying about, all their belongings being kept in large bags hung from posts. Their beds are made like tombs, surrounded by hides. Everyone sleeps naked, both men and women. The men go completely naked all the time, except for a buffalo robe covering. A great part of the women go naked like the men, with the difference that they wear a small, loose loincloth, about a hand-breadth wide and a span long, sewed to a girdle in front.[5] All the women have this kind of covering even when they wear a skirt, so that they are never embarrassed or keep their legs closed when they sit down, as all other Indian women do. Some of them wear a kind of shirt of antelope hide, well softened.

Vérendrye was similarly impressed when the Mandan chief demonstrated some European-style guile. The headman quickly realized that the crowd of Assiniboines who accompanied the French would soon consume the Mandans' entire winter supply of corn. He accordingly started a rumor that Mandan hunters had seen a war party of Sioux in the vicinity, and he ordered preparations for an attack. "The Assiniboines," wrote Vérendrye, "fell into the trap and quickly made up their minds to decamp, not wishing to have to fight. A Mandan chief, by a sign, made me understand that the rumor about the Sioux was merely to make the Assiniboines leave."

Unfortunately Vérendrye's Cree interpreter fled with the Assiniboines, and he was reduced thereafter to making himself understood by signs and gestures. He did learn by this means that there were five more Mandan villages on the river a day's journey away, and each was twice the size of the current outpost. The Indians also told him that a day's journey beyond the last of the Mandan villages were the towns of two tribes (evidently Hidatsa and Arikara) with whom the Mandans were at war. Lacking an interpreter, the French were certain to receive a hostile reception there. The Mandans also told him that white men with horses and armor lived at a great distance down the river—the journey there and back took all summer—and with that piece of intelligence Vérendrye seems to have realized that the Missouri would not lead him to the Western Sea. The white men of whom the Mandans spoke were almost certainly French in fur-trading posts on the Mississippi or Spanish in settlements on the Gulf of Mexico.

Low on trade goods and gunpowder and lacking an interpreter, Vérendrye decided to return to Fort La Reine to spend the winter. Fully expecting to return and resume his explorations, he left two voyageurs with the Mandans with instructions to learn all the regional languages so he would not have to rely on Indian interpreters. His party departed on December 13, 1738, having spent a mere week with the Mandans, and reached La Reine on February 10, 1739.

Although he had added immensely to the body of geographical knowledge about the North American continent, Vérendrye's report to the governor that winter was remarkably restrained. Reluctant to confess failure in finding the River of the West, he barely mentioned the Missouri. Nor could he enlarge upon the prospects for the fur trade, for the beaver he had seen on the shallow western rivers were smaller and with pelts inferior to the beaver that could be found in abundance around Lake Superior. Ironically his diffidence discouraged the French government from exploring the upper Missouri, whose tributaries (in present-day Montana and Wyoming) were rich in beaver and other fur-bearing animals. The government of the dissolute Louis XV was too shortsighted to pursue such an imperial vision in any case.

Louis-Joseph de la Vérendrye Resumes the Quest

Ill luck continued to dog Vérendrye's pursuit of his dream of finding an all-water route to the Western Sea. Furs that he had collected to finance an expedition were seized by his creditors. A year-long visit to Montreal and Quebec (1740–41) to secure support from the governor yielded little but obscure instructions. The governor ordered him to return to the Missouri and resume his search for the River of the West, even though by this time Vérendrye thought the Saskatchewan River held more promise of a water-route across the plains. When he returned to the West in the summer of 1741 prepared to lead another expedition to the Mandan villages, he found himself in the middle of another confrontation between the Cree-Assiniboine alliance and the Dakotas. Realizing that only he had the stature to maintain peace among the Indians, Vérendrye decided to remain at Fort La Reine and instead sent two of his sons to find the

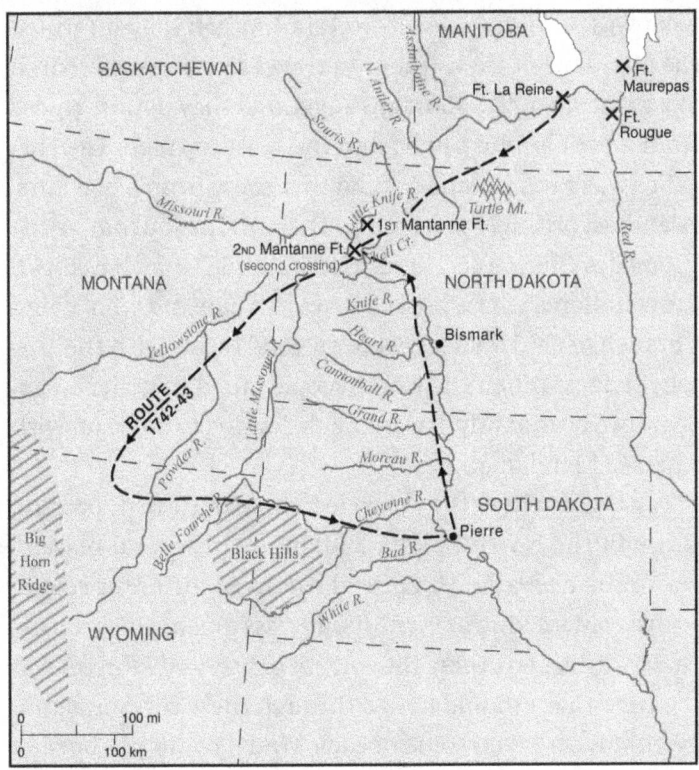

Map 6. Louis-Joseph de la Vérendrye's route to the West, 1742–43.

River of the West. The elder, Louis-Joseph, now endowed
with the title chevalier de la Vérendrye, was placed in command of the small party, consisting of his brother François
and two *engagés*. These four men would be absent for more
than a year, and they would push farther into the western
plains than any other French explorers. The only record we
have of the expedition is a letter, in the form of a "journal,"
sent by the chevalier to the governor of Canada, the mar-
quis de Beauharnois.

The party left Fort La Reine on April 29, 1742, and arrived
at the Mandan villages on May 19, the quickest trip yet on

what was becoming a well-trod trail. When they informed the Mandans of their intent to travel southwest in search of a great river, the Mandans suggested they obtain guides from a people who came from the West to trade. The chevalier was given to understand that these people had horses and accordingly referred to them in his journal as the "Gens des Chevaux." These "Horse People" may have been Crow Indians, whose language was Siouan and who, being a branch of the Hidatsas, were on good terms with the Missouri tribes. When the Horse People failed to make an appearance by mid-July, Louis-Joseph decided to move on with a pair of Mandan guides.

For twenty days they traveled west-southwest, passing through the North Dakota Badlands. "In several places," wrote the chevalier, "I noticed earths of different colors, such as blue, a kind of vermillion, grass green, glossy black, chalk white, and others the color of ochre. Had I foreseen at the time that I should not go through these regions again, I would have taken some of each kind. I could not burden myself, knowing that I had a very long way to travel." On August 11 they reached "the mountain of the Gens des Chevaux" (probably White Butte in southwestern North Dakota, the highest point in the state) and lit signal fires on it to attract any Indians in the vicinity. After a month of waiting they saw smoke signals to the southwest, and upon investigating, they came upon a village of what the chevalier called the "Beaux Hommes" (Handsome People). These were, in all likelihood, Cheyennes, for the French party's Mandan guide did not understand their language and expressed fear of them. The chevalier paid him off and let him return to his village. Although the Vérendrye brothers were familiar with the Algonquian Cree tongue, the dialect of the Handsome People was sufficiently strange that twenty days passed

6. The North Dakota Badlands, created by erosion of the Little Missouri River (in center of picture). National Park Service.

before they understood it well enough to make their wishes known. What they wanted was a new set of guides/interpreters for their southwestern trek.

The Beaux Hommes agreeably supplied them with guides, and the party resumed its journey. On the second day they passed through a village of "Petits Renards" (Little Foxes, a military clan of the Cheyennes) and a week later a village of the "Pioya" (Kiowas). The Frenchmen distributed presents in each village, and the Indians, with seemingly nothing better to do, joined the march—men, women, children, and dogs.

The small army of guides steered the French in a more southerly direction, and on October 17 they came at last to a village of the Gens des Chevaux. They found the Horse People in great distress, for all of their villages had recently been ransacked by the "Gens du Serpent" (Snake People), with great loss of life. "Snakes" was the common pejorative used by the Plains Indians to describe the Shoshones, a large tribe that resided in western Wyoming and Montana. Possessed of a reputation for ferocity similar to that of the Dakotas, the Shoshones were universally hated and feared. Although the Shoshone menace appeared to block any further exploration, the Horse People (with whom the French apparently had no difficulty communicating) indicated that there was a powerful tribe a short distance to the south who had no fear of the Snakes and might serve as guides.

In his journal the chevalier referred to this tribe as "Gens d'Arc" (People of the Bow). Since all the Plains Indians were equipped with bows and arrows, this description is not very helpful. However, when the French reached their village a few days later, the chief claimed to have knowledge of white men and spoke a few words that the Frenchmen recognized as Spanish. The chief also claimed that his people had massacred a Spanish expedition that had invaded their lands. Spanish archives record a massacre in 1720 of an expedition onto the central plains from Santa Fe. The Spanish identified the attackers as Pawnees, and it is likely that it was with this nation that the French brothers now resided.

On their way to the Pawnee village the Vérendrye brothers passed through "a very large village" of "Gens de la Belle Rivière." We do not know who these people were, but both the Plains Indians and early fur traders referred to the north fork of the Cheyenne River as "River Beautiful," and it is known today as the Belle Fourche (Beautiful Fork). The river arises in Wyoming west of the Black Hills, and its crossing supplies us with one of the few geographical landmarks of the Vérendrye brothers' trek.

The Pawnees, who viewed the Frenchmen (and their guns) as potential allies in a war against the Shoshones, agreed to supply guides for a resumption of their westward odyssey.

To the surprise and concern of the Frenchmen, the "guides" amounted to over two thousand warriors and their families (every village they encountered seemed to pick up and leave at will). For a month, wrote the chevalier, "We continued to march over magnificent prairies where wild animals were plentiful. At night there was nothing but songs and shouting, and scarcely anything was done, except that they came to weep upon our heads, to get us to accompany them in the war." Eager to reach the crest of the western mountains in order to get a glimpse of the Western Sea, the brothers agreed to stay with the war party, though they had no intention of getting involved in a fight.

On January 1, 1743, the Vérendryes came in sight of a range of snow-covered mountains, probably the Big Horns. Leaving the main party in a camp, with his brother to guard their personal baggage, Louis-Joseph advanced to the mountains with a small band of mounted warriors (this is his first mention of proceeding by horseback). He reached the foot of the range in mid-January but was unable to ascend it as he wished. Pawnee scouts had found an abandoned Shoshone village, and the Pawnee chief became concerned that the Snakes had outflanked him and were descending on his home villages. The Pawnee "army" began fleeing east in some disarray, and the Frenchmen had no choice but to abandon the search for the River of the West and return to Fort La Reine.

Now on horseback, the four Frenchmen arrived at an Arikara village on the Missouri River on March 19. On a hill near the village the chevalier buried a lead tablet bearing the arms of the king of France and the names of members of his party.[6] This procedure was a fairly common French method of claiming title to the entire watershed (La Salle had buried a tablet at the mouth of the Mississippi in laying claim to Louisiana). The group departed the Arikara village on April 2 and, after a sociable visit with the Mandans, arrived at Le Reine on July 2.

Although the expedition of the Vérendrye brothers added significantly to the geographical knowledge of the northern plains, the results were a major disappointment to the minister of marine in Paris. The brothers had not found a route to the Western Sea, and the chevalier's report offered scant hope of expanding the fur trade to the Missouri River, especially in view of the expense of overland transport from the river to the Lake of the Woods. (Although St. Louis would eventually become a major fur entrepot for the Missouri Valley, it was not founded until 1764, after the French had lost Canada.) As a measure of his displeasure the comte de Maurepas in 1744 relieved Vérendrye of his position as commandant of the western posts. The pioneer explorer died five years later, and his sons thereafter focused their fur trade interests on the Saskatchewan River. A half century would pass before another white man visited the Dakota prairies.

David Thompson, Fur Trader and Mapmaker

In the same year that Vérendrye was relieved of his command, King Louis XV became involved in a prolonged conflict with Great Britain that quickly spread to the New World and climaxed with the surrender of Canada to the British general, Lord Jeffrey Amherst, in September 1760. By the Peace of Paris that ended the war in 1763, France lost its North American empire. Britain took possession not only of Canada but also of the half of Louisiana that lay east of the Mississippi River. (Louisiana west of the Mississippi went to Spain, in partial compensation for Spain's loss of Florida to the British.) Thereafter, Britain became involved in a quarrel with its colonies on the Atlantic seaboard, a dispute that culminated in the American Revolution. Throughout this age of warfare the Hudson Bay Company and British fur merchants in Montreal continued to collect beaver pelts from the Indians in the woodlands north and west of Lake Superior, but they made no effort to trade south and west of the Great Lakes/Hudson Bay watersheds until after the warfare ended.

In 1784 a consortium of Scottish merchants in Montreal formed the Northwest Company to offer the western Indians an alternative to Hudson Bay as a market for their furs. Utilizing the Lake Superior–Lake Huron–Ottawa River route to Montreal, the Northwest Company greatly enlarged Vérendrye's post at the Grand Portage on Lake Superior and turned it into a major fur entrepot. Its agents, most of them of French ancestry, penetrated the woods south and west of Lake Superior, engaging the Indians of Wisconsin and Minnesota and penetrating as far west as Lake Winnipeg. The most energetic of all the Northwest Company's agents was a Scotsman, David Thompson, a surveyor and mapmaker by trade. He would be the first white man since the Vérendrye brothers to visit the Indian tribes of the Dakota prairies and leave a record of his travels. He would also be the last civilian to explore the northern plains. Further explorations for the next half century would be undertaken by the U.S. Army.

Born in Scotland, Thompson at the age of fourteen was employed as an apprentice clerk by the Hudson Bay Company and took ship to the company's Churchill Factory on the bay. He soon moved south to the York Factory at the mouth of the Nelson River, the terminus of the Indian trade route from Lake Winnipeg. There, at the age of twenty, he became an apprentice to Philip Turnor, the only professionally trained surveyor in western Canada. Inspired by this training, Thompson began surveying on his own, paying for his hobby by trading with the Indians. Over the next quarter-century Thomson surveyed and mapped the entire Canadian West, going as far north as Lake Athabaska (starting point for Alexander MacKenzie's 1789 journey to the Artic Ocean) and as far west as the mouth of the Columbia River.

Unfortunately the staid management of the Hudson Bay Company had little use for Thompson's cartographic services, and in 1797, after his service contract expired, Thompson paddled to Grand Portage and went to work for the Northwest Company. His first assignment, unencumbered by any need to collect furs, was to map the route from Lake Superior to Lake Winnipeg. After mapping the rivers that flowed into the western lake, he was to visit and determine the location of the Indian villages on the Missouri River, map the Red River, and, finally, determine the source of the Mississippi. The motive for this immense assignment was concern among the partners of the Northwest Company as to whether their western posts lay on Canadian or American soil. By the treaty of 1783 that ended the American Revolution, the international boundary west of Lake Superior was a line from the headwaters of the Mississippi to the northwest corner of the Lake of the Woods. But the fur traders well knew that the Mississippi lay far to the south of the Lake of the Woods and even of Rainy Lake. In 1792 the United States and Great Britain informally agreed on the 49th parallel as the boundary from the Lake of the Woods to the crest of the Rocky Mountains (an agreement formalized by the Convention of 1818). This naturally raised concerns among the Montreal businessmen about the true source of the Mississippi as well as the precise location of their western outposts. The assignment took Thompson on a journey of more than two thousand miles, which he made in ten months.

Thompson quickly made the survey of the well-marked canoe trail from Grand Portage to Lake Winnipeg, completing this task by August 1797. He then set out by canoe for the Northwest Company posts on the Assiniboine River. To reach the Mandan villages from there he had to proceed overland, for the Souris River, a tributary of the Assiniboine that dips into North Dakota, was too shallow for canoes at that time of year. The overland party, consisting of a French guide and interpreter who had lived for eight years with the Mandans and five French Canadians who carried goods for trade, departed the company post on November 28, 1797. Although Thompson had a horse to ride and two to carry his survey equipment, the rest of the party moved on foot. The Canadians had purchased thirty dogs from the Assiniboines, and each pair of dogs hauled a sled on which their trading goods were lashed. Thompson had little regard for the Canadians, who were illiterate and whose chief delight was in eating (each consuming, he claimed, eight pounds of fresh meat a day). He cared even less for their dogs. "They were all half dog," he confided to his journal, "half wolf, and always on the watch to devour everything they could get their teeth on; they did not willing[ly] work, and most of them had never hauled a flat sled, but the Canadians soon broke them in by constant flogging, in which they seemed to take great delight. When on the march the noise was intolerable, and made me keep two or three miles ahead."

Thompson's seeming lack of concern for the lateness of the season when they departed is in itself breathtaking. Not surprisingly, the travelers encountered below-zero temperatures and blizzard conditions as they made their way across the treeless prairie in December. Forced by snow and wind to hunker in tents for days at a time, the party reached the Mandan villages on December 30, a journey of thirty-three days that in summer would have taken ten. The Mandans received them hospitably, and each member of the party was given a bed in a Mandan house.

Like the elder Vérendrye, Thompson was impressed with the quality of the Mandans' fortifications and the spaciousness of their dwellings:

> On entering the door, on the left sits the master of the house and his wife, on a rude kind of sofa, covered with bison robes, and before [them] is the fire, in a hollow of a foot in depth, and at one side of the fire is a vase of their pottery, or two, containing pounded maize, which is frequently stirred with a stick, and now and then about a small spoonful of fine ashes put in, to act as salt, and [this] makes good pottage. When they boil meat it is with only water, and the broth is drunk. We saw no dried meat of any kind, and their houses are not adapted for curing meat by smoke, for although the fire is on one side of the house, and not under the aperture, yet there is not the least appearance of smoke, and the light from the aperture of the dome gave sufficient light within the house. Around the walls, frame bed places were fastened, the bottom three feet from the ground; covered with parchment skins of the bison with the hair on, except the front, which was open. For a bed was a bison robe, soft and comfortable.

Thompson observed that horses had stalls within the houses, an arrangement that both prevented theft by hostile tribes and kept the animals warm. In the winter the horses were fed corn, itself an indication of the abundance of vegetable food among the Mandans. Thompson marveled at the small number of horses kept by each family. "The chief with whom I lodged had only three." Whether this indicated the Mandans' disinclination to warfare, the limitations of winter lodging, or their reliance on vegetable gardens can only be guessed. Even in the winter, Thompson was impressed with the fecundity of their gardens. Their storage bins contained a large amount of Indian corn "of the small red kind," pumpkins (squash?), beans, and melons that "have been raised to their full size and flavour."

Thompson also found that the Indians had elaborate ways of entertaining themselves through the long winter evenings:

In the house of the chief in which I stayed, every evening, about two or three hours after sunset, about forty or fifty men assembled. They all stood; five or six of them were musicians, with a drum, tambour, rattle, and rude flutes. The dancing women were twenty-four young women of the age[s] of sixteen to twenty-five years. They all came in their common dress, and went into a place set apart for them to dress, and changed to a fine white dress of thin deerskins, with ornamented belts, which showed their shapes almost as clearly as a silk dress.

They formed two rows of twelve each, and about three feet apart. . . . When the music struck up, part of the men sang, and the women, keeping a straight line and respective distance, danced with a light step and slow graceful motion toward the musicians, until near to them, when the music and singing ceased; the women retired in regular line, keeping their faces toward the musicians. . . . Each dance lasted about ten minutes. There was no talking, the utmost decorum was kept; the men all silently went away; the dancing women retired to change their dress. They were all courtesans, a set of handsome, tempting women.

Thompson discovered, however, that the decorum was confined to the formal dance. Otherwise women were readily available: "The curse of the Mandans is an almost total want of chastity; this, the [French] men with me knew, and I found it was almost their sole motive for their journey hereto. The goods they brought, they sold at 50 to 60 percent above what they cost, and reserving enough to pay their debts and buy some corn, spent the rest on women. Therefore we could not preach chastity to them, and by experience they informed me that syphillis was common and mild."

Thompson spent three weeks making astronomical observations of the latitude and longitude of the Mandan villages. He and his party then departed for the Red River and their quest for the source of the Mississippi. The only company outpost that he found to be on American territory was Pembina on the Red River, one minute and thirty-six seconds south of the 49th parallel, a latitude reading confirmed twenty years later by the U.S. Army when it finally evicted the Canadians from American soil.

CHAPTER FOUR

Ventures under the American Flag, 1800–1837

E urope was at war in the year 1800. The war had begun with the French Revolution and the effort of a coalition of monarchies, led by Great Britain, to suppress it. In 1799 General Napoleon Bonaparte seized control of the French government and embarked on a war of conquest. By 1800 Spain, which had initially joined Britain's coalition of monarchies, wanted to switch sides. If it did so, however, Spain's ministers realized that their American empire would be a hostage to the British navy. Particularly vulnerable was the colony of Louisiana because its settlement and government were concentrated in the city of New Orleans. If the Royal Navy seized that port, the entire hinterland, from the Mississippi River to the Rocky Mountains, would fall into British hands. Accordingly Spain and France signed a secret treaty by which Spain ceded Louisiana to France, with the understanding that Napoleon would defend the colony from British attack. Although Spain probably viewed the transaction as a loan, with Louisiana to be returned to it at the end of the war, Napoleon saw it as the first step in a grand plan to recover the French empire in North America.

A lull in the European war in 1802 gave Napoleon an opportunity to send an army to occupy New Orleans. He instructed its commander to stop in Haiti on the way to suppress a slave rebellion led by the Negro general Toussaint L'Ouverture. The French army succeeded in temporarily pacifying the island but then succumbed to yellow fever. Napoleon's dream of New World empire was thus dashed by the bite of a lowly mosquito. Unable to defend Louisiana and ever in need of money to carry on his conquest of Europe, Napoleon decided to sell the colony. He asked his financial minister to summon the American ambassador, Robert R. Livingston. The American government had been informed of the transfer of Louisiana to France, and Secretary of State James Madison had instructed Livingston to warn the French against occupying New Orleans and, if possible, to secure American access to the port facilities.

Livingston had no authority to accept Napoleon's stunning offer to sell all of Louisiana for $15 million, but he agreed to it anyway. Livingston and Napoleon's ministers were on the verge of coming to terms in April 1803 when James Monroe, a special emissary from the United States, landed in Paris. President Thomas Jefferson and Secretary Madison had sent Monroe to reinforce Livingston with an offer to buy the port of New Orleans and as much of the Gulf Coast as France was willing to sell. Monroe immediately agreed with Livingston on the purchase of all of Louisiana, and the treaty of purchase was duly signed.

Although Monroe and Livingston had violated their instructions—told to buy the Gulf Coast, they had bought the Great Plains instead—President Jefferson was delighted with the acquisition of this "empire for liberty." The purchase doubled the size of the American republic, and, in Jefferson's view, ensured that the United States would remain, for the foreseeable future, a land of small farmers. Social equality and widespread property ownership, he felt, were the prerequisites for political democracy.

Lewis and Clark

Jefferson, in fact, had begun making plans for an American exploration of Louisiana even before he learned of the purchase. (Had the venture not been legitimized by the purchase, it would have amounted to a military invasion of Spanish soil.) In early 1803, he named his private secretary and Albemarle County (Virginia) neighbor Meriwether Lewis a captain in the U.S. Army and placed him in command of the military expedition. Lewis, in turn, named William Clark, younger brother of Revolutionary War general George Rogers Clark, second in command, and the president made Clark a lieutenant in the army. The two commanders departed for the West in July 1803, just as news of the treaty of purchase arrived in the nation's capital. The Spanish commander in St. Louis, however, had not received official word of the transfer and accordingly felt obliged to enforce standing orders to prevent strangers from wandering around in Spanish territory. Lewis and Clark accordingly set up camp in Illinois, across the river from St. Louis, and spent the winter gathering their force. The expedition ultimately consisted of four sergeants, twenty-two privates, and an equal number of river boatmen. Clark's Negro servant, York, rounded out the troop, which was placed under military orders and discipline.

Jefferson's instructions were to ascend the Missouri River to its source, find a passage across the Continental Divide, and follow westward-flowing waters to the Pacific. An

American ship captain had discovered the mouth of the Columbia River a decade earlier, thus establishing an American claim to the Pacific Northwest. In addition to mapping "the most direct and practicable water communication across the continent, for the purposes of commerce," Lewis and Clark were to impress upon the remote Indian tribes the "rising importance of the U. States" and persuade them to deal with American fur traders rather than the British. Finally, the explorers were to gather scientific data relative to the geography and climate of the country and to send back specimens of plants and animals.

Louisiana was formally transferred in the spring of 1804, and the party started up the Missouri on May 14 in three boats. The largest was a keelboat, a craft that would be the primary vehicle for the Missouri River fur trade for the next thirty years. It was fifty-five feet long and fifteen feet abeam. Drawing a mere three feet of water, it was round-bottomed, with a keel extending its entire length. It was equipped with a mast and square sail, but the primary means of propulsion against the Missouri's four-mile-an-hour spring current was poling. Two narrow catwalks extended along each gunwale of the vessel, each accommodating eight or ten men. Each man had a sturdy pole made of ash, with a ball at the end that fit against his shoulder. At the command of the boat's captain they plunged their poles into the river bottom and walked the length of the boat pushing it upstream. When each man reached the stern, he lifted his pole and dashed back to the bow to repeat the process. When the channel of the river lay close upon the bank, a party was put on shore to tow the keelboat with a line attached to the mast. The two other boats were pirogues, canoe-like rowboats propelled by three pairs of oars. Only two horses accompanied the party, walking along the shore and used only for hunting.

One day in late June, as the boatmen were passing the mouth of the Kaw River (present-day Kansas City), they encountered a party of traders coming downriver on two rafts loaded with buffalo hides. The leader was a trapper of mixed French and Indian stock named Charbonneau. He had been living for several years among the Mandans and was familiar with the language and culture of the upper Missouri tribes with whom Lewis and Clark expected to spend the winter. Lewis promptly hired him as guide and interpreter, and Charbonneau abandoned his erstwhile partners to join the northbound expedition.

They reached the Dakota prairies toward the end of August. Near the mouth of the Vermillion River Clark landed (by policy one of the two captains remained with the boats at all times) and climbed a hill that the Indians called "Mountain of Spirits." It was perfectly conical and built of earth and "loos pebbles." Although the Indians thought it had been man-made, Clark noticed that the ground around it was also full of round stones and concluded that the hill "was most probably the production of nature."[1] From the top of the mound, he wrote, "we beheld a most butiful landscape; Numerous herds of buffalo were seen feeding in various directions, the Plain to North N.W. and N.E. extends without interruption as far as can be seen."

Moving on to the mouth of the James River, they set fire to the prairie as a signal to any Indians in the vicinity to come in for friendly talk. A party of Yankton Dakota put in an appearance, and Lewis gave them gifts. Accompanied by a sergeant and a French interpreter who knew the Siouan language, Clark visited their village and was invited to dinner. "A fat dog was presented," he recorded in his journal, "as a mark of their great respect for the party of which [we] partook hartily and thought it good & well flavored."

7. The "Mountain of Spirits," eight miles north of the Missouri River. Today it is part of National Prairie. Photo by author.

At every stage of the journey the explorers marveled at the abundance, and occasional strangeness, of the wildlife. And mindful of Jefferson's instructions to satisfy the world's scientific curiosity, they wrote detailed descriptions in their journals. On September 1 they caught their first sight of a grizzly, which they called a "great white bear" because at a distance the gray tips of a grizzly's hair gave it a white appearance. A week later a hunting party came upon a village of prairie dogs (*petits chiens* to their French interpreter). They caught one by pouring water into their holes, skinned it, and cured the skin for dispatch to President Jefferson. On September 14, as Clark walked along the shore, he encountered and killed "a Buck Goat of this Countrey." He noted that it was about the size of a small deer with shorter horns and longer tail. This was the group's first description of the American pronghorn, an animal that resembles the African antelope although it is not related. Both Lewis and Clark would refer to the abundant pronghorns as "goats" throughout their trip, though Clark admitted that the animal "is more like the Antilope or Gazella of Africa than any other Species of Goat." Four days later, near the mouth of the White River, Clark was again hunting on the shore and "Killed a Prairie Wolf, about the size of a gray fox, bushy tail, head & ear like a wolf. Some fur. Burrows in the ground and barks like a small dog." This was the party's first acquaintance with a coyote. Clark had its skin cured and stretched for the benefit of President Jefferson.

Near the end of September the explorers came upon a village of the Arikara tribe situated on a large island in the middle of the river. It contained, by Lewis's estimate, more than five hundred warriors. These people, wrote Lewis, were "the best looking, most cleanly, most friendly and industrious Indians I saw anywhere on the voyage." The Arikaras, who would later prove most troublesome to fur traders using the river, were indeed in a sociable mood on this occasion, probably due to the heavy armament (the keelboat boasted a swivel cannon in its bow) and evident discipline of the expedition. The Indians loaded the explorers' boats with the produce of their fields — corn, squash, and beans — and Lewis presented the village headman with gifts of salt and sugar and a sun lens for ease in making fire.

The Arikaras had a custom, rather common among the Plains Indians, of honoring a guest by offering him a woman for the night. Lewis noted in his journal: "These women are handsomer than the Sioux; both of them [Arikaras and Sioux] are, however, disposed to be amorous, and our men found no difficulty in procuring companions for the night by means of the interpreters." Lewis also observed that "The black man, York, participated largely in these favors; for,

8. American pronghorn—"goats" to Lewis and Clark. U.S. Fish and Wildlife Service.

instead of inspiring any prejudice, his color seemed to procure him additional advantages from the Indians, who desired to preserve among them some memorial of their wonderful stranger." When York's "comrades" sought to break up one of these liaisons (whether from a misguided sense of propriety or a fear for his health is not clear), the woman's husband stood in the door of the lodge and "would permit no interruption until a reasonable time had elapsed." The two captains firmly refused to participate in such wantonness, but they had to admire the Arikaras' refusal of all offers of drink. The tribes they had met lower on the river had all begged the explorers for whiskey. The Arikaras, on the other hand, wrote Lewis, "were surprised that their father [President Jefferson] should present to them a liquor which would make them fools. . . . No man could be their friend who tried to lead them into such follies."

Before the explorers resumed their journey, they were treated to a sample of Indian compassion that was incomprehensible to the "civilized" whites. Lewis ordered the arrest of Private John Newman for "mutinous expressions." Lewis believed that griping of the sort attributed to Newman threatened morale and jeopardized the entire expedition. Newman was tried by court martial, convicted, and sentenced to receive seventy-five lashes on his "bear back." By military custom the brutal punishment was witnessed by the assembled corps. The village chief was among the group witnessing the occasion, and midway through the whipping he cried aloud in sympathy for the suffering Newman and begged that the punishment cease. Lewis, the commander, remained obdurate.

In late October the party at last reached the villages of the Mandan tribe. After the usual exchange of welcoming speeches and presents, Clark went in search of a site for winter encampment. He selected a well-wooded position about three miles from the main Mandan village. The soldiers began felling trees and building huts. Fort Mandan, as Lewis christened it, was built in a triangle, with a row of huts forming two sides and a wooden palisade, with walkway at the top for a sentry, across the front.

Food was plentiful through the early part of the winter. The Mandans showed the explorers how to build a brush entrapment for pronghorns, and in two days they captured "100 goats." The Mandans had stored their garden produce in pits dug next to their earthen lodges. The pits, about

9. A replica of Fort Mandan, showing barracks for soldiers and sentry post overlooking the stockade. Photo by author.

seven feet deep, were bottle-shaped, narrow at the top so they could be easily concealed in the event of an enemy raid and six feet wide at the bottom. Buffalo hides served as both floor and top covering. In mid-December Mandan scouts reported a buffalo herd in the vicinity, and the Indians chased them on horseback. Lewis and fifteen soldiers joined the hunt on foot and with their rifles killed ten. Because they had only one horse, Lewis and his men were able to carry only five carcasses back to the fort; the Indians took the remainder. It was the custom of the plains, the Indians explained, that kills must be shared, and a single hunter, regardless of how many buffalo he killed in a chase, was entitled to only a part of one.

When Lewis and Clark arrived at the Mandan villages, they had brought assurances of peace from their neighbors to the south, the Arikaras and Dakotas. The Mandans interpreted this as a promise of help if their villages were attacked. When a Dakota raiding party killed a solitary Mandan hunter in mid-December, Clark led a party in search of the marauders. He found them, gave them presents, and obtained a renewed pledge of peace. The mediation efforts added to the explorers' reputation, and the Mandans began to rely on them to resolve a variety of disputes.

Domestic quarrels occupied them for a good part of the winter. Although the Americans' own culture recognized few rights for women, Lewis and Clark noted, with apparent dismay, the extent to which Indian men treated their wives as beasts of burden. When a man, for instance, brought a load of corn to exchange for tobacco or gunpowder, it was his wife who carried the load on her back. Women were the exclusive gatherers of firewood, and the explorers witnessed almost daily a troop of them carrying what seemed like one-hundred-pound bundles for miles through the snow.

One day in early winter an Indian woman who had quarreled with her husband fled for safety to the hut of the interpreter, Charbonneau. The interpreter had two Indian wives. One of them, Sacajawea (Bird Woman), was a Shoshone who had been captured by the Hidatsas some years earlier and sold to the Frenchman. Charbonneau and his wives gave the woman refuge. After a few days she returned to her home, where her husband beat her badly and stabbed her three times with a knife. She fled back to the fort with her husband in pursuit, threatening to kill her for desertion, an action to which he was entitled under Mandan law. The sentry alerted Lewis, who sought to mediate the dispute. Lewis learned that the man was accusing his wife of sleeping with a soldier without his permission. Lewis assured him that no man under his command would "touch his squar, or the wife of any Indian." At that juncture "the Grand Chief of the nation arrived & lectured him," and the two departed, still arguing. A few weeks later the Indian returned to the fort, in company with his two wives, and expressed eagerness to be reconciled with Charbonneau, who had given his wife refuge. The Indians also came to rely on the soldiers for medicine. After mediating the misunderstanding caused by Charbonneau's kindness, Lewis received a woman with a child who had an abscess on his back. She offered as much corn as she could carry for some medicine, and Lewis obligingly treated the child.

By the end of January, with snow deep on the ground and daily temperatures well below zero, food became scarce. The Mandans understandably would part with their corn only for a price. At that point Lewis discovered the value of his blacksmith. The Indians, he wrote, "are extravagantly fond of sheet iron of which they form arrow-points and manufacture into instruments for scraping and dressing their buffalo robes." He thus allowed his blacksmith to cut up and sell an iron stove that had been "nearly birnt out." For each piece of iron four inches square the blacksmith received "seven or eight gallons of corn from the natives who appeared extremely pleased with the exchange." The Mandans also discovered that the blacksmith, with charcoal fire and bellows, could mend the metal cooking pots that they had obtained from fur traders. He did a brisk business repairing leaks and broken handles in exchange for corn.

In early February Clark took sixteen men and three pack-horses on a week-long hunting trip. He returned with forty deer, sixteen elk, and three buffalo bulls, but the animals were so close to starvation themselves that they yielded little meat. The main beneficiaries of the hunt, according to Lewis, were hungry wolves, "which are here very numerous." On February 11, 1805, Charbonneau's wife Sacajawea gave birth to a boy, whom they named Baptiste. Realizing that Sacajawea might be useful as a guide and interpreter when they reached the mountains, Lewis renewed his contract with Charbonneau and agreed to allow his seventeen-year-old wife and her child to join the expedition.

In mid-March Lewis's men cut down cottonwood trees and sawed them into planks for the construction of two new pirogues. Lewis clearly thought that these stout, maneuverable vessels would be more serviceable in attacking the shallow, swift-running waters at the head of the Missouri. Lewis sent the keelboat back to St. Louis with the skins of the animals they had killed for scientific purposes. He also sent plant specimens, an earthen pot of the type the Mandans used for cooking, a "Tin box containing insects, mice, etc.," and cages containing a live prairie dog, four prairie magpies, and a prairie chicken. In the return party were a half dozen soldiers, two French hunters, and the dishonored private, John Newman.

On April 7, 1805, the same day that the keelboat set out for St. Louis, the remainder of the expedition, now numbering thirty-two men plus Sacajawea and her child, embarked in the two new pirogues and "six small canoes." Two weeks later, on April 26, the explorers passed the mouth of the Yellowstone River (their translation of Roche Jaune, the name conferred on the stream by French fur traders) and began the ascent across the high plains to the Rocky Mountains.

The Missouri River is formed by the junction of three forks in western Montana, which the explorers named the Jefferson, the Madison, and the Gallatin. They made their way up the Jefferson, the westernmost fork, and near the head of that stream Sacajawea was reunited with her brother, a Shoshone chief. The Shoshones led them across the Continental Divide and supplied them with horses to reach the

10. The shallow Missouri River as seen from Fort Mandan.
Photo by author.

navigable waters of the Columbia. They spent the winter
camped near the mouth of that river, and in the spring of
1806 began to retrace their steps. On the eastern side of the
Continental Divide the party split in order to cover a wider swath of territory. Lewis and the main party planned to
explore the upper sources of the Missouri and then journey
down the river to the Mandan villages. Clark, with a party
of ten, including Charbonneau and Sacajawea, would move
south to the headwaters of the Yellowstone River (in present-day Yellowstone Park) and follow that stream to its junction with the Missouri. Clark reached the Missouri on August 3, and Lewis's party joined him four days later. Lewis
had been delayed by an altercation with a party of Blackfoot Indians at the head of the Missouri; the incident resulted in the death of one Indian, the only death by gunfight
on the entire trip.

The passage downriver was much less work but had miseries of its own. The men's clothing had long since worn out, and they dressed like Indians in buckskins. They complained that they could not cure the skins properly, however, because every time the party put to shore, it was visited by hoards of mosquitoes. "Thos troublesom insects" made it impossible to camp in the woods on shore, and they slept instead on sandbars in the middle of the river.

In the principal Mandan village on August 17, Lewis paid off Charbonneau for his services with enough trade goods for the interpreter to purchase a horse and a lodge in the village. The payment, according to Lewis, amounted to $500.33. Clark had grown much attached to Sacajawea's son, Baptiste, and offered to take him "and raise him in such a manner as I thought proper." Sacajawea declined to let him go because the boy, although nineteen months old, had not been weaned. She thought he might be ready to travel in a year, however. In fact, four years passed before Clark, then governor of the Louisiana Territory, took the boy to St. Louis for a formal education.

President Jefferson had instructed the explorers to bring an Indian leader back to the nation's capital so that upon his return he could report on the power, numbers, and wealth of the white man and his government. The explorers made inquiries among the Mandans, and one of their principal leaders, Shahaka, agreed to go provided they took along his wife and child, plus an interpreter and his family. Lewis ordered two canoes to be lashed together with poles to accommodate Shahaka's entourage and its baggage. Essential to the arrangement was a promise that the government would return Shahaka and his family the following year, a promise that would entail no end of difficulty and some loss of life.

Having made these arrangements, the party resumed its

journey downriver, pausing at the villages of the Arikaras and the Dakotas to reinforce the warning that the "father" in Washington insisted that they remain at peace with their neighbors on the plains. The Indians smiled and smoked their pipes; time would prove that the veiled threat had fallen on deaf ears. Although shallow water and sandbars were a constant problem at this time of year, the party made good time and landed in St. Louis on September 23, 1806.

Manuel Lisa, Fur Trader

The fur trade merchants of St. Louis listened excitedly to Lewis and Clark's tales of Rocky Mountain streams teeming with beaver, but they were still doing a good business with the Indians of the lower Missouri Valley and were not quite ready to risk capital on so distant an enterprise as the Rocky Mountains. There was one exception, however—a thirty-year-old entrepreneur of Spanish ancestry, Manuel Lisa. He was born in New Orleans or its environs, his father a functionary in the government of Spanish Louisiana. By 1796, when he was a mere twenty years old, Lisa was described as a "merchant of New Orleans" with a riverboat of his own and a branch store in Vincennes, soon to become the capital of the Indiana Territory. In 1799 he moved to St. Louis and purchased a house in town and a sixty-acre farm on the banks of the Missouri River.

The Spanish government of Louisiana tightly regulated the fur trade. It conferred monopolies on only two or three trading houses for trade with the neighboring tribes—the Osages, Kansas, Pawnees, and Dakotas (on the upper Des Moines River). Lisa, making himself the leader of a group of small merchants who were not favored with monopolies, published a plea for free trade and carried a petition to the intendant general in New Orleans asking for a change in government policy. In the spring of 1803 Lisa's continued agitation landed him in a St. Louis prison. He was free from jail and running his retail business when ownership of Louisiana passed into the hands of the United States. For Lisa the political transfer meant the arrival of free enterprise. When Lewis and Clark set up their camp on the Illinois side of the Mississippi in the fall of 1804, Lisa visited the encampment with an offer to provide supplies. He also found river boatmen for the expedition.

When Lewis and Clark returned in 1806, Lisa formed a partnership with merchants of the Illinois country (in Kaskaskia and Vincennes) to finance a trading and trapping expedition to the upper Missouri. By the spring of 1807 he had purchased two keelboats and recruited about fifty boatmen, many of them veterans of the Lewis and Clark expedition. They started up the river in April and by mid-July they had passed the mouth of the Big Sioux River and entered the country of the Dakotas. The young men of this tribe were probably on a midsummer buffalo hunt, and the traders passed through the region without seeing a single Indian.

The Arikaras, on the other hand, were another matter. Arriving at the first "Ree" village, Lisa saw two to three hundred warriors drawn up along the bank. They fired on the boats and ordered Lisa to land. He did so but told the Indians not to set foot on the boats. The Rees respected this command but raised their guns menacingly. Lisa responded by ordering his own men to arms and aiming his swivel-mounted cannons at the Indians. The Rees fell back in confusion and ultimately decided that a battle was not in their best interest. Lisa went ashore, smoked a pipe with them, and offered presents. The trading party then resumed its journey.

The aftermath came a few weeks later when the U.S. government's party, returning Shahaka and his entourage, arrived at the Ree village. To protect the Indian chief the parsimonious government had supplied a military detail of only fourteen soldiers. Accompanying them was a group of twenty-three traders who planned to establish a post among the Mandans. After some preliminary sparring, the Rees fired upon the passing boats, killing four men and wounding several others. The expedition fled back to St. Louis, and another year passed before Shahaka was returned to his people. Whether the Arikaras felt humiliated by Lisa's passage and desired revenge or whether, as Shahaka's interpreter believed, they were jealous of the courtesy given the Mandan chief remains uncertain. Missouri River fur traders approached the Ree villages with extreme caution ever after. The Mandans, though reported by Lewis and Clark to be the friendliest Indians in the West, also gave Lisa's party some anxious moments. Lisa proceeded alone through the first two villages, handing out presents while his boats stood offshore, ready to either fight or run. In the third village the chief rejected the presents Lisa presented to the council and demanded instead a quantity of gunpowder. Lisa stood firm. The chief eventually yielded, and the party passed on peacefully.

It was late October and time for winter camp by the time Lisa's party reached the mouth of the Yellowstone River. Lisa, profiting from information gleaned from Clark, turned up this river as far as the mouth of the Big Horn. There he built a winter post, which he named Fort Raymond. This was the heartland of the Crow Indians, who were reported to be the best curers of beaver skins of any tribe in the West. Skin preparation was important to ensure that the pelts arrived intact after a voyage downriver to New Orleans and a trip across the Atlantic. The beaver pelt was in demand in the markets of Europe and the American East Coast, not for the dark brown outer fur but for the fibrous underhair, which hatters pounded, mashed, and rolled into felting material for gentlemen's top hats. After spending the winter trapping and trading, Lisa returned to St. Louis in the spring of 1808 with two keelboats loaded to the gunwales with furs.

Lisa's success won over the cautious St. Louis fur merchants, and they joined him in forming the Missouri Fur Company in early 1809. Among the investors in the company was William Clark, Indian agent for the Louisiana Territory. To help finance an expedition to build a fur trading post among the Mandans the company entered into a contract with Louisiana's governor, Meriwether Lewis, to return Shahaka and his entourage to his village. Under the contract the government paid $7,000 for the escort duty and required the company to provide 120 men to protect the chief, 40 of whom had to be Americans and expert riflemen. This group, under the command of St. Louis merchant Pierre Chouteau, left St. Louis on May 17, 1809. A second, larger party, numbering about 190, departed a month later. This party, about half Americans and the rest French boatmen who had been recruited from as far as Detroit and Louisville, would construct the Mandan fort and replace the trappers at Fort Raymond.

Both parties suffered from rampant desertion as boatmen, accustomed to downriver runs on the Ohio and Mississippi, tired of battling the spring current of the Missouri. Even after the two groups joined, their combined numbers were fewer than two hundred. At the mouth of the James River a band of Teton Dakotas met them and treated them to a feast of roast dog, the standard menu for honored guests. Just below the Arikara villages Chouteau put ashore Shahaka's military guard with their sole cannon. The militia marched with fair military precision through the villages as the flotilla sailed by them on the river. Finding the Rees sufficiently intimidated, Chouteau seized the occasion to lecture them on their past misconduct and obtained promises of future friendship.

Chouteau and Lisa delivered the Mandan chief to his people and then pushed on to the main village of the Hidatsas, where they received a hospitable reception. Because the area around the village had been stripped of firewood and fodder, Lisa pushed ten miles farther upriver before looking for a suitable place to build his trading post. He selected a site just below the mouth of the Little Missouri River. Named Fort Mandan, it would serve as a trading center for the local tribes and a base for trapping expeditions up the Little Missouri and Yellowstone Rivers. The fort was triangular with a bastion at each of the three corners.

The news from the upper Missouri was disappointing. The Blackfoot Indians had attacked the trappers working in the area of the Three Forks and stolen their beaver pelts. Eight of the trappers were killed, and the rest had fled across the Continental Divide to seek refuge among the Shoshones, longtime enemies of the Blackfeet. Benito Vasquez, who was in charge of Fort Raymond, had closed up the fort and paddled to the Mandan villages to await the arrival of Chouteau and Lisa. He carried only fifteen beaver skins and ten buffalo robes, a miserable showing for a year's work. The Missouri Company partners who had made the upriver trip held a council and decided that Lisa and Chouteau would return to St. Louis to put together a new expedition the following spring. Andrew Henry, another partner who a decade later would play a prominent role in developing the Rocky Mountain fur trade, would lead a party of forty men to rebuild Fort Raymond and resume trapping on the upper Missouri.

Bad news continued to dampen the dreams of the Missouri Fur Company. President Jefferson's embargo on American trade, as retaliation for British and French depredations on American merchant vessels, had halted the export of beaver pelts and depressed prices. Lisa spent a year battling lawsuits and journeying as far as Detroit in search of new investors, and he was not able to mount a new expedition until the spring of 1811. The mission that year was to reinforce the garrison at Fort Mandan and locate Andrew Henry and his trappers, who had disappeared somewhere into the western mountains.

It was a small party—a medium-sized keelboat with twenty-one men engaged as crew. Also in the party were Charbonneau and Sacajawea, who had apparently come to St. Louis to retrieve their son, left the previous year in the care of now-governor William Clark. Lisa also took Henry M. Brackenridge on board as a "hunter." Pittsburgh-born and trained in the law (his lawyer father had played a prominent role in the Whisky Rebellion), Brackenridge was on a sightseeing tour before settling in New Orleans. His journal of the trip, published in 1814 as *Views of Louisiana*, is a priceless description of the river valley and its people.

Preparing for departure, Lisa had his first taste of competition from the man who would eventually dominate the Missouri River fur trade, John Jacob Astor. A German immigrant who had settled in New York, Astor had made his fortune in the fur trade of the eastern Great Lakes. By incorporating himself in 1808 as the American Fur Company, Astor was able to move into the western fur trade through wholly owned subsidiaries of his corporation. Utilizing one of these, the Pacific Fur Company, Astor planned to erect a trading post, Astoria, at the mouth of the Columbia River. In the spring of 1811 he sent two expeditions to build the post, one by sea and the other by land, following Lewis and Clark's route up the river. The overland Astorians managed to leave St. Louis several weeks before Lisa's party could get under way. It was composed of eighty men in four keelboats, and Lisa feared that it would, by dominating and thus humbling the Indians, render them vengeful when his own small party made an appearance—just as he himself had done four years earlier.

Departing St. Charles (a town across the Missouri River from St. Louis and famed for its low-priced female companionship) on April 2, Lisa hastened to catch up with the Astorians. The Astorians themselves were in a hurry, fearing that if Lisa passed them, he might turn the Indians against them. Lisa finally caught up with them on June 2, near the mouth of the Platte River, and the two leaders realized that cooperation was in their best interests. The Dakotas proved to be no problem, nor were the Rees. Arriving at the Mandan villages, where Lisa built a new Fort Mandan to replace the vulnerable one farther upriver (which had been repeatedly burglarized by the Hidatsas), Lisa entertained his first visitor, aging Shahaka. Brackenridge reported on Shahaka's plight in his journal:

> He is a fine looking Indian and very intelligent—his complexion fair, very little different from that of a white man much exposed to the sun. His wife had also accompanied him—has a good complexion and agreeable features. They had returned home loaded with presents, but have since fallen into disrepute from the extravagant tales which they related as to what they had witnessed; for the Mandan treat with ridicule the idea of there being a greater or more numerous people . . . than themselves. He . . . expressed a wish to come and live among the whites, and spoke sensibly of the insecurity, the ferocity of manners, and the ignorance, and state of society in which he was placed.

Andrew Henry, dressed in buckskins, appeared at the fort in September with a tale of harrowing escapes from the Blackfoot Indians and a bitterly cold winter in the mountains among the Shoshones. His men had found mountain streams teeming with beaver, however, and his canoes were jammed with ninety-pound packs of furs. Lisa's party, joined by Henry, returned to St. Louis in the fall, and the profits from Henry's hunt enabled Lisa and his partners to reorganize the Missouri Company with expanded capital. Ill fortune continued to dog the company, however. By the spring of 1812 Congress was preparing for war with Britain (it imposed a new trade embargo in April), and the partners were understandably reluctant to risk a large amount of trade merchandise in another upriver venture. As a result, Lisa's fourth trip to the Dakota prairies was smaller than he had hoped, carrying only $11,000 in trade goods in two keelboats.

One of the goals of this expedition was to establish a new trading post on the upper Missouri, and Lisa decided to locate it about halfway between the Arikara and Mandan villages, near the mouth of Hunkpapa Creek (just south of the present border between North and South Dakota). Completed in October, the post was Christened Fort Manuel. Trade with the Indians was initially quite brisk, but devastating war news soon rendered Lisa's position precarious. The United States had declared war in June, and the Indians of the western Great Lakes, under the leadership of the Shawnee chief Tecumseh, had aligned with the British. A combined Canadian-Indian force had seized Michillimackinac in the straits between Lakes Huron and Michigan. Fort Dearborn at the foot of Lake Michigan had been evacuated, and Detroit had surrendered to a British-Canadian army in August. The plains tribes sensed the tide of events and turned quite hostile. After the Dakotas seized one of the Missouri

Company's posts near the junction of the Big Sioux with the Missouri, Lisa packed up and fled for home. He arrived in St. Louis with only thirty-six packs of mixed furs and skins. With prices depressed by the war, the proceeds of the expedition could not have amounted to more than half the costs.

Lisa did manage a fifth venture up the Missouri in the spring of 1813 but met nothing but hostility. The traders upriver from Fort Manuel had either been killed or disappeared. The men at Fort Manuel had managed to collect some forty packs of beaver pelts, so Lisa packed them into his boats, closed the fort, and returned to St. Louis. Later that summer the partners dissolved the Missouri Fur Company. Ten years would pass before Americans would again appear in strength on the Dakota prairies.

Disaster on the Missouri: Mountain Men and the Arikaras

On February 13, 1822, the *St. Louis Missouri Gazette and Public Advertiser* carried an ad seeking one hundred men to ascend to the source of the Missouri River and remain there gathering furs for one, two, or three years. The advertisement was placed by Missouri businessman and lieutenant governor of the state, William H. Ashley. Volunteers were asked to report to Ashley's partner, Andrew Henry.

Ashley's ad was based on a new concept. To that point the fur trade, going back to the seventeenth century, had centered on the fixed post, located at some strategic crossroads in the wilderness, where Indians brought their skins and exchanged them for trade goods. Ashley's concept, based no doubt on Henry's experience in the mountains in 1811–13, was to employ his own trappers in the mountains and bring the furs all the way to St. Louis. The idea, still in its infancy, would evolve into the era of the "mountain man," the trapper residing semipermanently in the wilderness who would bring his furs to an annual summer "rendezvous" in the mountains, where Ashley would purchase them for shipment to St. Louis. Among those answering Ashley's ad was Jedediah Strong Smith, an itinerant farm laborer who had worked his way across the Midwest to St. Louis. Although he had never been up the Missouri nor ever trapped a fur-bearing animal, Jedediah Smith would become one of the greatest trailblazers in the history of the West—discoverer of the South Pass across the Continental Divide, a landmark on the Oregon Trail, and the first white man to make the overland trek to California.

An advance party led by Andrew Henry left St. Louis on April 3, 1822; a second boat, with Ashley and Smith aboard, left a month later. The two parties, numbering more than a hundred, jammed themselves aboard two large keelboats. Fort Atkinson at Council Bluffs, forty miles above the mouth of the Platte River, was the farthermost American military presence on the Missouri. Fort Kiowa at the mouth of the Bad River (just south of present-day Pierre), which had been built by Manuel Lisa after the war and was still occasionally visited by fur traders, was the last white habitation. A hundred miles beyond that lay the villages of the Arikaras, still regarded as potentially belligerent and generally unreliable.

The party passed through the Rees without incident and even managed to trade for some horses. While Ashley returned to St. Louis, Henry established a winter camp at the mouth of the Yellowstone River. The party realized the need for horses that winter, both for hunting and to pack beaver pelts. Early in 1823 Henry sent Smith to St. Louis to obtain trade goods to exchange for horses. Ashley and Smith returned upriver with ninety men in two keelboats, hoping to purchase a substantial number of horses from the Arikaras.

Arriving at the Ree villages on May 30, Ashley cautiously anchored his boats in the middle of the river and sent Smith ashore with a party to bargain for horses. A day passed in fruitless haggling, and that night an uproar broke out in the village. Boatmen had gone into the village looking for women, and one of them was killed in a fight. At dawn the Indians began shooting at Smith's party, which was camped on a sandbar. Smith tried to return the fire, but the Indians were too well concealed. Finding their position hopeless, Smith and what remained of his party leaped into the river and swam out to the keelboats. They left twelve dead on the beach. Eleven wounded (two of whom would die) made it to the boats with Smith. It was the most casualties by battle in the history of the western fur trade.

Ashley's volunteers were utterly demoralized. Half wanted to return home. Ashley gave them one of the keelboats, with instructions to leave their trade goods at Fort Kiowa and alert the army at Fort Atkinson (a second fort in present-day Nebraska) on their way. He sent Smith on foot to reach Andrew Henry and return with reinforcements. Learning of the attack, Colonel Henry Leavenworth, commander at Fort Atkinson, started north with six companies of infantry. The troops went by land; three keelboats tagged along with supplies and two cannons. Along the way several hundred Dakota warriors, always happy to fight the Rees, joined the expedition. As they neared the Ree villages, the mounted Dakotas dashed impulsively ahead and were met by mounted Arikaras. After an inconclusive fight, the Rees withdrew to their heavily fortified village. Unwilling to mount a frontal attack on the village, Leavenworth bombarded it with cannon, killing mostly women and children. The Arikaras abandoned their village during the night, and the Dakotas went home in disgust. Leavenworth had no choice but to return to Fort Atkinson. The effect of this comic-opera war was to make fierce enemies of the Arikaras and render the upper Missouri impassable for lightly armed fur traders for several years.

In the aftermath Henry returned to the Yellowstone, from which he would send his trappers to the forks of the Missouri. Ashley returned to St. Louis to supervise the business end of the trade, and Smith set out from Fort Kiowa to find a new route to the mountains, bypassing the Arikaras. He followed the Cheyenne River into southern Wyoming, crossed over to the North Platte, and followed that stream and its tributaries to the South Pass. He spent the next several years in the mountains, developing the trade route that would become the Oregon Trail and helping Ashley organize the rendezvous system that would revolutionize the Rocky Mountain fur trade.

Although the fur trade was no longer dependent upon the upper Missouri, the government felt obliged to pacify the Indians of the northern plains, who had been generally hostile and under British influence since the War of 1812. Until 1820 the Hudson Bay Company had the effrontery to maintain a post on American soil on the Red River. Its posts on the Assiniboine River, though on Canadian soil, continued to attract the trade of the Missouri River tribes. In 1824 Congress passed an act that appropriated money for a commission and its military escort to negotiate treaties of friendship with the Indian tribes along the Missouri River. President Monroe named General Henry Atkinson, commander of the army's Department of the West, to head the commission.

Atkinson spent the remainder of the year in St. Louis organizing the expedition, expected to number five hundred, and arranging for food stockpiles along the route.

An engineer by training, he also devised a system of slides and gears by which men, seated in the keelboat with feet on pedals, could turn paddlewheels on each side of the boat. This was far less work than poling, and it made for faster progress. The expedition assembled at Fort Atkinson in the spring of 1825—four hundred men in eight keelboats, with a mounted party of forty cavalry scouts proceeding along the riverbank. They departed on May 16. After stops to arrange treaties with various Nebraska tribes, the flotilla reached Fort Kiowa a month later, having doubled the pace of earlier keelboats. The commissioners waited several days while messengers brought the principal Dakota men back from their summer buffalo hunt, and the parties then signed a treaty that would serve as a model for agreements with tribes farther up the river. The Indians agreed to allow into their country traders who were duly licensed by the government and to cease any trade with "enemies of the United States"—that is, the British. The government, in turn, agreed to protect the Indians and to send only licensed traders into their midst.

The expedition reached the Arikara villages on July 15. To overawe the volatile Rees Atkinson arranged an elaborate parade of his infantry, cavalry, and artillery. Because of their past misdeeds he gave them only a few twists of tobacco rather than the usual presents of powder, lead, and trade goods. The Rees signed the proffered treaty, and Atkinson departed under the impression that the tribe would "behave well" in the future. Toward the end of July the expedition arrived among the Mandan villages and remained there for ten days, negotiating with representatives of the Mandans and Hidatsas, whose villages were strung out for seven miles along the river. At the mouth of the Yellowstone Atkinson signed a treaty with the Crows and then started for home. He held a final review of his brigade at Fort Atkinson on September 20 and then pushed on to St. Louis.

It was a remarkable feat of generalship. Atkinson had traveled to the upper Missouri and back in a single summer without losing a man or incurring damage to his boats. In his report to the War Department Atkinson advised that there was no need for an army post on the upper Missouri. He proved correct. The northern plains remained at peace for the next thirty years—until the government resurrected Indian hostility by forcing the sale of their lands and squeezing them onto reservations.

The American Fur Company

Manuel Lisa (who died in 1820) and other St. Louis merchants had continued to send small trading ventures to the upper Missouri in the decade after the War of 1812, but they struggled against British competition. In 1818 the United States and Great Britain agreed upon the 49th parallel of latitude as the U.S.-Canadian boundary from the Lake of the Woods to the Continental Divide. Two years later the Hudson Bay Company removed its Red River post northward to Lake Winnipeg, and those two actions ended British influence on the upper Missouri. British withdrawal, in turn, created a vacuum soon filled by American corporate enterprise—namely, the American Fur Company.

John Jacob Astor had retired in 1820, leaving day-to-day management of the company in the hands of his capable son, William, and his executive officer, Ramsey Crooks. Both continued Astor's policy of corporate expansion through wholly owned subsidiaries. In 1822 Crooks created a Western Department and absorbed a St. Louis company that gave him a foothold on the Missouri. Using tactics that would become standard among the "Robber Barons" of a half century later,

Crooks eliminated competition by purchasing rival companies or by lowering prices and taking short-term losses to drive them out of business. In 1826, for example, he absorbed a company headed by Manuel Lisa's one-time partner, Pierre Chouteau, and then placed the knowledgeable Chouteau in charge of the Western Department. By 1827 the American Fur Company had a monopoly of the Missouri River trade, a string of small outposts reaching as far as the Yellowstone, and the services of a group of experienced traders.

Over the next five years Crooks and Chouteau built a hierarchy of trading posts through the northern plains. The principal ones were Fort Union, established in 1829 at the mouth of the Yellowstone River, and Fort Pierre (christened in honor of Pierre Chouteau in 1832) on the Missouri, just below the mouth of the Cheyenne River. Each was a headquarters for local administrators and a collection point for skins received from fixed regional posts.

In the spring of 1832 Alexander Philip Maximilian, hereditary ruler of a minor German principality in the valley of the Rhine River and an inveterate traveler, visited Fort Pierre and left a description of it. The fort was built as a quadrangle, about one hundred yards on a side, with log pickets forming the outer wall. On the northeast and southwest corners were blockhouses that protruded beyond the picket wall and thus commanded the two entrances. The lower story of each blockhouse held cannon, while small arms served the upper story. The director's house was one story but had a fireplace in each room and glass windows. Along one wall of the fort were barracks for clerks, interpreters, and their families, totaling about one hundred persons. Along the other walls were storage rooms for trade goods, valued on the day of Maximilian's writing at $80,000, and furs obtained from the Indians. Outside the fort was a

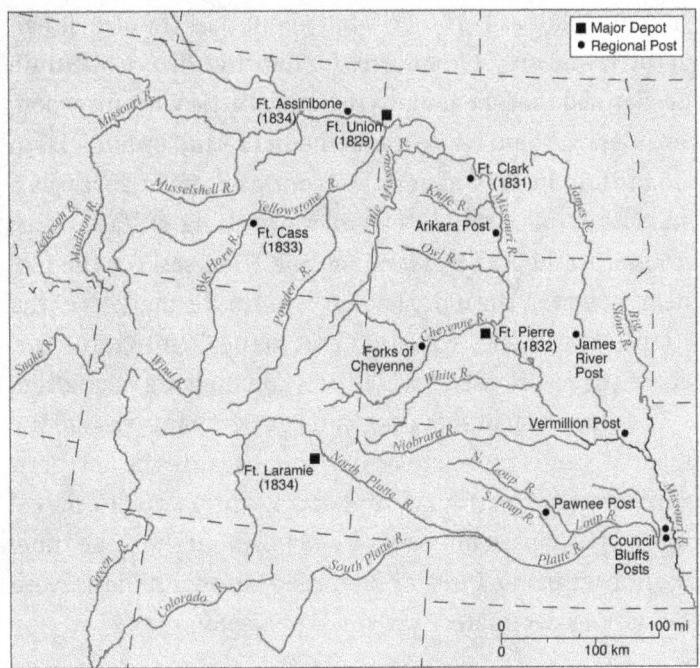

Map 7. The upper Missouri River fur trade, 1826–40.

pasture containing 150 dairy cows and 36 horses. "Indians, on foot and on horseback, were scattered all over the plain, and their singular stages for the dead were in great numbers near the Fort; immediately behind which the leather tents of the Sioux Indians, of the branches of the Tetons and the Yanktons, stood like a little village."

Subsidiary to the two administrative centers of Fort Union and Fort Pierre, the American Fur Company maintained a series of regional posts, extending into the heart of the Blackfoot country at the forks of the Missouri. The regional post in the northern plains was Fort Clark (established in 1831), situated among the Mandan villages about a mile from the enclosure built by Lewis and Clark. It was built on the same plan as Fort Pierre but about half the size. It had no cattle and only a few horses for hunting. Prince Maximilian claimed that the Indians regarded cattle with suspicion, considering them white man's medicine and prejudicial to the buffalo hunt. Outside the front gate of the fort was a "machine" (Maximilian's term) for packing buffalo skins, brought to the fort by Mandans and Hidatsas. For the moment, however, the hides had no value in the markets of the Atlantic coast. They were sent east to the farming frontier, where they were used for blankets and housing insulation.

The extension of the American Fur Company posts to the upper Missouri proved to be ill timed because the northern plains were trapped out of fur-bearing animals (with the exception perhaps of muskrats) by 1830. About the same time, by another ironic twist of fate, the Missouri Indians were themselves decimated by a small pox epidemic.

The Dreaded Pox—Again!

It came by steamboat. Although steamboats had been plying the western rivers since 1811, the novel craft was slow to reach the Missouri. Pilots regarded the river as too shallow for much of the year, laden with shifting sandbars and unseen deadheads. In 1819 an army expedition attempted to navigate the river in four steamboats, and only one got as far as Council Bluffs. A second one was wrecked on a snag, and the other two went aground in low water and tied up for the winter. Seeing the value of such craft in the fur trade, Pierre Chouteau ordered one specially built for the Missouri, with shallow draft and side-mounted paddle wheels for sharp turns. The *Yellowstone*, first of the American Fur Company's steamers, reached Fort Pierre in the summer of 1831 and made it to Fort Union the following year. Thereafter the company's steamboats made annual trips between April, when the ice broke on the river, and July, when the spring flood receded. The boats averaged two hundred feet in length and were capable of carrying five hundred tons of freight.

On April 17, 1837, the American Fur Company steamboat *St. Peter's* left St. Louis. Among the passengers was William N. Fulkerson, Indian agent for the Mandans. Shortly after the boat had passed the mouth of the Kaw River, a deckhand, described only as a "mulatto," came down with a fever. Since fevers, or "agues," were common on the river, the captain paid little mind. By the time the boat reached Council Bluffs, the man had broken out in small pox pustules, and several passengers had taken sick. The ill were put ashore, and the virus spread among the local Indians. About this time three Arikara women took passage upstream to return to their tribe, which had recently moved in among the Mandans and Hidatsas. By the time the vessel reached the Dakota agency at the mouth of the Big Sioux River three weeks later, the women were recovering from a mild strain of the virus, but the infection was still aboard. Trade goods left with the agency carried the virus among the Dakotas living nearby.

The *St. Peter's* docked at Fort Clark on June 19. François Chardon, a clerk in the fort, visited the boat but reported no sign of disease. The three Arikara women, seemingly recovered but still capable of transmitting the disease, disappeared into the Indian village. The boat departed for Fort Union the next day, and by the time it reached that agency, the virus had struck more passengers and crew. The epidemic spread to the Assiniboines and Blackfeet living in the vicinity and brought wholesale death. The captain of the *St. Peter's* put his sick people ashore and hurried back to St. Louis. He paused at Fort Clark on the way for only an hour to take on wood. Fulkerson remained on board and did not take up his duties at the Mandan agency.

On July 14 a "young Mandan" (Chardon's description) died in the village, and the epidemic spread like wildfire through the crowded and filthy Indian villages. Chardon recorded a dozen more deaths within a few days, and by the end of September the Mandan tribe, with seven-eighths of its people dead, had virtually ceased to exist. News of the plague reached St. Louis late in the year and prompted government inquiries and journalistic speculation. Legends finding the white man to blame have echoed in history books ever since. The legends rely primarily on a "blanket incident" recorded by Fulkerson after his return to his home in St. Louis. In a report sent to William Clark, Indian superintendent at St. Louis, Fulkerson claimed that the small pox was introduced to Fort Clark through a blanket stolen by an Indian from an infected crewman on the boat.[2]

The problem with the "blanket" explanation is timing. Death from small pox almost always occurs within eight to ten days after the onset of the disease. The death of the "young Mandan" occurred almost a month after the *St. Peter's* first docked at the fort. Moreover, Chardon went aboard the vessel at that time and found no evidence of sickness. A stolen blanket may indeed have played a role in the epidemic, but it could not account for the rapid spread of the disease among several villages. A more likely agency was the three Arikara women, recovering from a mild form of the disease but still infectious, as they wandered in search of their homes.

The U.S. commissioner for Indian affairs estimated that at least 17,200 of the Plains Indians died in the epidemic. As in 1780 the Dakotas were the least affected because of their nomadic lifestyle. By this time the Teton Sioux in particular lived far enough west of the Missouri that they had almost no contact with the Indians along the river. It was the village-dwelling river tribes who were the most devastated. The surviving Mandans, numbering only about sixty, merged with the Hidatsas and Arikaras, each of whom had suffered more than 50 percent losses. Within a few years the separate tribal identities of the three groups fused into one, and when the army set up the reservation system, the group docilely moved onto one at Fort Berthold, North Dakota, where their descendants remain today.

CHAPTER FIVE

From "Desert" to Gold Mine

Although for the past thirty years mapmakers had written "Great American Desert" across the Great Plains—a result of disparaging reports by military explorers in the 1820s—pioneers who had reached the valleys of the Big Sioux and Red Rivers in the 1850s knew that there was good land and adequate rainfall in the prairies immediately to the west. The lands along the Red River had already been settled by people of mixed Indian and white genes, known as Metis. The Metis were the product of mixed marriages, which had long been a feature of the fur trade. Both French voyageurs and British agents of the Northwest Company who wintered in the Indian country found that taking an Indian wife cemented exchanges with members of her tribe and provided them with much-valued helpmeets. An Indian wife not only taught her husband the customs and language of her people but she also provided him with dressed furs and such Indian garb as moccasins and snowshoes. Their children, Metis, tended to enter the fur trade and thus provided a new generation of mediators between eastern merchants and western tribesmen. When, after 1800, the furs became depleted in the lakes and rivers north of Lake Superior, the Metis moved into the Red River Valley south of Lake Winnipeg. Some remained in the fur trade, manning the canoes that carried the furs north along the river route that led to the British trading posts on Hudson Bay, but most became part-time farmers and buffalo hunters.

The southernmost—and perhaps the largest—Metis community on the Red River was Pembina, on the 49th parallel, which in 1818 became the boundary between the United States and Canada. By that date the settlement had a population of three hundred and boasted a Hudson Bay Company trading post. After a boundary survey the following year determined that Pembina lay within the United States, the company moved its trading post north to Fort Garry on the lower Red River. Deprived of access to a fur market, the Pembina settlers turned to farming and hunting. The prairies immediately to the west of the settlement teemed with buffalo, and over the next twenty years Pembina became the center of the buffalo hunt for the Metis of the entire Red River Valley.

As already noted, the Canadian and American West had largely become trapped out of fur-bearing animals by 1830. Providentially the shortage of furs coincided with a change in European fashion in men's hats. Silk from the Orient replaced beaver felt, and the price of beaver pelts fell dramatically. As a result of these twin events the Hudson Bay Company posts north of the border and the American Fur Company posts on the Missouri River dealt almost exclusively in buffalo hides after 1830. Although the hides had previously been regarded as of limited market value, easterners, in the course of the ensuing decade, discovered the value of buffalo robes as cold-weather covering. Eastern tanners converted the hides into robes for use in sleighs, as well as bedding, boots, and shoes. As a result, prime hides—those taken in winter when the animals' hair was thickest—fetched good prices in eastern markets such as New York and Montreal. At St. Louis a buffalo hide sold for about six dollars in the 1830s.

The Metis hunted buffalo in the summer for meat and in the winter for their hides. Regardless of the season buffalo cows were the preferred prey. Their meat was more tender (unless starving, the Plains Indians ate only the tongues of bulls), and their hides were more easily cured. The hunters had firearms, but these were clumsy, muzzle-loading weapons that fired a round lead ball. The inveterate traveler, Prince Maximillian, was dismayed when his party of mounted white hunters fired twenty bullets into a bull buffalo before it finally fell. He described the Indian method of shooting with considerable admiration:

> The Half Breed and the Indians are so skillful in this kind of hunting on horseback that they seldom have to fire several times at a buffalo. They do not put the gun to their shoulder, but extend both arms, and fire in this unusual manner as soon as they are within ten or fifteen paces of the animal. They are incredibly quick in loading; for they put no wadding to the charge, but let the ball (of which they generally have several in their mouth) run down to the powder, where it sticks, and is immediately discharged. With this rapid mode of firing these hunters of the prairie soon make a terrible slaughter in a herd of buffaloes.

The Metis buffalo harvest involved entire families, who gathered in Pembina in June for the summer hunt and in November for the winter hunt. In summer the women dried the buffalo meat for storage or made it into pemmican—bits of dried meat and berries held together by melted fat and stored in a bag fashioned from the animal's bladder. In winter the women cured the hides for market by scraping off the remnant meat, drying them before a fire, and rubbing them with brain matter to soften them. The families traveled to the hunt by two-wheeled carts of local origin (the famed "Red River Carts"), and the vehicles also served to carry home the proceeds of the hunt. In the 1820s each hunt that gathered in Pembina comprised five or six hundred carts; by the end of the 1830s that number had risen to a thousand.

Prior to 1840 the only market for buffalo hides, even for the American Metis at Pembina, was through the Hudson Bay Company's post at Fort Garry. The company's monopoly was broken, however, in 1844 when Pierre Chouteau's St. Louis trading company, which had dominated the Missouri River fur trade, opened a post at Pembina. Chouteau's company sent the buffalo hides overland to St. Paul using Red River carts. It was thus able to offer better prices for buffalo hides than the British company because its route to eastern markets was much shorter and its traveling season longer. As a result, it even attracted Metis hunters from the Canadian side of the border. The number of Red River carts traveling from Pembina to St. Paul increased from a mere 6 in 1844 to more than 1,400 twenty years later. Increasingly involved in the buffalo trade and less dependent on farming, the Metis population spread west from Pembina and established year-round settlements on Spirit Lake and the Missouri River. Thus when the first white pioneers reached the Red River Valley in the 1850s, they found the northern Dakota prairie peopled with scattered settlements but scarcely farmed. White pioneers, however, were reluctant to take up farming until the government cleared the Indian title.

Strangely enough, farmers were not the primary force urging government action. The impetus instead came from two groups of businessmen—railroad promoters and townsite speculators.

The Dakota Land Boom

In 1851 the federal government negotiated the Treaty of Fort Laramie with the Indians of the northern plains. The primary purpose of the treaty was to secure the safe passage of pioneers along the Oregon Trail, but the treaty also included a clause by which the Dakotas allowed a railroad to be built across their country. Over the next several years engineers, sent out by the governor of the Washington Territory, explored the region west of the Red River, looking for a suitable route for a railroad that would run from St. Paul to the mouth of the Columbia River. Members of the Minnesota Territorial Legislature became so excited about the wealth that railroads and settlement would bring to the Red River Valley that they spent much of their time granting charters to railroad and land companies and creating paper townsites. Commenting on the speculative mania that raged in St. Paul, a witty skeptic urged "that a small portion of the land be reserved for agriculture and not all be laid out in town lots."

In 1855 the U.S. Army abetted the railroad promoters by purchasing Fort Pierre from Pierre Chouteau and Company and turning it into a military garrison. In that same year the state of Iowa (itself only nine years old) founded Sioux City at the junction of the Big Sioux River and the Missouri. A year later the army established another military stronghold, Fort Randall, on the west bank of the Missouri about halfway between Sioux City and Pierre. By that date the impetus for townsite planning and railroad building had shifted from the Red River south to the Big Sioux and the Missouri.

The most important of the new townsite entrepreneurs was John Blair Smith Todd, a West Point graduate and member of a prominent Kentucky family (he was a cousin of Abraham Lincoln's wife, Mary Todd Lincoln). A member of the expeditionary force that had first occupied Fort Pierre and subsequently stationed at Fort Randall, Todd recognized the potential for white settlement along the Missouri River Valley. In 1856 he resigned his captaincy, formed a trading company in partnership with a St. Louis merchant, and secured the post of sutler to Fort Randall. A year later Todd learned that the federal government was negotiating with the Yankton Sioux for the cession of the triangle of land between the Big Sioux and the Missouri Rivers. Minnesota was then moving toward statehood with a proposed western boundary of the Red and Big Sioux Rivers. It was obvious to Todd that the Indian cession would thus be part of a new federal territory with land and townsite claims to be had for the taking. Todd quickly made himself the most prominent advocate of the treaty, and when the negotiations broke down, the Department of the Interior asked Todd to intercede.

In February 1855, with the help of two Frenchmen of mixed blood who were trusted by the Yanktons, Todd persuaded the Indians to sign a treaty ceding 14 million acres of land at the price of twelve cents an acre. Government payments would take the form of annuities (annual shipments of trade goods), tools and wagons needed for farming, and the establishment of Indian schools. While the treaty lay before the U.S. Senate awaiting ratification, Todd and his French partners organized the Upper Missouri Land Company to speculate in townsites. By the time the Senate ratified the treaty in April, the company's agents had identified and laid claim to eight sites, including Yankton, near the junction of the James River with the Missouri, which Todd hoped to make the capital of the yet-to-be-formed territory. On the day that news of ratification arrived, company agents floated logs across the river from the Nebraska shore and laid the foundations for twelve cabins on lots laid out by company surveyors.

Minnesota became a state in the course of that year, leaving the vast region west of the Big Sioux, rapidly filling with pioneers and speculators (the distinction between the two being quite blurred), without any government. Todd spent the winter of 1858–59 in Washington DC, lobbying for the creation of a new territory, upon which there was general agreement only on a name — "Dakota."

Dakota Territory

In 1858 Democrat James Buchanan was president, and Democrats controlled both houses of Congress. Southerners were the dominant voice in both the administration and Congress. As a result, whenever a group of westerners petitioned Congress for territorial organization — in addition to Dakota, the mining communities of Colorado and Nevada were seeking territorial status — southerners brought up the question of slavery. Because the westerners had no slaves, nor any interest in acquiring some, the petitions died in congressional committees.

Despite the governmental vacuum, town-building continued apace in the Missouri Valley. While Todd's land company was promoting the growth of Yankton, emigrants from Nebraska erected a store and a few houses at the junction of the Vermillion River with the Missouri, approximately halfway between Yankton and Sioux City. Between Yankton and this new community, Vermillion, a few Norwegian families took up farming in the summer of 1858. Norwegian emigrants soon joined them, driven from the old country—as the Irish had been—by the potato famine that engulfed much of Western Europe.

The biggest threat to John Todd's political ambitions and scheme to make Yankton the territorial capital was a settlement of Minnesota emigrants at Sioux Falls, some sixty miles northeast of Yankton on the Big Sioux River. The Minnesota Territorial Assembly had chartered the Dakota Land Company of St. Paul in 1857. The governor of the Minnesota Territory, a Democrat, was a director of the company, and many of the stockholders were Democratic members of the assembly. The company thus hoped to capitalize on the Democrats' control of the federal government to ease the establishment of a Dakota Territory with a Democratic governor and all the patronage that would entail. Besides government offices, the stockholders expected to profit from town building and railroad promotion. The company established a townsite at Sioux Falls in the fall of 1857, and speculators began buying up town lots. When Minnesota became a state the following year, Congress established its western boundary on a line of longitude from a point on the Minnesota River to the Iowa border. Because the line was a few miles east of the Big Sioux (though the lower boundary between Dakota and Iowa followed the river), the community of Sioux Falls fell within the as-yet-unorganized Dakota territory.

Confident of support from Minnesota's congressmen in 1859, the inhabitants of Sioux Falls, numbering no more than fifty, held an election for a territorial assembly. Committees from the town roamed the empty countryside casting fictitious ballots, so that the vote ultimately ran into the hundreds. The "squatter assembly" met during the autumn and elected a provisional governor of the Dakota "territory."

Adding to the assembly's claim of representing the inhabitants of Dakota was the presence of a few delegates from Pembina, the oldest of the Dakota settlements (a fur-trading post since 1819) on the Red River. Pembina's population of five hundred, about evenly divided between the Minnesota and Dakota sides of the river boundary, were mostly mixed-blood Metis. In addition to being commercially dependent on St. Paul, to which they sent buffalo skins and other frontier products, they had some hope, however slim, of becoming a river crossing point for a railroad running from St. Paul to the Pacific Coast. They thus sent petitions of their own for territorial status (in French, unfortunately, which few congressmen could read) and cooperated with Sioux Falls' grandiloquent pretensions.

Although it never received recognition from the Buchanan administration, the "squatter assembly" at Sioux Falls met periodically into 1860, passing laws that it had no way of enforcing. The assembly—and indeed the ambition of Sioux Falls to become capital of the territory—was doomed by the Republican victory in the election of 1860. The secession of the Lower South in the weeks following Lincoln's election left Republicans in control of Congress even before Lincoln was inaugurated as president. And that broke the logjam that had left Dakota, Colorado, and Nevada in governmental limbo.

Furthering democracy was not the only, nor even the most important, motive for erecting territories in the West. Since 1856 Republican platforms had endorsed the idea of giving away the public lands in 160-acre parcels to settlers who would actually live on them and farm them (thus the term "Homestead Act"). The plan was part of the Republicans' appeal (important in the early years of the party) to farmers and factory workers. The establishment of territorial governments was further inducement to the eastern poor to take up farms in the West, and with the Democratic Party dominated by southern aristocrats, it was a near certainty that western farmers would vote Republican. Significantly the most ardent advocate for the territorial organic acts of 1861, Representative Galusha Grow of Pennsylvania, was also the "father of the Homestead Act" of 1862. Other proponents of the organic acts were Republican congressmen committed to the construction of transcontinental railroads, whether following the central route from Omaha to San Francisco or the northern route from St. Paul to the Columbia River. Government for security and settlers as customers were vital to the success of any railroad across the plains.

On February 26, 1861 — a scant week before Lincoln was inaugurated president — bills were introduced into the Senate organizing the Dakota, Colorado, and Nevada territories. They contained no reference to slavery. Avoidance of that cantankerous issue eased their passage, to the satisfaction of Republicans. The remaining Democrats in Congress were likewise satisfied, for it meant that the people of the territories would themselves decide the issue, a position that the Democratic leader Stephen A. Douglas had been championing for a decade. The bills slipped through both houses with a minimum of debate and became law on March 1. Some have considered the Republicans' seeming acceptance of "popular sovereignty" a conciliatory effort to save the Union, but partisan motives were more likely — that is, the electoral debts owed to emigrant farmers seeking free land and to eastern financiers seeking governmental support for a transcontinental railroad.

President Lincoln ignored John Todd's political ambitions, fearing perhaps that to name Todd governor would leave himself open to a charge of nepotism. Lincoln's choice for

11. The Capitol of Dakota Territory in Yankton. The original
structure burned in 1883, and this replica currently resides in
Riverside Park. Photo by author.

governor of the Dakota Territory was instead Dr. William
Jayne, his neighbor and family physician in Springfield who
was also the brother-in-law of Illinois's powerful Republican
senator, Lyman Trumbull. Adopting the "spoils system" pioneered by Andrew Jackson, Lincoln filled the other territorial offices—secretary, attorney general, judges—with young
men who were protégés or relatives of influential members
of the Republican Party. Most of these ambitious young men
regarded the posts as mere stepping-stones to political ad-
vancement; some did not bother to journey to the territory. The citizenry consequently treated the territorial government with well-merited indifference.

Not knowing where the territorial capital might be located, Lincoln's appointees gathered in Sioux City, Iowa. There
in May 1861 they learned that Governor Jayne had chosen

Yankton as capital—at the request, it was rumored, of Mrs. Lincoln that he favor "Captain Todd's town." When the officials traipsed ashore at Yankton's steamboat landing, they found a community of fewer than three hundred souls living in log cabins. Most were young men engaged in buying and selling town lots or seeking government office. The principal building, located on Broadway, the town's main street, was the Ash Hotel, where one could obtain the rudiments of frontier existence—a bed, whiskey, and a meal prepared by the wife of the hotel's proprietor. The hotel's "rooms" were actually semiprivate compartments of a large hall subdivided by blankets and skins. Outside of the hotel lodging was so scarce that Governor Jayne had to share a bed with the attorney general for the first six months.

As so often happened in territorial politics, the principal issue before the first legislature, when it met in early 1862, was the choice of a permanent capital. Sioux Falls, Pembina, and Vermillion challenged Yankton for the honor. Moses Armstrong, a Minnesota émigré who would become leader of the Democratic opposition in Dakota, wrote that "excitement ran to a high pitch during a few days on the last stages of the bill" to make Yankton the permanent capital. "A little blood was shed, much whiskey drunk, a few eyes blacked, revolvers drawn, and some running done." A coup to move the capital to Vermillion was turned aside, local factions realigned themselves, and Yankton remained the capital.

The Civil War, which had begun with the firing on Fort Sumter in April 1861, had little immediate impact on the Dakota Territory. In the fall of 1861 Governor Jayne established three recruiting stations in the territory, and a total of seventy-two Dakotans enlisted that winter. They mustered at Yankton just as the army regulars, who had been manning the frontier forts, were sent to the Union army

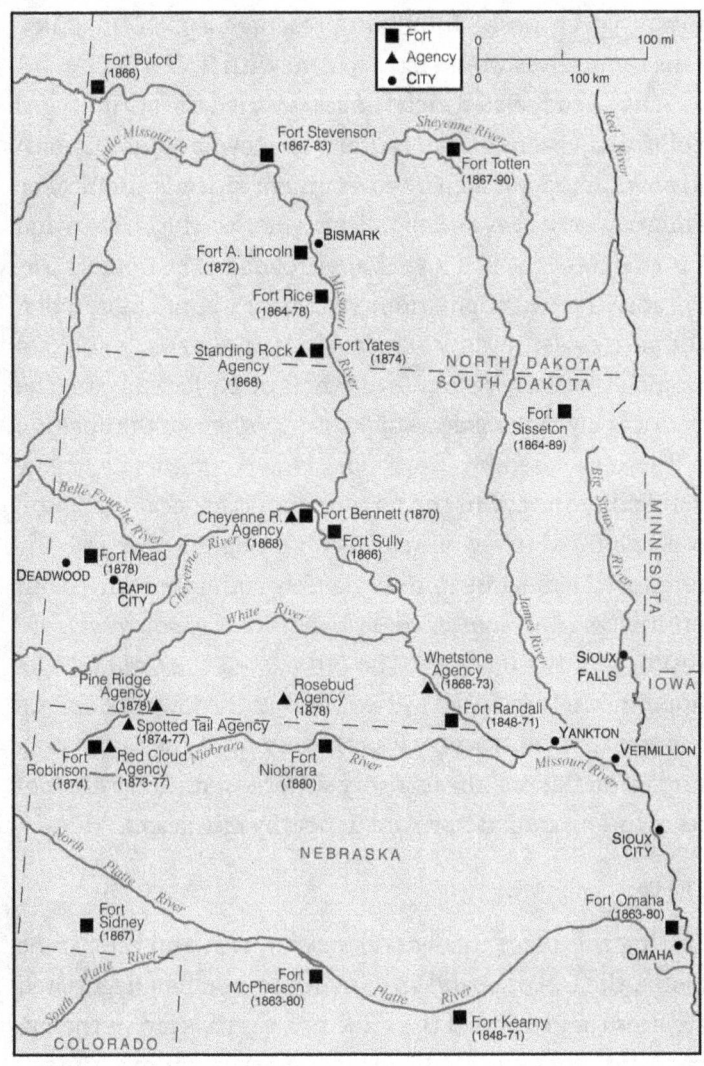

Map 8. The northern plains in the mid-nineteenth century.

invading Tennessee. If Indians presented a problem, Dakotans themselves would have to deal with it.

Slavery and related racial issues revealed the beginning of political divisions in the territory. The towns of the Missouri River Valley, populated by government officials and Yankee émigrés, were heavily Republican, whereas the farmers and fur traders of the Red River Valley tended to be Democratic. Because the two populations were nearly equal in number, the parties were evenly matched in 1861–62, though Dakota would eventually become overwhelmingly Republican. The political division made its appearance when, at the opening of the 1862 assembly, Governor Jayne recommended a law abolishing slavery in the territory, an issue that was purely academic since no one had as yet brought a slave into the territory. Democrats in the assembly countered with a bill prohibiting "persons of color," whether slave or free, from residing in the territory. The bill passed the Council (the upper house) but failed by two votes in the lower house. Although that controversy was the extent of the Civil War's impact on Dakota, the territory suffered a military crisis of its own—an Indian uprising in nearby Minnesota.

The First Sioux War

During the 1850s the federal government and the Santee Sioux, the Dakota band still in Minnesota, had negotiated treaties that confined the tribe to a reservation in the upper Minnesota River Valley. Under pressure from white settlers the government gradually reduced the size of the reserve and pushed the Indians onto the arid prairies at the source of the river. Discontent over this series of seeming betrayals reached the flashpoint when the federal government, distracted by the war in the East, failed to provide promised trade goods annuities and food supplies. Led by one of the most respected Dakota chiefs, Little Crow, the Indians attacked settlers' farms throughout the river valley, overran and massacred the inhabitants of one Indian agency, and laid siege to the town of New Ulm. Although the governor of Minnesota, with help from the U.S. Army, suppressed the uprising and hanged thirty-eight of its leaders, repercussions of the fight rattled across the Dakota prairies for the next two years.

Although the Yanktons living in the Dakota Territory remained neutral, the Santees, fleeing the military repression in Minnesota, raided farms in the Big Sioux and Red River Valleys on their way to refuge on the high plains. Upon learning of the attack on New Ulm, the residents of Sioux Falls abandoned their town altogether and fled to the Missouri River settlements. The Indians moved in and burned most of the buildings. Yankton built a sod fort and a stockade to serve as refuge in case of Indian attack, and every man went about his business armed with a rifle. To reinforce the military presence in Minnesota and Dakota, the War Department created a Department of the Northwest in September 1862 and placed in command General John Pope, recently dismissed commander of the Army of the Potomac.[1]

The Indian raids also discouraged new settlers from moving to the Dakota prairies, and Iowa's colonizing agencies did their best to further depreciate Dakota's reputation. In early 1863 Moses Armstrong, serving as the assembly Speaker, wrote that "a crazy panic has fallen upon the Norwegian settlement, and many are loading their teams to leave the territory." He begged the army to send a detachment "*immediately* to steady the nerves of the people and prevent an impending stampede." General Pope's helpful advice to the War Department was to prohibit settlement in Dakota until the Indian problem had been solved.

In the summer of 1863 General Pope devised a pincer strategy to capture the Santees who continued to harass the Dakota settlements. General Henry H. Sibley, the Minnesota politician-turned-military-commander who had pursued the Santees as far as the headwaters of the Red River, was ordered to continue westward to the Missouri. Pope ordered General Alfred Sully to proceed up the Missouri from Fort Pierre and intercept the retreating Indians. Low water held up Sully's advance until September, however, and in the meantime Sibley fought a few minor skirmishes, reached the river, and returned to Minnesota. In early September Sully learned that a band of migrating Santees was in the valley of the James River south of Sibley's route. He marched his force of 2,200 northeastward from Pierre and fought a bloody battle with the Indians at Whitestone Hill (near present-day Ellendale, North Dakota). The remaining Santees fled to their brethren west of the Missouri or crossed into Canada. The following spring, 1864, General Sully led an expedition up the Missouri as far as the mouth of the Yellowstone River and established a line of military outposts to ensure peace and protect river traffic.

The reaction of whites in Dakota to the military expeditions was mixed. They were initially outraged when they learned that General Pope's quartermasters had purchased supplies for Sully's expeditions in Sioux City, Iowa, rather than in the Dakota communities, and they fretted about the image of Dakota as a war-torn territory. The expeditions, on the other hand, greatly increased steamboat traffic on the Missouri, and farmers in the vicinity of the new military posts eagerly sought contracts to supply them with beef, pork, and cornmeal. In 1865 Congress appropriated funds to build three roads into the territory—military roads, in theory, but of vast economic importance in opening new lands away from the rivers. Little growth could be expected, however, until the Indian warfare was brought formally to an end. That was the task to which Governor Newton Edmunds set himself.

Edmunds was a New England Yankee who had come to Dakota as a clerk in the office of the territory's surveyor general, George Hill. Technically in charge of land surveys, Hill had turned his office into a real estate sales agency with himself as chief beneficiary. Through colorful speeches and pamphlets Hill also undertook to persuade the outside world that Dakota was quite habitable. Using Hill's influence as a springboard, Edmunds made friends of Dakota's federal officials, including Governor Jayne. Aiming for the governorship in 1863, when Jayne, who preferred Washington to Yankton, was elected territorial delegate, Edmunds capitalized on the residents' desire for a governor who was an actual resident of the territory. After Jayne wrote a glowing recommendation to both President Lincoln and Senator Trumbull, Lincoln named Edmunds as Jayne's successor in March 1863.

In messages to the assembly in 1864 and 1865 Edmunds denounced military campaigns against the Indians as expensive and ineffective; worse—they gave Dakota a bad name and impeded settlement. Edmunds also benefited from a division of opinion in Washington regarding whether the Indian question should be handled "peacefully" by the Interior Department or "militarily" by the War Department. The Democratic-led assembly, which supported Edmunds's demands for tribal peace, created a Peace Commission and named Moses Armstrong its secretary. After General Sully's second expedition failed to punish—or even find—any hostile Indians, the army gave Edmunds and Armstrong permission to talk to the Indians in October 1865. Edmunds summoned a council of the various Dakota bands—Yanktons, Brules, Oglalas, Miniconjous—more than sixteen thousand Indians in all. By the ensuing treaty the Indians agreed to cease hostilities, not impede the overland trails, and eventually settle on reservations.[2] That agreement brought peace to the Dakota frontier for nearly a decade (until gold was discovered in the Black Hills), and with war drums silent, the flow of emigrants resumed. By 1870 the population of the territory stood at fourteen thousand. Good rains and crop yields in 1868–70 also helped, but the main impetus to both population growth and economic growth was the arrival of the railroads.

Iron Rails across the Plains

The idea of a transcontinental railroad that would tie the nation together from Atlantic to Pacific had percolated in Congress throughout the 1850s. The choice of a route from the Mississippi Valley to the West, however, became embroiled in the sectional rivalry. Secession of the South in 1861 removed that obstacle, and in 1862 Congress chartered the Union Pacific Railroad to build a line west from Omaha, which, it was anticipated, would itself soon be connected by rail to Chicago and thence to the East Coast. To subsidize construction of a rail line through territory then inhabited only by Indians and a few gold miners, Congress gave the railroad title to alternate sections (much like a checkerboard) of public lands to a distance of ten miles on each side of the roadway. It also gave the railroad $16,000 in U.S. bonds for every mile of track completed.

Congress was even more generous two years later when it chartered the Northern Pacific Railroad to build a line on a more northerly route from Lake Superior to the north Pacific coast, letting the railroad choose between the mouth of the Columbia River and Puget Sound. It granted the railroad alternate sections of public lands to a distance of twenty miles on each side of the track in the state of Minnesota and forty miles in the territories to the west. When the Northern Pacific finally "proved up" its claims in the 1870s, it found itself in possession of nearly 25 percent of all the land in North Dakota. The railroad received title to the land, however, only after it had earned it by laying track. Obtaining financing for construction took time, and it was six years before the Northern Pacific began putting down track across Minnesota.

In the meantime the Chicago and North Western line, relying on the support of local communities that wanted rail service instead of a federal land grant, was the first to reach the Dakota Territory. In expectation of becoming the link between Chicago and the Union Pacific terminus at Omaha, the North Western built a line across Iowa to Council Bluffs. It then sent a spur north along the Missouri River to Sioux City, reaching that river port in 1868. The arrival of a railroad in Sioux City created much excitement in the Dakota Territory, and the legislature promptly chartered a number of railroad companies to build a line up the river valley from Sioux City to Yankton. Most companies existed only on paper, but by 1871 the Dakota Southern became the first to obtain enough eastern capital to begin construction. On the board of directors of the Dakota Southern were several public officials, including ex-governor Edmunds and Delegate Moses Armstrong, who received shares of stock in exchange for their influence. After the Dakota Southern reached Yankton in early 1873, it was discovered that the road had been funded primarily by bonds issued by Yankton County, putting the county in debt without the citizens' knowledge, and the ensuing legal controversies dampened further local investment in railroads. The Dakota Southern was eventually taken over by the North Western, which extended the line up the river to Bismarck in the mid-1870s.

In 1870 the land-rich, capital-shy Northern Pacific finally found a financial angel in Jay Cooke, a Philadelphia banker who had helped finance the Civil War by marketing the bonds of the federal government. By that date the railroad's exploration parties had settled on Duluth (where Cooke had a substantial investment in city lots) as the eastern terminal, and both the Columbia River and Puget Sound as the western terminals. Determining that the railroad's land grant provided a good basis for credit, Cooke issued to the Northern Pacific a $100 million land grant mortgage payable in thirty years. Cooke in return received Northern Pacific bonds in this amount, which he planned to sell to investors in Europe, as well as Philadelphia and New York.

Armed with this capital, the Northern Pacific purchased a half interest in a rail line being built between Duluth and St. Paul and began construction from a station on that line, some twenty miles west of Duluth. With ample rock and timber from its right-of-way and a steady supply of steel rails from both Duluth and St. Paul the Northern Pacific reached the Red River in the spring of 1872. Its terminus was named Fargo in honor of one of its directors, who had been prominent in prewar western stagecoaching. On June 7 the first steam locomotive to enter the Dakota Territory crossed the river on a wooden trestle. Construction went rapidly across the Dakota prairie, and by the time winter snows halted work, the line was a mere thirty miles from the Missouri River.

The line was extended to the Missouri and opened to rail traffic on June 4, 1873, and freight traveled from there by steamboat to the Montana Territory. The directors named the rail terminal on the east bank of the Missouri "Bismarck" in honor of the chancellor of Germany and in hopes of attracting German immigrants to the railroad's lands. Only a week after construction reached the Missouri, a survey team departed from the village of Mandan on the west bank of the river to explore a route to the Montana border. Because the government had promised the western railroads protection from the Indians, the survey team had a heavy escort of ten companies of infantry, nineteen companies of cavalry, and eighty-five Indian scouts. Starting at the Heart River opposite Bismarck, the survey followed that stream and its tributaries into the North Dakota Badlands. They found a suitable crossing for the Little Missouri River and then halted the survey, some 205 miles west of Bismarck.

At that point disaster struck. The Franco-Prussian War, which broke out in the very year that Jay Cooke had agreed to finance construction of the Northern Pacific, disrupted Europe's financial system and blasted any hope that Cooke had of selling railroad bonds on the Continent. At the same time the capital demands of other railroad and factory construction made it difficult for him to market Northern Pacific bonds in New York and Philadelphia. With debt mounting due to the railroad's construction costs, uneasy depositors began withdrawing funds. On September 18, 1873, the banking house of Jay Cooke and Company, the nation's largest, declared bankruptcy. Its downfall triggered a panic on the Stock Exchange—which came to be known as the Panic of 1873—and banks across the company closed their doors. It was the most widespread financial disaster in the nation's history to that time, and the ensuing depression lasted for nearly the rest of the decade. Construction of the Northern Pacific, which itself went into receivership, ceased for the next four years.

The Black Hills Gold Rush

The one segment of the Dakota Territory that prospered through the depression of the mid-1870s was the Black Hills. Lying just to the west of the South Dakota Badlands, the pine-covered hills seemed black to early explorers, and thus their name. The westward migrating Dakota bands deemed the hills sacred (though they themselves had reached the hills little more than a half-century earlier) and discouraged white pioneers from entering them. As a result, the hills became the subject of rumors and legends, many of which involved the prospect of gold, especially since gold had been discovered in other mountainous regions of the West. After 1868, when the hills became part of a "permanent" Dakota reservation (which extended from the Missouri River to the Big Horn Mountains of Wyoming), the army prohibited exploration parties from entering the hills. That did not stop individual prospectors from following streams into the hills with equipment-laden donkeys, however, and tales of gold strikes circulated throughout the country.

In the summer of 1874 the government sought to stifle the speculation by sending a scientific expedition to explore the hills and report on any mineral wealth. Accompanying the scientists was a force of 1,200 men from the Seventh Cavalry Regiment, commanded by Lieutenant Colonel George Armstrong Custer. The expedition left Fort Abraham Lincoln (near Bismarck) on July 2 with a supply train of 110 wagons and 300 cattle. Custer was so enchanted by the beauty of the hills and their potential for cattle ranching that he lost sight of the purpose of the expedition, which was to produce an essentially negative report that would discourage settlement. He became particularly excited when his men discovered flakes of gold in French Creek in the southern part of the hills. (The mining camp that sprang up along the creek was later named Custer City in the colonel's honor.) Upon his return to Bismarck on August 22 Custer reported that his men had found gold "in numerous localities that are termed gulches," and he had reason to believe that the hillsides contained veins of gold-laden quartz.

With that dramatic announcement the rush was on. Overnight Yankton and Sioux City became outfitting centers for goldseekers in need of wagons, mules, and camping equipment. Sidney, Nebraska, and Cheyenne, both stops on the Union Pacific, also became centers for stocking expeditions into the hills. Miners coming from the gold fields in the West were forced to organize for protection as the Dakota tribes of Montana and Wyoming harassed the expeditions and killed any miner found alone. Ignoring the Indians for the moment, the army made sporadic efforts through 1875 to evict the prospectors from the hills. It stationed a company of infantry and two of cavalry at Custer City, but the miners simply crept into hidden valleys and continued their prospecting. In November President Ulysses S. Grant, recognizing that army deserters were adding to the ranks of prospectors, ordered the army to withdraw. By the end of the year the population of the Black Hills had reached an estimated fifteen thousand.

Some time in the late autumn of 1875 a party of prospectors found a bounty of gold flakes in the sands of Whitewood Creek in the northern part of the hills, and a new rush was underway. Custer City became virtually a ghost town in a matter of days. The creek valley was choked with fallen trees, likely the result of a windstorm, and the mining camp that sprang up there was given the name of Deadwood. By the early summer of 1876 the population of the valley numbered several thousand. The town itself had more than a

12. Deadwood in 1876. Photo courtesy of the State Archives of the South Dakota State Historical Society.

hundred stores and taverns, many of them operating out of tents. Among the goldseekers thronging into Deadwood in the summer of 1876 were two of the most famous figures in western lore, "Wild Bill" Hickok and "Calamity Jane."

The "Dead Man's Hand"

His parents christened him James Butler Hickok when he entered this world on May 27, 1837, the fourth of seven children. The Hickoks were Illinois farmers, and at age nineteen James went to Kansas to try his own hand at farming. Farm routine failed to satisfy his longing for adventure, and in 1859 he joined the gold rush to Pike's Peak in Colorado. During the Civil War he was employed by the army as wagonmaster and scout, tasked with chasing Confederate guerillas through Missouri and Arkansas. He earned a reputation as an expert shot with a pistol and apparently caused enough grief among southern sympathizers that some pursued him even after the fighting ended.

On July 27, 1865, the Springfield, Missouri, newspaper, the *Weekly Patriot*, reported that Hickok had killed one David Tutt in a duel in the town square, noting that Hickok was known in southwest Missouri as "Wild Bill." This was the first public reference to his famed nickname. The sobriquet seems to have been applied throughout the West to almost anyone handy with a gun. Hickok's biographer, Joseph G. Rosa, has counted more than thirty "Wild Bills" in the West prior to 1870. Although there is no evidence that Hickok personally sought fame or notoriety (unlike "Buffalo Bill" Cody), the legend makers of magazines and dime novels found his occasional gunfights irresistible. The lead article in the February 1867 issue of *Harper's New Monthly Magazine* was titled "Wild Bill." The author was Colonel George Ward Nichols, who had purportedly ridden with Hickok during the war. Though highly colored and largely fictional, the article made Hickok's name known throughout the West. The man and the myth thereafter became almost inseparable.

The writers of dime novels who elaborated the Hickok legend in the last quarter of the nineteenth century claimed that he had killed more than a hundred men in gunfights. Joseph Rosa has found a written record of no more than ten, and in most cases Hickok was acting in self-defense. A year after his duel in the public square in Springfield, Hickok was involved in a gunfight in Nebraska in which two men died. He was indicted for manslaughter, but the jury concluded he had acted in self-defense. In 1869, while serving as acting sheriff of Hays City, Kansas, Hickok killed a man who was shooting up the town. Two years later, in April 1871, Abilene, Kansas—the wildest of the early "cow towns"—made him city marshal, with apparently a carte

13. "Wild Bill" Hickok. Photo courtesy of the State Archives of the South Dakota State Historical Society.

blanche to maintain peace. A few months later he shot and killed two Texas cowboys who had challenged him, and that was his last known gunfight. The following December, after the Texas cattle trail riders had all gone home, the city fathers of Abilene replaced Hickok with a less combative lawman. He surfaced again in 1873–74 as part of Buffalo Bill Cody's touring company, "Scouts of the Plains," a cast that included eight "Sioux Indians." Hickok proved to be a poor actor, however, and disliked living out of a suitcase. By 1875 he was in and around Cheyenne, where he was remembered as a quiet, gentlemanly fellow who frequented the gambling halls.

For several years Hickok had maintained a correspondence with Agnes Lake Thatcher, whom he had first met in Abilene when she passed through the town as part of a theater troupe. The two were married in St. Louis in March 1876, and after a brief honeymoon Hickok returned to Cheyenne with intent to join the gold rush to the Black Hills. In June he joined a party that was headed for Deadwood. In addition to prospectors, the party included gamblers, saloon keepers, and fourteen "ladies of easy virtue." At a roadside "ranch," which offered camping facilities, a bar, and dancing, another "easy lady" joined the party. She also had the ability to drive a team of mules as well as any man, "with a black snake whip and lots of cussing," according to western storytellers. She was called Calamity Jane.

Her name was actually Martha Canary, born in rural Missouri in 1856. In 1864 her family joined the rush to the newly discovered gold fields of Montana. Her mother died two years later and her father a year after that. Martha was thus orphaned at the age of twelve, far removed from relatives, friends, or a comforting childhood environment. She grew up wandering and begging through the Union Pacific railroad towns of Wyoming. In this environment she became a young woman of lax morals with an addiction to alcohol. It is not clear when she earned the nickname "Calamity Jane," but the source of it is rather simple. "Jane" was a generic word for females, as in "Jane Doe." In the West the appellation "Calamity" was conferred on anyone, man or woman, who drank heavily and grew loud, boisterous, and profane. In addition to Wyoming's Martha Canary, Nebraska, Colorado, and Montana each boasted a "Calamity Jane" of their own during the 1870s.

By the early 1870s Jane was working as a dance hall girl in the "road ranches" that sprang up along Wyoming's cattle trails. Never one to lay roots for long, she joined nearly every military or scientific expedition that passed up the trail, working as a teamster or cook. When accompanying an army expedition, she dressed as a man to avoid detection by the commander, no doubt with the complicity of some of the common soldiers. In the summer of 1876 the army decided to end the Indian harassment of the miners in the Black Hills. It sent two expeditions to drive the western Dakota bands back onto their reservations in Montana and Wyoming. One, commanded by George Custer (now with the brevet rank of major general), would meet disaster at the Little Big Horn on June 25. Martha joined the other expedition, commanded by General George Crook, which fought a band of Indians led by Crazy Horse at Rosebud Creek (a tributary of the Yellowstone in northern Wyoming) on June 17. Calamity Jane had been with the army a few days at the time of the battle, and after discovering her, General Crook sent her back to Laramie with the wounded after the battle. She encountered Hickok's expedition en route and promptly joined it, still garbed in male attire. When the party arrived in Deadwood on July 12, Hickok and others loaned her money to buy a dress so she could resume her calling as a dance hall girl. There is no evidence that the two were anything but casual acquaintances over the following three weeks.

On the afternoon of August 2 Hickok was playing poker with friends in Nuttall & Mann's Number 10 Saloon when

14. Calamity Jane. Photo courtesy of the State Archives of the South
Dakota State Historical Society.

he was shot through the back of the head by one Jack Mc-Call. Other than perhaps a desire by McCall for gunfighter fame, no one has ever ferreted out his motives. McCall fled the saloon and leaped onto a horse tethered outside. The saddle turned over and spilled him onto the street because the owner had loosened the cinch straps in the August heat. McCall was then arrested by an irate citizenry. Hickok had died instantly, but his friends were acute enough to observe the cards he held in his poker hand. It was two pairs, aces and eights, all black, known ever after as the "dead man's hand."[3]

The next day Hickok was buried under a tree at the edge of town. A large crowd attended, but no one mentioned the presence of Calamity Jane. In 1879, after the town established a public cemetery on Mount Moriah, Hickok's body was removed to that grave site, where it remains today, one of the major tourist attractions of the Black Hills. In the years after Hickok's death Calamity Jane got her alcoholism more or less under control and made a career of riding and shooting in Wild West shows. When she died in 1903, some Deadwood boosters, organized as the Society of Black Hills Pioneers, brought her to Deadwood and buried her on Mount Moriah next to Wild Bill Hickok. Legend triumphed in the end.

Jack McCall was tried for murder before a coroner's jury in Deadwood. The jury, apparently believing McCall's excuse that he was seeking revenge for a brother Hickok had killed in Kansas (for which there is no evidence in court records or newspapers), found him not guilty. McCall hastily departed for Wyoming, trailed by a friend of Hickok's, George May, who was furious at the verdict. In a tavern in Laramie, May heard McCall boast publicly that he had gotten away with Hickok's murder. May obtained a bench warrant, and a deputy U.S. marshal arrested McCall. He was taken to Yankton to be tried for murder in a U.S. district court.

The court had jurisdiction because the murder had occurred on an Indian reservation, and there was no double jeopardy because the Deadwood court had been illegitimate for the same reason. McCall was found guilty and hanged in Yankton on March 1, 1877.

The Mining Frontier

In 1877, while the high plains Dakota tribes were on the run following the Battle of the Little Big Horn (Crazy Horse surrendered that summer, and Sitting Bull fled to Canada), Siouan bands living in the Dakota Territory sold the Black Hills portion of their reservation to the federal government. The territorial government organized the hills into a new county, and the elected mining camp leaders in Custer City and Deadwood became municipal governments. Mining camp law, originating in European custom and honed in the lead mines of Missouri and Illinois and the gold fields of California, was now enshrined in federal and territorial statute. Under the law a group of prospectors could form a mining district, typically extending for two or three miles along a creek bed. The district could make up its own laws, providing they did not conflict with those of the territory. Individual claims, usually about one hundred yards in length, had to be clearly marked and recorded with an officer of the mining district.

The deposits of gold-bearing sand or gravel in a creek bed were called placers, and that became the name of the method of gold extraction as a mixture of water and sand was swirled in a shallow pan to separate the sand from the heavier gold. The flecks of gold were moved with a finger or moistened toothpick and stored in a leather bag, usually made from a bull's scrotum (cloth, no matter how fine the weave, was too porous to hold gold dust). The customary price of gold at the mines was twenty dollars an ounce, and miners treated their bags as money at that rate in exchanging them for groceries, tools, or liquor. Cooperating groups of miners increased the scale of production by using perforated boxes ("rockers") that could be rocked back and forth to separate the gold and increased their water supply with dams and sluices.

As in California, the surface wealth in the Black Hills was skimmed off within a year or so, and investors sought eastern capital to search for and mine the quartz lodes on the hillsides. Once a lode was discovered, the quartz vein was broken free with blasting powder and picks. The rocks were then sent to a mill where an eight-hundred-pound stamp pounded them into a powder that was washed through a fine sieve and then passed over copper tables smeared with mercury. The mercury held onto the gold flakes while the mud washed on. By the end of 1877 about three hundred stamp mills were operating in Deadwood and the surrounding area.

The largest and most productive of the Black Hills gold mines was the Homestake, some three miles southwest of Deadwood in another valley. The city that grew up around it was named Lead (pronounced as the verb "[to] lead" because it referred to indicators of a gold-bearing quartz vein on a hillside). Homestake's story began in April 1876, when the brothers Moses and Fred Manuel discovered a vein of very rich quartz ore. They apparently had enough capital to mine the claim and build a ten-stamp mill in Lead. Like most prospectors, the Manuels were never sure of the future value of their claim and were inclined to accept "a bird in the hand." When an agent of California mining investor George Hearst appeared in Lead, they sold their mine for $70,000.

Hearst brought in steam-driven diamond-bit drills and bought out neighboring claims throughout the valley. His drillers followed the lode and its tributaries several hundred feet underground and thousands of feet horizontally. In 1883 a cave-in dropped part of the town of Lead into the two-hundred-foot level of the mine, and eventually the entire business district of the city had to be moved because it rested on the decaying timber props of the mine. In 1888 the mine produced 243,355 tons of ore that yielded $3.68 in gold per ton. After labor and milling costs, the profit to the owners was $292,000. By that date George Hearst had used his fortune to buy a seat in the U.S. Senate from California. A decade later proceeds from the Homestake financed the newspaper publishing empire of George's son, William Randolph Hearst. While all other mines in the Black Hills have long since shut down, the Homestake continues in operation today, largely due to the rising world price of gold.

CHAPTER SIX

Prairie Farms and Statehood

L ike many American farmers, then and today, the
Northern Pacific Railroad, after the fall of the house
of Cooke, was land rich and cash poor. Although the
railroad had reached Bismarck before the Panic of 1873, few
farmers had taken up its lands west of the Red River. If the
railroad were to pay interest on its bonds, meet operating
expenses, and finance future construction, it had to promote settlement and traffic along the line. James B. Power,
the railroad's chief land agent, thought he had a solution.
In October 1873, a scant month after Cooke's bankruptcy
triggered the financial panic, Power announced that the
company would accept its own bonds from investors at par
value in exchange for railroad land. Because of the panic
Northern Pacific bonds had dropped to less than forty cents
on the dollar. Speculators and bondholders leaped at the
chance, and over the next year Power disposed of nearly half
a million acres of railroad land, most of it in the Red River
Valley. The problem was that most of the purchasers were
eastern capitalists, anxious to recover their investment in

railroad bonds; few had any intention of taking up farming in the West.

In 1875 Power had another idea: highly capitalized, large-
scale farms operated by local tenants or employees—farms,
in short, modeled on the eastern factories. He persuaded
George W. Cass, president of the railroad, to exchange some
of his semiworthless stocks and bonds (the railroad was by
then in receivership) for five thousand acres of land about
halfway between Fargo and Jamestown. Benjamin P. Cheney,
a member of the board, reached a similar agreement, and
the two executives made Power their local agent. Although
bringing the land under cultivation was part of the agreement, neither the Cass-Cheney partnership nor Power knew
how to bring that about. They considered putting tenants on
individual tracts but found no one willing to rent when government land could be had for the price of a land office fee.

In 1876 Power had yet another brainstorm. He hired Oli-
ver Dalrymple to manage the Cass and Cheney farms, with
the added enticement that Dalrymple could purchase additional lands for his own use. Dalrymple was one of those
opportunistic individuals that nineteenth-century Americans idolized. A school administrator and lawyer by turns,
he had successfully farmed 2,000 acres of wheat in southern
Minnesota and was looking for new worlds to conquer. The
challenge of managing a factory-style farming operation
in Dakota with ample capital backing appealed to him. In
Minnesota he found the men he needed, as well as the livestock and equipment for large-scale farming. He arrived in
the newly founded town of Casselton in April, and before
spring was out he had plowed and planted 1,280 acres of
wheat. While the crop was growing, he built dormitories
and equipment sheds on each of the two farms and broke
an additional 3,200 acres of prairie sod. The following year

he purchased six sections of railroad land in the Casselton area for his own use and made plans to break 5,000 acres a year until he had 30,000 acres in wheat crop. By 1877, after being in operation only a year, Dalrymple was employing fifty men at seed time and nearly a hundred at harvest. The capital investment included eighty horses, twenty-six sod-breaking plows, forty cross plows, sixty harrows, twenty-one seeders, thirty harvesters, five steam-driven threshers, and thirty wagons to carry the grain to the railroad elevators.

Dalrymple's financial success induced other Northern Pacific bondholders and stockholders to exchange their paper for square-mile-sized lands in the West, to be managed by westerners experienced in wheat culture and (ideally) blessed with leadership skills. The Dalrymple-managed farms thus became a model for the bonanza farms that dominated northern Dakota agriculture between the Red River and the James in the decade after 1876. To promote his concept of industrial farms Power mastered the art of drawing attention to the region to encourage both investors and farmer-employees. In September 1878 President Rutherford B. Hayes, having read Power's glowing account of bonanza farming, made a special trip to Casselton to view the mass-production harvesting operation. A month later *Frank Leslie's Illustrated Magazine* ran an article on the novel use of farm machinery, with awe-inspiring sketches, and for the next several year reporters from eastern magazines and newspapers produced enthusiastic articles on bonanza farming. Power saw to it that many of the articles were reproduced in the European press; Scandinavian and German immigrants added to both the bonanza workforce and the number of homesteaders taking up government lands along the railroad right-of-way.

An improving economy, which increased freight revenues

and eliminated much of its bonded debt through land sales, allowed the Northern Pacific to resume construction west of the Missouri, and in 1879 it reached the Montana border. By that date another empire builder had entered the picture in the northern plains—James J. Hill. Canadian-born, Hill landed in St. Paul in 1856 at the age of seventeen. By the end of the war he had become a shipping agent who arranged freight for railroad companies, and in 1870 he formed a partnership to operate a steamboat line on the Red River. That, in turn, led to the dream of a rail line to complement his steamboat traffic. While others were building east-west railroads across Minnesota, Hill fixed his eye on a north-south line connecting St. Paul with the lower Red River Valley. In 1878 he purchased the grandly named St. Paul and Pacific, a spur of the Northern Pacific that reached only into the North Woods. The St. Paul and Pacific had inherited a land grant from the state of Minnesota and had been rendered an orphan by the bankruptcy of the Northern Pacific. Within a year Hill extended the line down the Red River Valley to the town of St. Vincent on the Canadian border. There he linked up with a spur that the Canadian Pacific had obligingly constructed south from Winnipeg. Hill's railroad could now carry Canadian wheat from the prairie provinces to the mills of Minneapolis, and he never again had trouble obtaining private financing.

In 1880 Hill's railroad, rechristened the St. Paul, Minneapolis, and Manitoba, bridged the Red River at Grand Forks and began building west across Dakota to Devil's Lake (Spirit Lake today). In the following year he enticed James B. Power into his employ. Because much of the railroad's unsold acreage from its original Minnesota land grant lay in the Minnesota counties along the Red River, Power simply redirected his promotional tactics to the lower portion of the valley. He sold a few bonanza farms to eastern investors, but his main thrust was Scandinavian immigrants and midwestern farmers. He offered to carry potential settlers from any point in the United States to a station along the Manitoba's route for ten dollars a person. Homesteaders with large families, household goods, and farm equipment were able to rent entire boxcars for a few dollars. In 1884 Hill, having bestowed upon his railroad the name Great Northern, announced plans to build a road all the way to Puget Sound on the Pacific. He had no difficulty obtaining financing and surveyed much of the route across the high plains himself. His construction crews made it across the Dakota Territory from Devil's Lake to the Montana border in a single season (April to November 1887), laying 643 miles of track. While his main crew pushed on across the mountains to the Pacific, which it reached in 1893, Hill built spur lines in Dakota, north and south of his main line, opening up the most remote areas to settlement.

The Northern Pacific also built spur lines and employed the same tactics as Hill in luring Scandinavian and German immigrants to take up both railroad and government lands along its right-of-way. By 1889, when the territory was ready for statehood, much of the land east of the Missouri River was under cultivation.

The Uprooted

At the end of the Middle Ages, when centralized monarchies emerged from the Viking clans, two kingdoms ruled the five Scandinavian peoples, Denmark-Norway (which included Iceland) and Sweden-Finland. Despite periodic movements for independence, it was not until the twentieth century that five separate nations emerged: Norway separated itself from Sweden in 1905; Finland dissolved a union with Russia in

1918; and Iceland declared independence from Denmark in 1944. Upon emigration to America, however, these five peoples had great similarities. Located in the northernmost part of Europe with few cities, vast stretches of spruce forest, and surrounded by water, the Scandinavians possessed certain skills that they brought to America—farming, lumbering, fishing, and sailing. The five nationalities also shared two important cultural traditions—language (with the exception of Finnish) and religion. As is the case today, Norwegians and Swedes understood one another quite well, and they could both handle Danish, despite its guttural German-influenced inflections. Most Icelanders knew Danish, although it is not their native language. All five peoples were predominantly Lutheran, though there remained long-standing rifts between high church (orthodox) and low church (pietist) adherents, and these schisms continued in America.

Norwegians were the first ethnic group to enter the Dakota Territory. Driven from the Old Country by overpopulation on limited land, they landed in Minnesota and migrated across the Red River some time around 1870. They clung to the river valleys rather than the uplands because the lowlands provided timber for log houses (they shunned sod houses if possible), rich grass for dairy cattle, and the opportunity to supplement the food stocks by fishing. They occupied the valleys of the Sheyenne and Goose Rivers, both tributaries of the Red, and the two valleys are still "Norwegian country" today.

With more tillable land and labor-intensive industries (e.g., glass making), Sweden did not suffer the population pressure of Norway; consequently most Swedes who came to Dakota in the late nineteenth century were second or even third-generation migrants from Minnesota, Wisconsin, and Illinois. Lacking any strong national identity, they sprinkled themselves throughout the rural landscape. Danes and Finns trickled in toward the end of the century, most of them from the lumbering and mining communities of Michigan, Wisconsin, and Minnesota.

One of the most interesting ethnic groups to populate Dakota in the last quarter of the century was the Black Sea Germans. Theirs was an odyssey of promise and betrayal. In the mid-eighteenth century Empress Catherine the Great of Russia invited German-speaking people to settle the fertile grasslands of the lower Volga River Valley. As enticements she offered them freedom of religion and exemption from compulsory military service. Some thirty thousand German peasants and craftsmen answered the call. Catherine's grandson, Tsar Alexander I, continued the policy after 1801, and during the Napoleonic wars thousands more Germans fled to the lands bordering the Black Sea. About half were Lutheran, a third Catholic, and the remainder pietists, such as Mennonites. In 1871 Tsar Alexander II revoked the colonists' privileges, notably the exemption from military service. German families began moving to America the following year, and after tarrying in the Midwest, most made their way by rail to Yankton in 1873. The first immigrants gradually pushed northward up the valley of the James River and eventually met and merged with another German-Russian immigrant stream coming south from Winnipeg. Wheat farmers on the Russian steppes, the Black Sea Germans chose to settle on the relatively level, treeless plains between Devil's Lake and the Missouri River. While American land sale practices distributed their holdings fairly evenly around the countryside, the Germans built their farm homes in close proximity to one another, thereby establishing communities of similar religious belief and Old Country village origins.

The Sod-House Frontier

The standard farm house on the treeless prairie was made of sod, usually some twenty feet long and sixteen feet wide. Using a plow, a farmer turned over furrows on about a half-acre of ground where the prairie grass roots were thickest. He took care to make the furrows of even width and depth so that the walls of the cabin would be straight and smooth. The sod was then cut into bricks three feet long. He outlined the house by placing the first layer of bricks in line around the four sides, leaving an opening for the door. He then laid the sod as a bricklayer would, filling the joints with clay. The roof was framed with cottonwood poles obtained from a nearby streambed. The railroads brought some pine lumber from the woodlands of Minnesota and Wisconsin, but only the settlers with a bit of capital could afford such a luxury. The cottonwood rafters were covered by a sheet of brush and prairie grass, and the whole was made weatherproof with another layer of sod.

Having provided his family with shelter at minimal capital cost, the pioneer put what money he had into tools. His first need was access to a plow that could break the prairie sod. The steel plow developed by John Deere in the 1840s was billed as "the plow that broke the plains," but it was nothing of the sort. The prairie sod was such a thick tangle of roots that reached deep into the soil that it could not be broken by a plow drawn by a single horse steered by a single farmer. Toolmakers on the Illinois prairies developed the breaking plow around the year 1820. This ungainly instrument consisted of a wooden beam, ten or twelve feet long, resting on small, sturdy wheels in front and holding a massive steel share and mould board in the rear. Drawn by a yoke of six oxen or four draft horses, the prairie breaker could turn a furrow thirty inches wide and about four inches deep. It required two men, one to drive the team and the other to guide the plow. They could turn about three acres in a day, with frequent stops to sharpen the cutting edge of the share. The prairie breaker was thus a specialized service, and the breaking crew normally charged a farmer two or three dollars an acre. Once the prairie was broken, the farmer had to plow a cross-furrow with his own horse and plow in order to break the sod further before he could plant seeds.

The prairie farmer planted only wheat and a small vegetable garden for his family. He obtained hay for his livestock on the open prairie—that is, unoccupied land owned by the government or a railroad. For new arrivals haying—cutting the prairie grass with a scythe and raking by hand—was a family project. Horse-driven mowing machines had been invented before the Civil War, and one could be purchased in the 1870s for $125. A farmer unable to muster that amount could rent a mower for $5 or $6 a day. He would ride out onto the prairie and cut a swath around a patch of grass he wanted. This amounted to a claim that was respected by others. After cutting the hay, he gathered it using a horse-drawn revolving wooden rake. Haying was often a community project where farmers helped one another, as they did in the threshing season.

Perhaps the biggest technological advance of the 1870s was the invention of barbed wire. Because cattle simply walked through strands of ordinary wire, farmers had tried tying hooks on the wire to deter the animals. It was Joseph F. Glidden of DeKalb, Illinois, who invented a machine that would entwine two strands of wire and place a barb at each of the interstices. He patented his invention in 1874 and entered into a contract with an eastern wire manufacturer for mass production. Too expensive for ordinary farmers in the

1870s—$20 a hundred pounds—it came within their reach by the mid-1880s at $4.20 a hundred pounds.

The final bit of technology needed to farm the Great Plains was the windmill. European windmills were gigantic wooden fans (reminiscent of those at which Don Quixote tilted his lance) designed for power that turned millstones to grind grain. On the plains they were needed to draw water, and that presented a different sort of problem. Because the plains consisted of dirt and gravel laid down by wind and water erosion of the Rocky Mountains, the water table usually lay about two hundred feet below the surface. It could be reached by drilling a narrow shaft and lining it with pipe. Water was drawn less by power than rapid repetition of a cylinder pump. This, in turn, required a fast-moving fan of light metal only about eight feet in diameter. Such a windmill had been developed before the Civil War and was initially used on the plains to pump water for railroad locomotives. Because watercourses on the plains were few and far apart and winds never-failing, a well and windmill were essential to every farm family. Mass production reduced the price, and by the 1880s the landscape was dotted with windmills and strung with barbed wire.

Improvements in farm technology allowed a homesteader on the prairie to subsist, but nothing could alleviate the drudgery and isolation of life on the sod-house frontier. Farmers' wives, in particular, often suffered from loneliness and despair. They seldom left the home and might have gone months or even years without seeing another woman. Their days were hard and long—caring for the children, planting and weeding the garden, making soap, sewing clothing, cooking, and cleaning. One oft-told story involved a farmer who brought his wife to the state asylum in Yankton. Explaining his wife's sad mental condition to the superintendent, the mystified farmer remarked, "I don't know what would drive her crazy, Doc. She ain't been off the farm in twenty years."

The Range Cattle Frontier

Spring wheat, technology, and migrant farmers brought the land east of the Missouri River under cultivation and sprinkled the countryside with market towns and cities, but the land west of the Missouri was another matter. With an average rainfall of only eighteen inches, the region was too arid for crop cultivation prior to the advent of dry farming and irrigation in the twentieth century. The short-grass prairie, on the other hand, was quite nutritious, as the vast herds of buffalo attested. Once the buffalo herds were virtually annihilated by indiscriminate slaughter in the 1870s, the land seemed prime for cattle raising.

The range cattle industry originated in southern Texas while the region was still part of Mexico. Ranchers, using Spanish strains of cattle, developed longhorns, a breed that could survive on the open prairie with little or no care. The cattle not only survived but also reproduced abundantly. After Texas became part of the Union, the surplus cattle were driven to New Orleans, and the meat was shipped north from there by steamboat. In 1865, because of the high price of beef during the war, several Texas cattlemen drove their herds overland to railheads in southwest Missouri. Because of their inexperience they suffered losses on the way, and they met resistance from Indians in Oklahoma and farmers in Missouri. The man who perfected the cattle drive was an Illinois rancher, Joseph G. McCoy.

In 1867 McCoy visited Kansas seeking a terminus for a cattle trail that would cross public lands and shallower rivers. He decided upon the village of Abilene, a whistle-stop on the Kansas Pacific Railroad. The settlement consisted of a dozen rude huts and was eager for investment. McCoy contracted with the railroad for a favorable shipping rate and built pens capable of holding three thousand cattle. He also financed a hotel and a saloon to accommodate the trail riders. McCoy was too shrewd to ride the dusty trail himself; he simply made Texans aware of the potential in Abilene. The first herds sent to Abilene yielded a nice profit to Texas ranchers, and the cattle drive became an annual event. In 1871 the Santa Fe Railroad, building southwest from Kansas City, offered a shorter route for the trail drivers. Its terminals—successively Newton, Wichita, and Dodge City—became the new "cow towns" of the West.

By the late 1870s stockmen discovered that the cattle, left to feed a while before being shipped east by train, grew fat on the lush prairie grasses of Kansas and Nebraska. Texas thereafter became more of a breeding ground and the northern plains a feeding ground. The government's need to provide beef for the reservation Indians brought cattle ranching to the Dakota Territory. Its contracts for the Sioux reservations alone amounted to more than 26 million pounds per year. A contractor for a Sioux agency could expect a net profit of around $100,000 per year. As railroads spread across the territory in the late 1870s, an eastern market opened up for the range cattle industry. With the development of the refrigerated rail car, live cattle from the plains had to be sent no farther east than Sioux City or Omaha, and the processed meat could be shipped from there to the East Coast. The difficulty was that Texas longhorns, even when fattened on prairie grass, were too rangy and tough for eastern tastes. They needed to be interbred with, or even replaced by, British strains. Long known as "beefeaters," the people of the British Isles had bred the world's finest beef cattle, English Herefords ("whitefaces") and Scots Anguses ("black cattle").

Two familiar empire builders pioneered the breeding experiments in the early 1880s that would make western Dakota cattle country—James J. Hill and James B. Power.

Hill, who combined scientific curiosity with financial genius, began experimenting with cattle breeding and large-scale feeding in the 1870s on farms he owned in Minnesota. Using stock improved by shorthorn and Angus bulls imported from Britain, Hill demonstrated that a bushel of wheat, which sold for $0.55 at a flour mill, could yield the equivalent of $0.82 when fed to beef cattle. Power, who acquired six thousand acres in the Sheyenne River Valley southwest of Fargo about the same time, complemented Hill's findings. Recognizing that the soil was too poor and the climate too dry for normal agriculture, Power simply turned cattle onto the prairie. His holdings were scattered among twenty-one government sections, with public land in between. He could thus utilize a huge area of grazing lands without having to purchase it. By 1885 he had 230 cattle, all of purebred or mixed British strains, 75 horses of French stock, 250 English-bred sheep, and 130 Berkshire hogs. Other ranchers developed similar methods, and by 1880 the Dakota Territory boasted more than 140,000 head of cattle, although that was still only a third of the number being raised in Wyoming and Montana, where the entire territory was given over to cattle range.

High prices in the early 1880s, due to government beef contracts for the Indian reservations, meant that a rancher who purchased young Texas cattle at a relatively low price could make an enormous profit. Territorial immigration agencies in Dakota and Wyoming published pamphlets with tables showing profits of 30 to 40 percent annually. Coinciding with the bonanza fever in eastern Dakota, the ranching fever in the West attracted eastern investors. Bankers and businessmen in Boston, New York, and Philadelphia formed cattle companies to purchase and manage ranches in the West.

Because the cattle were expected to range widely over the public lands, both the federal and territorial governments hastily imposed regulations to preserve order. The federal government prohibited fencing of the public domain, but it had no objection to cattle grazing or hay cutting on public lands so long as the lands were available to all. The territories passed laws regulating the branding of cattle because the mark of a rancher burned onto the animal's hide was the only sign of ownership. The laws required that all brands be registered with the county, and cattle could be branded only during the summer roundup. A calf was given the same brand as its mother. Adults roaming without a brand were sent to the county corral and sold at auction. Severe punishment awaited any rogue who altered a brand. Even so the larger ranchers designed brands that could not easily be altered.

One of the most famous easterners who became a cattleman in the 1880s was Theodore Roosevelt, who had worked as a ranch hand as a youth when he had been devoted to building his physique. Scion of a wealthy New York family, he went west in 1883 to buy a ranch in the Dakota Territory. He actually bought two ranches, the Elkhorn and the Chimney Butte, in the valley of the Little Missouri River (a region known as the North Dakota Badlands today). He wisely retained the previous owners as his ranch managers, and they remained lifelong friends. (He gave them government jobs when president.) In his autobiography Roosevelt described his life as a rancher:

> I enjoyed life to the full. After the first year I built on the Elkhorn ranch a long, low ranch-house of hewn logs,

15. The ranch house on Theodore Roosevelt's Maltese Cross Ranch. Photo by author.

with a veranda, and with, in addition to the other rooms, a bedroom for myself, and a sitting-room with a big fireplace. I got out a rocking-chair—I am very fond of rocking-chairs—and enough books to fill two or three shelves, and a rubber bathtub so that I could get a bath. And then I do not see how anyone could have lived more comfortably. We had buffalo-robes and bearskins of our own killing.

In his autobiography Roosevelt devoted most of the space on his ranching experience to the roundup, clearly the most exciting time of the year. His own brand was the Maltese Cross, referred to locally as "maltee cross," he explained, "as the general impression along the Little Missouri was that 'Maltese' must be a plural."

Roosevelt's description of his life on the cattle frontier has been accepted by most biographers, but ranchers who knew him best were more cautious in their appraisal. One of his cattlemen neighbors wrote: "He didn't know a thing about cattle; he could not catch his own horse out of the cavvy. Roosevelt took part in only one roundup—that of 1885, and here he was simply in the way. He was willing to help but a nuisance anywhere you put him. He didn't have a cowman in his outfit, although he had some who made pretty good hands."

Roosevelt's ranching experience—and indeed that of many others—lasted only three years. The winter of 1886–87 lingers on in memory today. From November to February blizzard followed blizzard until the snow lay five feet deep on the open prairie. Cattle that sought refuge in ravines simply drowned in the snow. Temperatures plummeted to forty or fifty degrees below zero. The cattle, expected to survive the winter on the open range, died by the thousands. Losses of 40 to 60 percent of a ranch's herd were common. Roosevelt sold out and returned east, and so did many others. Such selloffs only exacerbated the problem, for the panicky sale of entire herds caused prices in the stockyards of Chicago, Omaha, and Kansas City to collapse. Adding to the problem was a severe drought the following summer in the corn belt states, Iowa and Illinois, causing a drop in demand for feeder cattle. By midsummer a well-bred steer from Dakota fetched only about three dollars a hundred weight, while a Texas longhorn went for about two dollars.

The disastrous year brought an end to the cattle range era. The ranchers who survived worked on a smaller scale; they fenced in their lands, turned exclusively to short-horned breeds, and stored hay for winter feeding. They also found that spring calving was the most reliable operation and sent their yearlings to the corn belt states for fattening.

By 1880 there were three centers of population in the Dakota Territory, and each had a profound distrust of the inhabitants of the other two. The southeast, with Yankton as its political center, was the most heavily populated. The Black Hills was second in population. The third region, to the north, consisted of two ribbons of settlement—the Red River Valley and the lands along the Northern Pacific right-of-way from Fargo to Bismarck. The only contact among the three was by stagecoach. It took two and a half days, traveling day and night, to get from Bismarck to Rapid City on the edge of the Hills. The trip from Yankton to the Hills took nearly a week. The sections had different economic bases and different political outlooks. The southeast was solidly Republican, reflecting its dependence on government offices that had been filled by successive Republican administrations beginning with Lincoln. Both the Black Hills and the north tended to elect Democrats to local offices, probably more out of hostility to the Yankton oligarchy than appreciation of the national Democratic Party.

The most elementary division in the territory, however, was north-south. Because both railroad and telegraph lines ran east and west for the most part, there was little communication or cultural interchange between north and south. The Black Hills was dependent for supplies on the Missouri River towns, and they, in turn, were tied commercially to Sioux City and Chicago. The Red River Valley had traditional economic ties with Winnipeg to the north and St. Paul to the east. Completion of the Northern Pacific line tied the north even more firmly to St. Paul and Minneapolis. The northern population was growing rapidly by 1880, but the area was still regarded as a frontier. Despite reapportionment in the

Territorial Assembly, the north held only seven seats out of a total of thirty-six. As a result, the main thrust of northern opinion in the 1880s was for separation. Southern leaders instead worked for statehood—partly because the politically ambitious wanted to throw off the federal yoke and partly out of apprehension over moves in Congress to make the Black Hills into a separate territory. The south's drive for statehood, however, received an early setback when the Democrats won control of Congress in the election of 1882, presaging their capture of the presidency with Grover Cleveland in 1884. National Democrats were in no hurry to add Dakota to the Union, for it meant two additional Republican senators (four if the territory were split into two states) and a majority of Republicans in the state's House delegation.

By the mid-1880s the statehood party, centered in the southeast, numbered only about two hundred active members, but they were the economic elite of the territory. The group included politicians, merchants, land agents, and professional men, especially lawyers. Most of them had migrated to Dakota from New England, New York, or the upper Midwest. They summoned conventions and drafted state constitutions in 1883 and again in 1885, hoping to prod Congress into action on statehood. Significantly two of their leaders, Gideon C. Moody, political boss of the Black Hills, and Richard F. Pettigrew, Republican boss of Sioux Falls and the Big Sioux Valley, became U.S. senators after statehood was achieved in 1889.

Railroads were the principal opponents of statehood, in part because they found Congress easier to manipulate than the Territorial Assembly. Through their lobbies in Washington they had considerable influence over appointments to territorial offices. The last five governors of the Dakota Territory, for example, had been railroad men. The railroads also had reason to fear popularly elected state governors and assemblies. The Granger movement in the Midwest and the Farmers' Alliance in the plains states were advocating government regulation of railroad freight rates and other practices that hurt railroad users. In Congress the opposition to statehood included Minnesota senators and representatives of both parties. Minnesota politicians had long regarded Dakota's territorial government as a convenient graveyard for their surplus party hacks.

The most interesting feature of the statehood controversy was the utter indifference of most Dakota voters. Statehood, after all, brought new responsibilities, particularly in the realm of finance. For the territory the federal government paid the salaries of most officials and financed the construction of roads and river improvements. With statehood all of these expenses would fall on taxpayers. Sensing this general apathy, the statehood forces timed their conventions for the spring and fall planting and harvesting seasons when the rural population was too busy to participate in meetings.

Democratic control of either Congress or the presidency stalled the statehood movement until 1888, when the Republicans nominated Benjamin Harrison for president. As a U.S. senator from Indiana, Harrison had secured the appointment of his close friend Arthur C. Mellette as head of the land office in Watertown in the valley of the Big Sioux River. Mellette became a leader of the statehood movement (and later first governor of South Dakota), while Harrison in the Senate gained national stature with a fight for Dakota's admission to the Union. In addition to nominating Harrison, the Republican national convention in 1888 adopted a platform favoring the admission of North and South Dakota, as well as any other territories that might qualify. After the Republicans won both the presidency and control of Congress in the election, the division of the territory and the admission of two states were all but inevitable.

Even before the election Democrats in Congress had proposed the admission of four territories—Dakota, Washington, Montana, and New Mexico. They figured that New Mexico, with its large Hispanic population, would vote Democratic and that Washington might go Democratic in the future, thus maintaining a balance between the political parties. The scheme depended on forcing the Dakotas to come in as a single state, and that died with the Republican victory in the election. Sentiment within the Dakota Territory so clearly favored separation that even Dakota Democrats dropped their opposition to it. In addition, the admission of New Mexico was not popular nationally. As a result, early in 1889 the Lame Duck Congress approved an Omnibus Bill authorizing the two Dakotas (divided at approximately the 46th parallel of latitude), Montana, and Washington to draft constitutions preparatory to statehood. President Cleveland signed the bill into law a few days before leaving office.

The South Dakota convention already had extensive experience at drafting constitutions, and it simply consolidated earlier drafts drawn up in 1885 and 1888. These, in turn, drew heavily upon the constitution of Minnesota, copying the institutions of a state immediately to the east having become fairly standard practice in western constitution making.

North Dakota was another story. The Farmers' Alliance had made great headway among the stricken farmers of the territory following the disastrous winter of 1886–87. As in the other plains states, the Alliance attracted a variety of reformers, many of whom would appear at the formation of the People's Party in Omaha in 1892. Among the reforms being bruited was a state railroad commission, taxes on corporations, government loans for seed purchases, adoption of the Australian (secret) ballot, women's suffrage, prohibition of spirituous liquors, and abolition of the territorial immigration bureau on grounds that North Dakota could not support any more inhabitants.

A fall in wheat prices in the late 1880s added to the rural distress, and as a result the Alliance was able to recruit Scandinavian and German farmers who had previously voted solidly Republican. The convention that met in Bismarck in the summer of 1889 to draft a state constitution was accordingly dominated by Alliance men, and the document it crafted was perhaps the most liberal of any in the nation. With the abuses of the Yankton government firmly in mind, North Dakota limited the appropriations power of the state assembly and restricted the powers of the governor. Among specific reforms inserted in the state constitution were a mechanism for arbitrating labor disputes, restrictions on child labor, the Australian ballot, and statewide prohibition. Among reforms considered but not adopted were a unicameral legislature and a popular referendum on certain legislation, both features of the Progressive movement that was to sweep the country after the turn of the century. The ascendancy of the Farmers' Alliance and the liberal state constitution that it drafted paved the way for the Nonpartisan League, which would dominate North Dakota politics for the first quarter of the twentieth century.

CHAPTER SEVEN

The Road to Wounded Knee

Until the middle of the nineteenth century the U.S. government believed it had "solved" the Indian "problem" by removing the eastern tribes west of the Middle Border (i.e., to Nebraska, Kansas, and Oklahoma). Occasionally the government reserved small tracts of land for the eastern tribes—an entire county for the peaceable Menominee of Wisconsin, for instance—but there was no general policy relative to Indian reservations prior to 1850. White land hunger, as so often happened, forced the government to develop a plan. By midcentury farmers in Iowa and Missouri coveted the rich lands occupied by the transplanted Indians west of the Missouri River and demanded that the government concentrate the Indians' holdings so whites could move onto the vacated parcels of land.

In response, the commissioner of Indian affairs in Washington developed a plan for small, well-defined Indian "colonies" where the tribes would be concentrated. In establishing such colonies, the government would protect the Indians from rum sellers and disease while teaching them how to survive in a white, Christian civilization. With the support of Congress the Indian Affairs Bureau negotiated a series of treaties by which the tribes that had been moved west in the 1820s and 1830s ceded 13 million acres of land in exchange for annuities and small reservations in eastern Kansas and the Indian Territory (Oklahoma). Whites poured across the Missouri River, and the government formally organized the Kansas and Nebraska territories in 1854.

The Great Sioux Reservation

In the late 1860s, following the First Sioux War, General William Tecumseh Sherman, military commander in the West, sought to apply the reservation concept to the tribes of the northern plains. He was driven primarily by the need to secure pioneers on the overland trails from Indian attacks and open the way for construction of the Union Pacific Railroad. In the summer of 1868 army messengers rode into Indian camps throughout the plains inviting the Dakotas, Cheyennes, Kiowas, Pawnees, and other western tribes to a conference at Fort Laramie. When some Indians declined to participate—such as Red Cloud, holed up in the Big Horn Mountains—the army threatened force. The treaty signed that summer created a Sioux reservation that seemed ample enough. It extended from the Missouri River west to the Big Horn Mountains and to the south as far as the Nebraska-Dakota border. The northern limit was the line of latitude that would later divide North and South Dakota.

The reservation was unfortunately too generous to withstand the rapacious white frontier. Two events of the early 1870s doomed the Dakota tribes' hope of preserving their ancestral lands and culture: the great buffalo hunt and the Black Hills gold rush. Buffalo hides had long been sent east by fur traders, to be made into blankets and robes. In 1871 an eastern tannery developed a technology for tanning buffalo hides that required a different process from that of tanning cow hides. The result was a new industry since buffalo were a cheaper source of leather than cattle. Hundreds of "hide hunters," armed with repeating rifles, spread out over the plains, slaughtering the animals for their hides, leaving the carcasses to rot in the sun. Within a decade they had virtually obliterated the vast herds that had numbered in the millions. A scientific expedition in 1883 counted a mere two hundred buffalo grazing on the prairies of the West.

The effect on Indian culture was devastating. Deprived of their primary source of food and housing, the Dakotas became dependent on government handouts. The new situation confined them to the reservation, whether they willed it or not, for an attempt at breakout meant hunger and military harassment. "All our people now were settling down in square gray houses, scattered here and there across this hungry land," recalled Black Elk of the Teton Sioux Reservation in the 1880s. "Hunger was among us often now, for much of what the Great Father in Washington sent us must have been stolen by Washichus [white Indian agents] who were crazy to get money. There were many lies, but we could not eat them."

The discovery of gold in Montana, which induced the government to reopen the Bozeman Trail and order the Sioux out of the Powder River Valley in 1875, together with the Black Hills gold rush, triggered the Second Sioux War, which climaxed at the Little Big Horn in July 1876. Sitting Bull and Crazy Horse, the war chiefs of the Dakotas, fled military retaliation with their followers to Canada, and the government negotiated a revision of reservation boundaries with the Dakota tribes that had not been involved in the war. By a treaty signed in 1878 the Dakotas ceded eastern Wyoming and the Black Hills (a triangle of land bordered on the north by the Belle Fourche River and on the south by the Cheyenne). On the much shrunken reservation the Dakotas reported to six Indian agencies for administrative purposes and food rations. On the Missouri River the Hunkpapas, Sans Arcs, and Miniconjous drew rations at the Standing Rock Agency (on the present North Dakota border) and the Cheyenne Agency (near the junction of that river with the Missouri). The Oglalas enrolled at Pine Ridge, near the Nebraska border, and the Brules at Rosebud on the edge of the Badlands.

Over the next three years the army rounded up the Dakota clans that had been living in northern Dakota and Wyoming and forced them onto the reservation. In the summer of 1881 Sitting Bull and Crazy Horse, driven by hunger and Canadian pressure, crossed the international border with their 2,500 followers and surrendered to the army. The two leaders were imprisoned (Crazy Horse soon to be killed by his jailers), and the rest of the band was placed on the reservation. The reservation then numbered about sixteen thousand Indians.

The Reformers

During the 1870s conscience-stricken easterners began a movement to reform government Indian policy, particularly to ensure more honest and humane treatment of the western tribes. Most of the reformers came from New England and New York, regions that had dispatched their resident Indians some two hundred years earlier; few had ever encountered a "real" Indian. They were characteristic of nineteenth-century reformers—business and professional people, pillars of their communities, deeply religious Protestants. In 1882 they formed an Indian Rights Association, which, like the prewar Antislavery Society, quickly formed

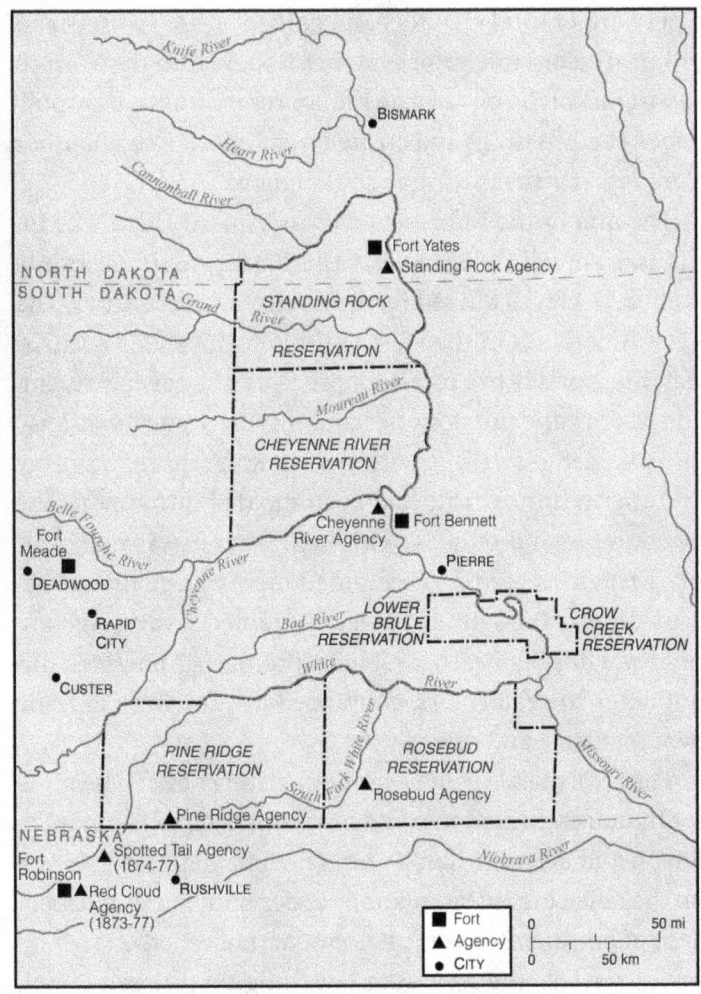

Map 9. The Sioux reservations.

a network of local chapters and gained access to press and pulpit. The organization sent fact finders into the West to report on conditions on the Indian reservations; they published their findings and created a commotion that neither Congress nor the executive could ignore.

The aim of the reformers was to "Americanize" the Indians, in much the same way that European immigrants had been Americanized in the course of the century. The ideal American, in the view of the reformers, led a Christian life, notably by Protestant precepts (they deeply resented the Catholic missionaries among the western Indians), and pursued his calling with the Puritan ethic of industry and thrift. Immigrants had been molded into Americans by churches and schools, with help from newspapers and magazines. The Indians presented more of a challenge because, it was thought, they were untamed savages and animal-worshiping heathens. Such "problems," however, did not deter the reformers, convinced as they were of their own rectitude and superiority.

The reformers' agenda was not entirely new; some ideas for Indian assimilation could be traced back to Thomas Jefferson and even William Penn. The first step was to break up the tribal organizations and render individuals independent of one another, for Americanization relied on free individuals—obedience to the law, religion (i.e., salvation), land ownership, and labor all required individual decision making. When this first step was accomplished—presumably by government agents, schools, and Protestant missionaries—the reservations could be abolished; Indian families could take up homesteads and live side by side with white farmers. Like many reformations, whether social, political, or religious, the concept seemed grand on paper. Implementation was another matter.

The treaties that established the Dakota reservation promised each Indian family beef, bacon, flour, coffee, and clothing to assure subsistence until they could provide for themselves by farming. The government also provided financial assistance in erecting clapboard houses in place of the buffalo-skin tepees, and government agents attempted to disperse the families throughout the reservation. To encourage farming the Indian Bureau (now under the Interior Department instead of the War Department) furnished seeds, implements, and instructors to teach the art of horticulture. Indians who resisted—and there were many, for in the Indian culture gardening was women's work—were threatened with a reduction in rations. But the threat worked two ways. If they succeeded in cultivating large fields and raising surplus crops, the Indians feared they would be dropped from the ration rolls. The former war leader Red Cloud spoke for many when he told an Indian agent, "The Great Spirit did not make us to work. He made us to hunt and fish." And he added, with irrefutable logic, "The white man owes us a living for the lands he has taken from us." As many white farmers had already discovered, the climate of the region west of the Missouri River was not conducive to eastern-style horticulture. Those families that did scatter out over the reservation to till the soil saw their corn and other crops burn up and blow away in late-summer droughts.

As white farmers had already learned, the country west of the Missouri was better suited to ranching than farming, and government agents, to their credit, recognized that the Dakotas might adapt readily to the life of cattlemen. In 1879 the Indian Bureau distributed about three thousand head of cattle among the Dakota agencies, and the Indians, superb horsemen, turned into excellent cowboys. They took good care of the cattle, and the herds increased yearly. But the government never provided enough breeding stock to produce a herd that exceeded the Indians' own needs, and the experiment faltered in the terrible winter of 1886–87. The Dakotas weathered that disaster more successfully than Theodore Roosevelt and other white ranchers, losing only 30 percent of their herds while white cattlemen suffered 50 to 75 percent losses. The Dakotas would ultimately prove to be quite capable cattlemen, but the 1886–87 setback worsened the psychological depression spreading across the reservation.

Perhaps nothing contributed more to the psychic degeneration of the Dakotas than the Indian Bureau's war on tribalism and its leaders. Because the Indian agents treated each family as a self-sufficient unit, the tribal council simply withered away. Young men who had previously earned status through war and the hunt joined the Indian Police. That earned them a certain amount of respect, as well as steady employment, but it also co-opted them as government servants. The tribal leaders—chiefs to the whites—were the principal targets of the government attack. And it was the most confusing to the Indians because of its inconsistency. The main weapon was the practice of distributing rations directly to each family rather than providing them in bulk to the chiefs for redistribution, as had formerly been the practice. Yet when the agents had to implement a particularly unpopular policy, they did so through the reigning chief at each agency. Even more confusing to the average Indian was the government's tendency to cater to the chiefs who had given it the most trouble. At the Pine Ridge Agency, the government provided the Oglala chief Red Cloud with a shiny black carriage, built a frame house for his family that was more imposing than the agent's own, and periodically sent him to Washington for a visit with the president.

The medicine men were another target of the government's war on tribalism. These shamans, who combined the role of physician and spiritual leader, had traditionally passed on their lore of rituals and herbal medicines to selected acolytes of the next generation. Prompted by the reformers, the Indian Bureau in 1883 published a "List of Indian Offenses." Among the "crimes" for which an Indian could be hauled before the Court of Indian Offenses was providing people with spiritual counsel or practicing heathen rituals. Silenced, the shamans retired and passed away without passing on their lore to apprentices.

The hardest blow to Indian morale was the prohibition, also in 1883, of the Sun Dance, a summer ritual/festival that dated back to the Dakotas' pre-Columbian forebearers. It was the centerpiece of the Indians' ritualistic religion and the heart of their value system. Prohibiting this ceremony left the Dakotas spiritually adrift and utterly demoralized. Missionaries sought to fill the void with Christian teachings, but for all the converts they made, they alienated many more by pouring ridicule on old Indian beliefs.

The Dawes Severalty Act

The reformers' program of breaking down tribalism and turning the Indians into independent farmers had barely begun when the reformers and their allies in Congress pushed ahead with the severalty program. Much of the political support for breaking up the Indian reservations into individually owned farms came from land-hungry white farmers and ranchers. Government agents estimated that even if each Indian family were given a homestead of 160 acres, there would be about 9 million acres in the Great Sioux Reservation left over. This surplus would provide homesteads and ranches for thousands of white migrants with additional room for road and rail communication between eastern Dakota and the booming Black Hills.

Congress could not resist the twin pressures of reformers and land boomers, and in 1887 it passed the Dawes General Allotment Act. The act applied to all the western tribes except the five "civilized" tribes that had been moved to Oklahoma in the 1830s. It authorized the Indian Bureau to give the head of each Indian family 160 acres of land, with lesser amounts to single adults. The Indians were allowed to select their own plots, so they could take advantage of any improvements they might already have made. The allotments were held in trust for twenty-five years before ownership was turned over to the Indian or his heirs. During that period the Indian could not sell or otherwise alienate the land—the reformers' way of protecting the Indian from his own moral weakness. When his land ownership was confirmed, the Indian was entitled to American citizenship. Reservation lands that were not taken up by Indians could be sold to whites, with the proceeds going to the Indian agencies, presumably for the Indians' benefit.

In 1888 Congress passed a law attempting to apply the principles of the Dawes Act to the Sioux Reservation, except it reversed the procedure. The government negotiated the cession of the 9 million surplus acres first and confined the Indian allotments to six separate reservations surrounding the existing agencies. Government agents then told the Indians that they could subdivide their holdings at their own pace. The Dakotas realized that they had been robbed, and at each agency they met to resist the law. For the better part of a year a military commission headed by Major General George Crook traveled among the Dakotas applying the army's familiar tactics of divide and conquer. The commission feasted and cajoled the more pliable Indian leaders, and when some of the Indians signed agreements, they warned the others to join or lose everything. By the summer of 1889 the commission had obtained the signatures of the three-fourths majority it needed to ratify the agreement. But Crook left behind a divided and demoralized people, bewildered by government betrayal and angry with one another for allowing it to happen. These were the conditions that gave rise to the Ghost Dance and the ultimate tragedy at Wounded Knee.

The Dakotas were certainly not alone in experiencing the social disorganization caused by government policies in the 1880s. In early 1889 Wovoka, a medicine man among the Paiutes of Nevada, had a vision in which he visited a new world, a world free of the white man's domination, a world in which the spirits of the Indian dead would be resurrected and the buffalo would again roam the plains. In the vision the Great Spirit designated Wovoka his representative on earth to lead his people out of bondage. It was, in fact, an interesting amalgam of Christian and pagan mythology, reminiscent of the preaching of Tecumseh's brother, The Prophet, among the Ohio tribes in the years prior to the War of 1812. Wovoka's revelation included instructions for the performance of a new ceremonial dance, the Ghost Dance, as preparation for the resurrection of the dead and the dawn of a new day. When his teachings attracted delegations from other mountain tribes, Wovoka was able to show them the scars on his hands where, so he claimed, white men had nailed him to a cross.

During the winter of 1889–90 conditions worsened for the demoralized Dakotas. Expecting them to have become farmers overnight, the Indian Bureau cut their rations. Hunger, even starvation, stalked their tepees, and epidemics of measles, influenza, and whooping cough swept through their villages. In March two Sioux pilgrims, Short Bull and Kicking Bear, returned to Pine Ridge from a visit to Nevada to spread the word of the new Messiah. In addition to teaching the Ghost Dance the two pilgrims showed their converts how to make a special garment to be worn for the dance, a Ghost Shirt, which they contended would protect converts from white men's bullets.

A midsummer drought that burned up planted crops added to the hardship and to the ranks of Ghost Dance converts. The religion spread to other agencies, but it centered at Pine Ridge, where Indians abandoned their cabins, set up tents in cottonwood groves, and danced hypnotically around sacred trees. As in the evangelical camp meetings of early nineteenth-century Appalachia, some fell to the ground in rapture, experienced visions of the promised land, and awakened in time to pass the Word onto others.

Experienced agents on most Dakota reservations tolerated the dance as a harmless outlet for Indian frustration, but Pine Ridge was another story. The agent there, Daniel F. Royer, was a prime example of the evils of the spoils system. A pharmacist from Alpena, South Dakota, who had fallen on hard times, Royer had wangled appointment as Indian agent in hopes of recouping his finances. Inexperienced and prone to panic, he had earned the Sioux name of "Young-Man-Afraid-of-Indians." He tried to stop the dances, claiming they were relics of barbarism, and ordered the dancers back to their cabins. Some laughed at him; most ignored him. By the fall of 1890 Royer was bombarding his superiors with requests for army intervention. By then the turbulence at Pine Ridge had aroused concern among neighboring white farmers, and in November President Benjamin Harrison ordered the army, now commanded by Major General Nelson A. Miles, to intervene. General Miles sent about five thousand men into western South Dakota.

The arrival of a military detachment at Pine Ridge caused

16. The South Dakota Badlands, ideal location for an Indian hideaway. Carol M. Highsmith's America, Library of Congress, Prints and Photographs Division.

the Ghost Dancers to organize in support of their faith. Led by Short Bull and Kicking Bear, they fled into the Badlands, some three thousand strong, and fortified an elevated tableland that soon became known as the "Stronghold."

Wounded Knee

General Miles had no wish to attack the Stronghold, an action that would have been costly indeed, and fervently hoped to calm the uprising with minimum force. That hope was unfortunately dashed by trigger-happy hotheads on both sides. At the Standing Rock Reservation on the North Dakota border Indian agent James McLaughlin had watched tolerantly as the Ghost Dance cult spread through the Hunkpapa Sioux during the autumn of 1890. The leader of the Hunkpapas, the aging war chief Sitting Bull, had become an icon among white Americans by participating in Buffalo Bill's

Wild West Show, but that had also cost him some stature among the Dakotas. Sitting Bull's attitude toward the Ghost Dance remains uncertain, but he may have encouraged the cult in an effort to restore his authority. Agent McLaughlin noted that the cult was centered at Sitting Bull's village on the Grand River, thirty miles south of the agency.

Hearing a rumor that Sitting Bull planned to lead his people south to join the Brule and Oglala dancers at the Stronghold, McLaughlin decided it was time to act. To defuse the incipient uprising he planned to arrest Sitting Bull and jail him in some distant place until the dance fever subsided. On December 15 he sent a force of forty-three Indian policemen, backed up by a troop of cavalry, to make a dawn arrest. The police made the arrest, but while they were saddling Sitting Bull's horse (a gift from Buffalo Bill), armed cultists wearing Ghost Shirts surrounded them. A shot was fired, most likely by a panicky policeman, and a brief fight ensued. When the cavalry arrived, they found Sitting Bull and seven of his followers dead around the cabin. Inside were four dead and three wounded policemen, two of whom died later. Word of this unfortunate incident spread through the Dakotas, and tension between the army and the Indians neared the breaking point. Another intended arrest brought on the ultimate tragedy.

A band of Miniconjou Dakotas lived on the south side of the Cheyenne River, ten miles up from its fork with the Belle Fourche. They were thus part of the Cheyenne River Reservation until its shrinkage in 1889 had left them outside its new boundaries. The leader of the band, Big Foot, had understandably been one of the most outspoken opponents of government policies, and he encouraged his followers to take up the Ghost Dance. The combination earned him a place on General Miles's list of troublemakers.

At Pine Ridge the aged and government-seduced Red Cloud had refused to join the Ghost Dancers and, indeed, viewed the turmoil as potentially disastrous for the Indians. Learning that Big Foot was having second thoughts about the Ghost Dance, Red Cloud invited him and his Miniconjous to the Pine Ridge Agency, apparently in the hope that he would add to the moderates there. To sweeten the invitation Red Cloud offered the Miniconjous two hundred horses. Big Foot, who in any event needed to be near an agency to receive rations, started south toward Pine Ridge. En route he was joined by about 40 Hunkpapa dancers escaping the melee at Sitting Bull's cabin. Big Foot's band then numbered about 350, 230 of whom were women and children.

Assuming that Big Foot was headed for the Stronghold to join forces with the Oglala and Brule dancers, General Miles stationed army units on the edge of the Badlands to intercept him. He set up headquarters in Rapid City but failed to find Big Foot because the latter was fifty miles to the east, heading for Pine Ridge. On December 28 a squadron of the Seventh Cavalry encountered his band while on routine patrol. Big Foot, ill with pneumonia and being carried in a wagon, put up no resistance and allowed the soldiers to guide his band to their camp, which lay on Wounded Knee Creek, about twenty miles northeast of the Pine Ridge Agency. That evening the remainder of the Seventh Cavalry Regiment, five hundred strong, rode into the camp. It was George Custer's old regiment, decimated at the Little Big Horn, now commanded by Colonel James W. Forsyth.

Dawn broke on December 29 to reveal a prospect of impending doom. The Indian camp was completely surrounded by mounted cavalry, backed on a nearby rise by four Hotchkiss guns, each capable of firing two-pound explosive shells at the rate of fifty a minute. No one on either side wanted or expected a fight. The Indians were badly outnumbered and burdened with women and children. Forsyth was so far from expecting a battle that he had allowed his soldiers to crowd so closely upon the Indians that they were a danger to one another in any uncontrolled shooting. Colonel Forsyth, nevertheless, had orders to disarm the band of Indians, and that almost surely meant trouble. Not only was a gun the most treasured possession of an Indian man, but also many feared that if they surrendered their weapons, they would be slaughtered.

The Indian men appeared to be unarmed (though some had rifles hidden under their robes), so Forsyth asked them to go into their tepees and bring out their guns. They returned with two aged guns, insisting that this was the extent of their arsenal. Forsyth then detailed squads of troopers to search the tepees. They turned up thirty-eight guns, many of them hidden under blankets that the Indian women lay upon. Most were old pieces of doubtful utility. Only a few were the repeating Winchesters that the soldiers had seen when they first stopped Big Foot's column. It was going to be necessary to search the warriors themselves.

While the village search was underway a medicine man had begun dancing around, blowing on an eagle-bone whistle, urging the Indians to fight while assuring them that their Ghost Shirts would protect them. Since none of the cavalry officers spoke the Siouan language, they regarded the antics of the dancer with mild amusement. The soldiers began a body search of the warriors present and recovered a couple of rifles and some ammunition. At that juncture a young man whom his fellow Indians had long considered crazy (he was also deaf) drew a rifle from his blanket and held it over his head, demanding money for its surrender. Two soldiers seized him, and in the ensuing scuffle the firearm discharged. The medicine man then threw a handful of dirt into the air as a signal, and a knot of Indians dropped their blankets revealing Winchester repeaters. Both sides fired at once, and the battle that no one expected was on.

The fight was initially a murderous melee fought at close quarters with pistols, knives, and clubs. Big Foot and the band of headmen around him died in the first volley of cavalry carbines. But most of the mounted soldiers held their fire for fear of hitting their comrades involved in the battle. With guns empty the Indians broke off the fight and ran for their tepees, apparently to get more guns and ammunition. At that point the Hotchkiss guns opened up on the Indian encampment, indiscriminately killing men, women, and children. The fight lasted less than an hour, but when the smoke cleared 146 Indians lay dead on the field: 84 men, 44 women, and 18 children. Fifty-one wounded were admitted to the hospital at Pine Ridge, of whom 7 died. Another 20 or 30 had fled the scene and were never accounted for. The Seventh Cavalry suffered 25 dead and 39 wounded.

The ultimate irony was that General Miles's offers of peace and leniency had induced the Oglala and Brule dancers in the Stronghold to abandon their fort and proceed to Pine Ridge. When they learned of the massacre, they reversed themselves and fled north toward the Cheyenne River. They were joined in flight by Red Cloud and the previously peaceful residents of Pine Ridge. General Miles had no difficulty locating this band of Indians, which now numbered close to four thousand. Anxious to avoid any further bloodshed, he sent into the camp a handful of his most level-headed officers, among them a youthful captain named John J. Pershing.

General Miles, whom the Indians themselves trusted, pledged that there would be no reprisal if the Indians returned to their agencies and that their rations would be

increased. He also responded to one of the Indians' key grievances by promising that the corrupt civilian sub-agents on
the reservations would be replaced by army officers whom
the Indians knew and trusted. Impressed by these guaran-
tees and aware of the ever-tightening ring of military com-
bat units around them, the Indians surrendered on January 15, 1891. Thus ended the four hundred years of conflict
between cultures that had begun with Columbus's discovery of America.

In another ironic coincidence, the U.S. Census Bureau in
1890 announced that it could no longer identify any part of
the West that contained fewer than two people per square
mile, its definition of "frontier." The American frontier, which
had begun with the landing of the English at Jamestown
in 1607, had ended. North and South Dakota were now, for
better or worse, part of American civilization.

After the West Was Won: Farming the Indian Lands

By the terms of the Dawes Act of 1889 the federal government
had acquired 9 million acres of Dakota reservation land to
be opened for settlement under the terms of the Homestead
Act. The Indians were allowed to take individual 160-acre
allotments if they wished to avoid being relocated to one
of the six diminished reservations. The government could
then open any remaining land to homesteaders, charging
the white pioneers a fee at the time of entry, with the money
allotted to the support of the Dakota people. The fee would
expire after ten years, and settlers thereafter could take up
their 160-acre plots for the cost of filing a claim. Contrary
to government expectations, settlers did not rush to occupy the South Dakota lands west of the Missouri. A drought
lasting several years in the early 1890s and a nationwide depression from 1893 to 1897 were the principal constraints.

After 1900, however, a combination of government advertising and railroad promotion triggered the last great American land rush.

Nearly all of the pioneer farmers were destined for grievous disappointment. The main problem was rainfall. Average annual precipitation declined steadily as one moved west, from 21 inches a year in lands along the Missouri River to 13.66 inches at the Wyoming border. Those amounts were enough to sustain crops of wheat, but the averages were deceptive. Precipitation fell below average 40 percent of the time, 60 percent in the northwestern counties. That meant crop failures just about every other year. Another problem was that the unglaciated lands west of the river differed greatly from the land to the east. Most of the land in the west river country contained what modern analysts call a gumbo soil—that is, a high percentage of clay and little organic humus to preserve water and nutrients. It tended to clump when wet and turn hard when dry; in short, it was difficult to cultivate and, without fertilizer, prone to scanty yields.

Day-to-day life was also more difficult than on earlier frontiers. Except for the Badlands, most of which lay within the newly crafted Indian reservations, the land was flat, treeless, and psychologically depressing. Some migrants built sod houses, as they had on the eastern prairies, but most built tar-paper shacks, which could be erected more quickly and at little more expense. Cheap lumber from the pine forests of Wisconsin and Minnesota, milled in St. Louis and shipped west by rail, could be had in every hamlet that was served by a railroad. A settler could purchase an assortment of 2x4 studs, 2x6 rafters, 1x6 boards, a few rolls of tar paper, and some nails; haul these materials to his claim; and erect a shack in a few days. Insulation consisted of a layer of dead air between the boards that held the outer and inner coatings of tar paper. "Tar-paper homesteaders" had their choice of red or blue for the interior walls. Because the blue was heavier and thus more expensive, it was regarded as a sign of wealth and status. Edith Ammons, who had come west with her sister to homestead, wrote, "Blue paper on the walls was as much a sign of class on the frontier as blue blood in Boston."

The lack of water was a constant problem. Creeks were few and far between and often dried up in the summer. Hand-dug wells were not practicable because the water table in the plains lay so far beneath the surface. Few homesteaders could afford the drills and piping needed to sustain a windmill. Most resorted to building an earthen dam in a draw at the lower end of their property. Spring rains created a pool that in normal years might last through the summer. In the winter the family survived on melted snow. Because water was so precious, it was constantly recycled. The same tub of water furnished baths for three or four family members; the soapy water was then used to clean floors or launder work clothing.

Good rains for the first decade of the twentieth century produced bumper crops and characteristic frontier optimism. Then the drought struck in 1910 and last for five years. Fields turned bleak and dry. Water holes dried up. Realizing that this frontier was more hostile to settlement than any earlier one, many homesteaders abandoned their claims and village merchants their businesses, moving back to a region with a kinder climate. Some west river counties lost half their populations, others lost a fourth to a third. At Fort Pierre, noted one departing farmwife, "so many wagons were ahead of us that we had to wait two or three days for our turn at the ferry" across the Missouri.

17. A prairie homestead in the west river country. Built in 1909 by homesteaders Edgar and Alice Brown, this is the only original sod house in the West that is still extant. Photo by author.

The rains returned during the years of World War I, and the prices of agricultural products rose dramatically. Professors at South Dakota State College had also been experimenting with new drought-resistant crops. In 1915 they reported good yields of alfalfa on their experimental plots, and newspapers urged farmers to give the nitrogen-producing crop a chance. They also had success with new types of forage crops imported from Russia and China. These successes led to some tentative experiments with dairy cows. With the introduction of farm machinery and chemical fertilizers the modest prosperity continued through the 1920s. But the war had also brought new expectations. Young men returned from the army unwilling to resume the drab life and ceaseless labor of farming the plains. Families who had taken advantage of war profits to purchase an automobile moved back to the towns and cities of the East in search of better jobs. The depopulation of the western counties re-sumed in the 1920s and continues in both North and South Dakota to the present day. Those who decided to stay in the west country took pride in themselves for "sticking" to the good work of farming. They came to relish the challenge that the land posed and regarded themselves as more self-reliant and independent than soft, job-dependent easterners. That cultural attitude, too, has survived to the present day.

CHAPTER EIGHT

Political Prairie Fires, 1890–1920

The North Dakota state constitution of 1889 was arguably the first legislative victory for the agrarian revolt that culminated in the formation of the People's Party in 1891–92. The Farmers' Alliance had made great headway among North Dakota voters during the hard times of the late 1880s, and Alliance men dominated the constitutional convention that met in Bismarck in the summer of 1889. The document they crafted was perhaps the most liberal of any state constitution in the nation. Among the reforms it incorporated were a mechanism for arbitrating labor disputes, restrictions on child labor, the secret ballot,[1] statewide prohibition of spirituous liquors, and provision for a popularly elected board of railroad commissioners to regulate railroad fares and shipping rates. Implementing the reforms envisioned by the constitution was another matter, however. Republicans had been the dominant political party in the Dakota Territory since the Civil War, and voters in both of the new states returned Republican governors and legislatures in the first state elections in 1889. In both states farmers' grievances against out-of-state corporations and railroads were not given voice until the formation of the People's Party.

Dakota Populism

During the 1870s Minneapolis succeeded Chicago as the flour-milling center of the United States. The reason was a change in methods of wheat farming and a consequent revolution in milling machinery. On the prairies of Illinois and Iowa farmers sowed winter wheat, a strain that came to the United States from Europe. Farmers scattered seeds in late summer, and the young plants spent the winter under a bed of snow. The plants matured in the spring, and the grain was harvested in June or July. This method did not work on the northern plains, where the winter was much colder and the snow was often insufficient to cover the budding stalks of grain. Spring wheat, sown in the spring and harvested in late summer, was a likely alternative for the farmers of Minnesota and the Dakotas, but it presented milling problems. Spring wheat had a brittle, rust-colored bran husk that shattered into tiny particles in the milling process and discolored the flour. Minneapolis millers solved the problem in the 1870s by installing French-invented "middlings purifiers" that filtered out the bran and produced a superior grade of white flour that found favor in both the eastern United States and Europe.

By 1880 spring wheat was the crop of choice among farmers of western Minnesota and the Dakotas, but that brought a new set of problems. Although some wheat was exported through the port of Duluth, the Minneapolis millers had a virtual monopoly of domestic production, and they were thus able to control the price. Between the farmers on the Dakota frontier and the millers was a host of middlemen, notably owners of grain storage elevators and the railroads. A farmer dealt directly only with his local elevator operator. The price he received for his grain depended on the elevator operator's estimate of its quality, or grade. Higher grades yielded more flour at the mill. The operator's estimate was largely guesswork, and he often succumbed to the temptation to underrate the grain when paying the farmer and then raise the grade when selling it to the miller. The railroads who hauled the grain had abuses of their own. They charged a standard "transit fee" for a carload of grain, regardless of the distance traveled. The Dakota farmer thus paid for shipping all the way to Chicago, even though his grain traveled no farther than Duluth or Minneapolis. The railroads also owned many of the grain storage elevators and sometimes refused to furnish cars to farmers who wanted to ship their wheat directly to the millers.

Through the 1880s the Farmers' Alliance attempted to set up local, farmer-owned co-op elevators, but nearly all failed owing to the farmers' inexperience in marketing and opposition from the railroads and the milling corporations. In 1891 North Dakota Alliance men secured passage of a bill that would force railroads to cease discriminating against farmer-owned elevators, but the governor vetoed it. The Alliance then conceived the idea of a single, state-owned storage elevator situated at the millers' doorstep—that is, in either Minneapolis or Duluth. For the idea to materialize, however, the Alliance needed a stronger political organization. That came from out of state in the form of the People's Party.

Though angry and frustrated almost beyond endurance, the Dakota wheat farmers, many of them morally conservative Scandinavians, were not the most radical, or even the most vocal, of farm protestors. On the Great Plains, Kansas, where orators were urging farmers to "raise less corn and more hell," was the center of the farm revolt, and the best-organized force was the Texas-born Southern Alliance. The Southern Alliance had entered politics in 1890, seeking to gain control of the Democratic Party in the South by requiring congressional candidates to swear fealty to the Alliance program. Although the Alliance helped elect a number of congressmen, its candidates did nothing to promote rural interests when they arrived in Washington. Seeing the need for an independent third party, delegates from the various alliances, joined by some labor organizations, met in Cincinnati in May 1891 to form the People's Party. The meeting endorsed a series of proposals that would become the core of the Populist movement: relief of the rural credit crunch by the government's resumption of the coinage of silver and the issue of legal-tender paper money; government ownership and operation of all railroads; election of the president, vice president, and U.S. senators by popular vote; and adoption nationally of the Australian (secret) ballot.

That same spring, 1891, South Dakota Alliance men calling themselves Independents joined with Democrats in the state legislature to elect James H. Kyle to the U.S. Senate. A Congregational minister from Aberdeen, Kyle was a popular orator given to attacks on corporate wealth and the milling monopoly. In Washington, Kyle, who described himself as an "Indecrat," joined Populist William A. Peffer, who was elected by the Kansas legislature about the same time.

The year 1892 was a presidential election year, and Populists regarded the candidates of both of the two major parties, Republican Benjamin Harrison and Democrat Grover Cleveland, as lackeys of the eastern business establishment. The People's Party accordingly held a convention of its own in Omaha and nominated a longtime advocate of government paper money, James B. Weaver. In the fall election

Weaver picked up a few electoral votes in Kansas and the Rocky Mountain states, where Populists "fused" with "Free Silver Democrats." In North Dakota Populists and Democrats formed a similar alliance. A third-party convention met in advance of the state Democratic convention and made nominations for presidential electors, state officers, and congressional candidates. The Democrats then met and endorsed the Populist nominees, except for the state's three presidential electors. The Democrats supported both Cleveland and Weaver electors. The Alliance-Populist-Democrat fusion endorsed the Populist platform approved by the Omaha convention, and it also promised North Dakota farmers state-owned grain storage elevators at freight terminals.

The strategy worked. North Dakota voters elected a Populist governor, Eli Shortridge, and won other state executive offices. The state's three electoral votes were split, one each to Cleveland, Harrison, and Weaver. Republicans managed to reelect the state's lone congressman and retained their majority in the legislature, but the party was badly fragmented. Fusionists, on the other hand, were disciplined by a lifetime of opposition and able to attract the votes of Republican mavericks. In its 1893 session the legislature passed a resolution asking Congress to adopt a graduated income tax and a resolution requesting an amendment to the U.S. Constitution for the popular election of U.S. senators. Most significant, the legislature approved a bill to construct a state-owned elevator in either Minnesota (Minneapolis or Duluth) or Wisconsin (Superior). Unfortunately the act contained a fatal clause, due largely to the legislative inexperience of the farm bloc. The statute required that Minnesota or Wisconsin cede to North Dakota "absolute civil jurisdiction over the tract of land" on which the elevator was to be built. The purpose was to ensure that the elevator managers use North Dakota's wheat-grading standards rather than the arbitrary ones of the millers. Since neither Minnesota nor Wisconsin could be expected to comply with this requirement, it rendered the statute a dead letter.

In South Dakota the farm bloc (still calling itself Independents) preferred to retain its ideological purity rather than fuse with Democrats. Henry Loucks, the Independents' candidate for governor in 1890, led the South Dakota delegation to the Omaha convention and became its permanent chairman. He promoted Senator Kyle as presidential nominee but lost to Iowa's Weaver. That, however, was the extent of South Dakota Populism in 1892. The state Republican platform in that year cynically favored a popularly elected railroad commission, a postal savings bank for the thrifty poor, and government coinage of silver. The Republican candidate for governor was a member of the Farmers' Alliance and an ardent temperance advocate. Not surprisingly, the Republicans swept the state offices and gave the state electoral vote to Benjamin Harrison. They used the same strategy two years later and actually increased the Republican majority in the legislature. By 1895 the lower house of the South Dakota assembly had only twenty-four Independents and but a single Democrat.

By 1896, however, a severe depression that had begun with the Panic of 1893 split both of the major political parties and gave new life to the Populists. The Populist demand for the "free and unlimited coinage of silver" had strong appeal in the Rocky Mountain states because it promised silver miners a new market for their product. In the Democratic convention of that presidential election year western Democrats captured the party under the leadership of Nebraska journalist William Jennings Bryan with his cry of "free silver." Although bimetalism was the only feature of the Omaha platform endorsed by Bryan, the Populist convention voted for fusion and endorsed the nomination of Bryan. In South Dakota both Independents and Democrats, weakened by a succession of defeats, were ready for fusion, and both were heartened by a split in the state Republican Party.

The Republicans, it will be remembered, had endorsed "free silver" in 1892 and again in 1894, while regarding it as a harmless gesture (the nation's president, Grover Cleveland, was a conservative "gold Democrat"). With the onset of the depression, however, some South Dakota Republicans concluded that an expansion of the money supply might benefit their constituency—large-scale farmers and village merchants. Leading this group of "Silver Republicans" was the state's senior U.S. senator, Richard Pettigrew, a Sioux Falls lawyer. When the Republican national convention in June 1896 committed the party to the gold standard (i.e., all government-issued money and bonds exchangeable for gold coin), thirty-four delegates, including Senator Pettigrew, bolted the convention. Pettigrew and other defectors subsequently endorsed Bryan and "free silver."

In Huron, South Dakota, the Populists met with the Silver Republicans to work out a common cause of action. Senator Pettigrew declared himself a Populist, and the meeting voted overwhelmingly in favor of fusion with the Democrats on the national ticket. It nominated for governor Andrew E. Lee, a Vermillion merchant who, as mayor of the city, had denounced the milling monopoly and endorsed "free silver." The state Democrats then met and endorsed the Populist/ Silver Republican candidates for state offices and Congress. In the election that year nearly 90 percent of the registered voters cast ballots, the largest electoral turnout in South Dakota history. Although an electoral revolution seemed imminent, the state's basic conservatism held quite firm.

Bryan carried the state over Republican nominee William McKinley by a scant 183 votes. Lee defeated the regular Republican candidate for governor by a little over 200 votes. The fusionists gained control of the state legislature by a slim margin and won the state's two seats in Congress, but most of the state executive offices went to Republicans. In the national election Republican William McKinley easily defeated Bryan, for whom Populism's embrace had proved to be a kiss of death.

The result in South Dakota, as might be expected, was mixed. The "Indecrat" Senator Kyle, sensing the national trend against Populism, declared his support for the McKinley administration and was reelected by a strange combination of Republicans and confused Populists. In its 1897 session the legislature authorized a railroad commission with power to establish maximum rate schedules, but the railroads took it to court and had it declared unconstitutional. The lone achievement from the standpoint of the Populists was the passage of an amendment to the state constitution providing for the initiative (initiation of laws by popular petition) and the referendum (popular vote on laws submitted to the voters by the legislature). That was the end of Populism in South Dakota. Although Lee was reelected governor in 1898, the voters returned solid Republican majorities to the legislature. The return of prosperity and the outbreak of war with Spain that year ended public concern with the issues raised by the People's Party. The Republicans swept the state in the election of 1900.

North Dakota's brief flirtation with Populism ended with the legislative session of 1893. The state returned to Republican control in 1894 and voted for McKinley over Bryan in 1896. It was about this time — some contemporary writers thought it even a few years earlier — that the North Dakota

Republican Party, and hence the state, fell under the thumb of a political boss, Alexander McKenzie. The uncertainty about the origin of McKenzie's ascendancy was due to the man's penchant for secrecy, his preference for invisibility. "Never write a letter," he once advised a colleague. "Walk across the state if necessary, but never write a letter. Sure, what you say goes up in smoke, but what you *write* is before you always." McKenzie had come to the Dakota Territory in the 1870s as a track-laying foreman on the Northern Pacific Railroad. He settled in Bismarck in 1873, and the following year he was elected sheriff of Burleigh County, a position he held for the next twelve years. His connection with the railroad enabled him to speculate in choice city lots, and by 1883, when he first came to public attention, he reportedly owned $250,000 worth of land in Bismarck.

In 1883 the legislature engaged in one of its periodic battles over removal of the capital from Yankton. The legislature set up a commission to consider alternate sites, and McKenzie wangled a seat on it. As a result of McKenzie's influence, the city of Bismarck offered the territorial government $100,000 in cash and 320 acres of land on which to build a capitol. The source of the cash is uncertain, but most of the land was part of the Northern Pacific land grant. After numerous ballots Bismarck won the prize, largely because the southern counties (Black Hills versus the Missouri River communities) could not agree on a common choice. The legislature compensated some of the losers by promising to build state universities at Grand Forks and Vermillion and an agricultural college at Fargo. The main result of this imbroglio was to further the movement for a division into two states. After 1883 South Dakota constitutional conventions met in Pierre, while North Dakota's adherents met in Bismarck. The further result was to solidify McKenzie's reputation as the backstairs orchestrator of North Dakota politics. Although few ordinary citizens ever saw him, a half-whispered reference to the "McKenzie Ring," according to one contemporary chronicler, "evoked a picture of almost magical power and influence, beside which governors and legislators were of little consequence."

The sources of McKenzie's power were two—the Minneapolis milling fraternity, which supplied him with funds, and the railroads, which supplied his "ring" with free passes. State officials and members of the legislature who cooperated with him—McKenzie was seldom forceful and never violent—received free passes for all railroad travel, whether in state or as distant as Chicago. It was bribery but of a subtle sort for which there was no law. During the 1890s McKenzie became a member of the Republican national party committee, a position that gave him control of most of the federal patronage in the state. McKenzie maintained a suite in St. Paul's Merchants Hotel, where North Dakota legislators gathered periodically to discuss strategy. To that extent the Twin Cities became the political, as well as commercial, capital of North Dakota.

We have only negative evidence for McKenzie's influence and "stand pat" conservatism. The governor of the state in the late 1890s was a former leader in the Farmers' Alliance, but he proposed not a single reform of the sort the Populists had wanted. The Republican governor in office from 1901 to 1904 ignored completely the tide of Progressivism that was sweeping the country in those years, often led by Republicans such as Theodore Roosevelt and Robert M. La Follette. In his first message to the legislature he declared, "Much legislation . . . is to be avoided. To use the words of [House of Representatives] Speaker [Thomas B. 'Czar'] Reed, 'If you don't know what to do, do nothing.'"

Dakota Progressivism

Historians generally agree that the Progressive movement can be dated from 1901, when Theodore Roosevelt became president upon the assassination of William McKinley and Robert M. La Follette was elected governor of Wisconsin. La Follette was a Republican "Insurgent" who objected to the control of the party—and hence the state—by bosses (notably Philetus Sawyer, who held office as U.S. senator through his control of the state legislature) rather than the will of the people. The thrust of La Follette's program, and that of other state reformers, was to eliminate "invisible government" and restore the average voter to his rightful place at the foundation of the political system, as he supposedly had been in the days of Jefferson, Jackson, and Lincoln. La Follette's methods included the primary election, which would give voters a voice in the nomination of candidates, as well as the initiative and referendum and popular election of U.S. senators. The Progressives' economic program included government regulation of railroad rates, elimination of corrupt practices such as free passes, income and inheritance taxes that would ensure a more equitable distribution of wealth, and workers' compensation insurance for injuries on the job. Because of opposition from Republican "Stalwarts" in the Wisconsin legislature, La Follette was able to obtain passage of nothing more than a primary law before departing for the U.S. Senate in 1907. His successors, however, managed to enact most of the Progressive program, which became a model for other states as the "Wisconsin idea." La Follette was popular in South Dakota. His brother William was a resident of the state and a prominent "Silver Republican" in the 1890s. La Follette's "insurgency" in Wisconsin thus became a model for malcontents who thought South Dakota had fallen under boss rule.

Although he lacked the mystique of North Dakota's McKenzie, Alfred B. Kittredge headed a clique of lawyers who allegedly met secretly in a room of the Locke Hotel in Pierre and drafted laws that the legislature simply ratified. Kittredge was a Republican national committeeman, chief dispenser of patronage for the McKinley administration, and general counsel for the Milwaukee Railroad. His cronies had as clients the Chicago and North Western Railroad, the Standard Oil Company, and assorted insurance companies.

South Dakota's "Insurgent" was Coe I. Crawford, a lawyer from Huron who had served as South Dakota's attorney general and had unsuccessfully run for Congress in 1896. After his hopes for a U.S. Senate seat upon Kyle's death in 1901 were dashed by the governor's appointment of Kittredge, Crawford laid plans to run for governor. He announced his candidacy in 1903 with a claim that machine politicians and their corporate backers were invisibly running the state. He endorsed a primary law and other Progressive reforms. He failed, as La Follette had in his first run for governor, because the party machine held firm control of the nominating convention. La Follette visited the state in 1905 and met privately with Crawford and his following, offering organizational advice. In 1906 the Progressives won control of the Republican convention, nominating Crawford for governor and endorsing electoral reform and railroad regulation.

In its 1907 session the legislature enacted a primary law, outlawed railroad passes, established a railroad passenger rate of two and a half cents per mile, created a pure food and drug commission, and authorized funds for free textbooks in public schools. Interestingly the primary law allowed voters to choose candidates for the U.S. Senate, even though their votes did not count because the choice was made by the legislature until 1916. In 1908 Crawford defeated Kittredge in the primary, and the legislature duly sent him to Washington to join La Follette and Iowa's Albert B. Cummings as a reform bloc in what Progressives had dubbed "the millionaires' club."

The Progressives continued to dominate South Dakota politics despite a rift in their ranks after 1910—a split that divided Republican Progressives nationally—involving the presidential ambitions of Theodore Roosevelt and Bob La Follette. William Howard Taft, Roosevelt's successor in the election of 1908, had alienated Progressives by his stance on the protective tariff and conservation issues. In 1910 Roosevelt broke with his one-time protégé and announced his candidacy for the Republican nomination in 1912. Once regarded as a "trust buster," Roosevelt, in a program he styled the "New Nationalism," proposed to regulate giant corporations rather than "bust" them. La Follette regarded this as too pro-business and announced his own candidacy for the Republican nomination. In the Republican national convention of 1912 the South Dakota delegation divided its ballots evenly between La Follette and Roosevelt. When the Stalwart-dominated convention renominated Taft, Roosevelt bolted and formed a new third party, the Progressives. In the election Roosevelt carried South Dakota by ten thousand votes, although Democrat Woodrow Wilson was the national winner.

The Progressive movement in South Dakota reached its pinnacle with the election of Peter Norbeck as governor in 1916. Republican Progressives controlled the legislature in alliance with Wilson Democrats. In its 1917 session the legislature adopted a rural credits plan that allowed the state to make loans to farmers, and it set up committees to examine the feasibility of other state enterprises recommended by the governor—state hail insurance on farm crops, state-owned coal mines, state-owned grain elevators, and state power-generating plants on the Missouri River. It also approved workers' compensation on the Wisconsin model and a law giving effect to a state constitutional amendment prohibiting the manufacture and sale of alcoholic beverages. The most sweeping proposal of all was a law permitting the state to enter any business enterprise it desired within certain financial limits. At that heady moment the South Dakota Progressives ran headlong into an even more radical political prairie fire, North Dakota's Nonpartisan League.

The Nonpartisan League

Despite McKenzie's armlock on the state, North Dakota was not immune to the tide of Progressive thought that was sweeping the nation. Like the young La Follette in Wisconsin, young Republicans whose ambitions had been thwarted by the McKenzie machine began spreading Progressive ideals, notably that of the direct primary. The miniscule Democratic Party also caught the mood of the times. In 1906 it nominated John Burke, the son of Irish immigrants, for governor on a platform that declared, "The political affairs of the state of North Dakota are controlled by the railroads." Popular support for the Progressives was centered in the eastern part of the state, where Scandinavians were dominant (the same was true in Wisconsin and Minnesota), while the Republican conservatives' main support lay among the German-Russian settlements of the west.

Burke's chances of breaking McKenzie's stranglehold on the state improved markedly in the spring of 1906 with the publication of a series of articles titled "The Looting of Alaska" in the progressive magazine *Appleton's* by muckraking journalist Rex Beach. Beach told of a gigantic conspiracy organized by McKenzie in 1900 to get control of gold claims held by Europeans (most of them Swedes) in Alaska. Federal officials broke up the conspiracy, but McKenzie fled the territory before he could be brought to trial. He was later arrested in California and sentenced to a year in jail. He was pardoned by President McKinley after North Dakota's U.S. senators interceded on his behalf. Beach called McKenzie "the biggest 'hidden' politician in the whole Northwest" and quoted McKenzie as saying, "Give me a bunch of Swedes, and I'll drive them like sheep." Later that year Beach turned his articles into a novel, The Spoilers, and North Dakota's Progressive and Democratic papers serialized the juiciest parts of the plot.[2] Burke was thus able to make political corruption and "boss rule" the centerpiece of his campaign, and he had great appeal to European-born, particularly Scandinavian, voters. Burke won the election, and the Democratic-Insurgent coalition won control of the lower house of the legislature.

Although conservative Republicans remained in control of the state senate, the legislature enacted a direct-primary law in 1907, including a provision for voters to express a preference for U.S. senator. Alexander McKenzie, who had always preferred to exercise control through subtle means, realized that the primary law would end his control of electoral candidates—and hence his political power; he resigned as Republican national committeeman that year. Conservatives remained a force in North Dakota politics for the next decade, but the discipline vanished. For example, Asle J. Gronna, the first North Dakota congressman to become a national figure, was a McKenzie choice when elected to the House of Representatives in 1904. In Congress he befriended Progressives such as La Follette and George Norris of Nebraska and voted in favor of both federal railroad regulation and the Pure Food and Drug Act, the centerpieces of Theodore Roosevelt's presidency.

Even in its prime the McKenzie machine had not been averse to progress, so long as "progress" did not threaten its control of the state. It approved, for example, the expansion of the state's colleges. A university whose boundaries were as broad as those of the state was at the heart of the "Wisconsin idea," and Progressives liked the notion of government by informed professionals. The University of North Dakota at Grand Forks, which was established in 1884 and had only twenty students upon statehood five years later, grew exponentially in the early years of the Progressive movement. Between 1899 and 1905 it opened schools of law, engineering, medicine, and education. In those same years the Agricultural College at Fargo added departments of engineering, education, veterinary medicine, and pharmacy.

In 1910 Burke was reelected for a second term, and a combination of Republican Progressives and Democrats finally won control of both houses of the legislature. In its next session the legislature adopted the entire panoply of Progressive legislation: the prohibition of railroad passes, a presidential primary, the regulation of lobbyists, and workers' compensation for injuries on the job. Grain elevator abuses remained the most important issue to the farmers of North Dakota, however, and by 1911 the best solution seemed to be a state-owned elevator located either in North Dakota or in the Twin Cities, the terminal point of most wheat shipments. State financing for such a radical (critics called it "socialist") experiment required an amendment to the state constitution, and that, in turn, had to win approval over the course of two sessions of the legislature and a referendum by the voters. An amendment to construct an elevator in Minnesota or Wisconsin survived this process in 1909–12 and a second amendment for a state-owned elevator located in North Dakota won approval in 1911–14.

In the election of 1912 the Republicans adopted the strategy that had successfully kept Populism at bay in the 1890s: they adopted a Progressive platform with no intention of carrying any of it into law. And it worked again. Republican Louis B. Hanna defeated John Burke in the gubernatorial canvass, and Republicans regained control of the legislature. Hanna publicly supported the amendments authorizing a state-owned grain elevator, but when the legislature created a state board of control to plan the construction of one, he loaded it with opponents of the idea. In early 1915 the board issued a six-hundred-page report opposing the project. It pointed out that an elevator built in Minnesota or Wisconsin would, despite North Dakota ownership, be subject to the wheat-grading standards of those states. It recommended leasing an elevator instead of building one. Armed with this report the legislature soundly defeated a bill authorizing the construction of a state elevator. The legislative session coincided with a meeting of a farm organization in Bismarck, and angry farmers milled through the halls of the capitol during the legislative debate. One story that circulated among the angry throng was that of a Republican legislator, arguing with constituents late into the night, who had impetuously told them to "go home and slop the hogs and leave the lawmaking to us." Whether apocryphal or not, the disparaging remark typified the politicians' disdain for rural interests. It helped ignite yet another political firestorm.

The catalyst was a thirty-five-year-old Minnesota-born farmer, Arthur C. Townley. Townley had failed as a farmer due to a combination of bad weather and price manipulation by commodity speculators in Minneapolis and Chicago. In 1913 he became an organizer for the state Socialist Party, whose tactics focused on personal appeals to farmers in their rural homes. Townley also found that a specific program of legislation had more appeal than abstruse ideology. Finally, he discovered that a party organizer won a friendlier reception if he was accompanied by a person of local eminence that his audience knew and respected.

In the spring of 1915, following the defeat of the grain elevator bill, Townley quit the Socialist Party and set out to form a protest movement of his own that eventually termed itself the Nonpartisan League (NPL). It was a revolutionary idea because it recognized the weakness of third parties in the United States and the dangers of fusion with one of the major political parties. Townley instead would capitalize on the newly invented primary to gain control of one of the established political parties, and since North Dakota was essentially a one-party state, his natural target was the Republicans. His method was to enlist members, regardless of their previous political affiliation, in an organization with specific farm-oriented goals:

State ownership of terminal elevators and flour mills

State inspection of grain quality

State hail insurance and taxes based on acreage rather than farm improvements

Nonprofit rural credit banks

None of the planks in the platform was new, and that was its appeal. They had been discussed for two decades and received the approval of most farmers. Townley and a few friends began visiting farm homesteads that spring to enlist members. The membership fee was $2.50 a year (later raised to $6), and with his first receipts Townley, who had crisscrossed the countryside by horse and buggy, bought a Model T Ford to improve his mobility. With subsequent receipts he began hiring recruiters, most of whom were Socialists experienced in personal-contact organizing. Training consisted of sending a novice to spend a few days in the company of a veteran before striking out on his own. One veteran recalled a typical hortatory sendoff for new recruiters: "Find out the damn fool's hobby and then talk it. If he likes religion, talk Jesus Christ; if he is against the government, damn the Democrats; if he is afraid of whiskey, preach Prohibition; if he wants to talk hogs, talk hogs—talk anything he'll listen to, but talk, talk, until you get his God-damn John Hancock to a check for six dollars."

With a fleet of NPL-owned Model Ts, Townley's organizers were able to blanket the state by early summer. Recognizing the need for centralized leadership, Townley ceased his own canvassing and established an NPL headquarters in Fargo. In September 1915 he founded a newspaper, the *Nonpartisan Leader*, and with that the shadow movement became a political force that could not be ignored. Sprightly written, the *Leader* gave North Dakota farmers a blend of muckraking exposé and homely wisdom. Cartoonist John M. Baer kept the state chuckling over his depictions of the "old gang" (i.e., the Republican establishment) as overweight, bowler-hatted, diamond-ringed capitalists.

By early 1916 League membership stood at more than twenty-five thousand, and Townley was ready to take aim at the Republican primary, scheduled for June in that election year. On Washington's birthday, February 22, Townley called for precinct-level caucuses to meet and select delegates for a state nominating convention to be held in Fargo on March 29. Across the state farmers met in rural schoolhouses, town halls, and churches to pledge allegiance to NPL's narrow set of goals and elect delegates who reflected those beliefs. With little or no education in politics, they rejected mercenary office seekers and sent to Fargo their most respected neighbors. The forty-nine delegates who convened in Fargo on March 29 were wise enough to recognize their inexperience, and they turned to Townley for advice. Townley, in turn, relied on the social connections of NPL general counsel William Lemke. As a result the convention nominated for governor Lynn J. Frazier, a Red River Valley farmer who had been a classmate of Lemke's at the University of North Dakota and had a history of leadership in farm organizations. For attorney general the convention chose William Langer, a graduate of the University of North Dakota Law School and another friend of Lemke's. As a county attorney Langer had taken on the mighty Northern Pacific Railroad and won a court decision forcing the railroad to pay taxes on the grain elevators and lumber companies it owned along its right-of-way.

In the June primary campaign Frazier and other statewide candidates rode in a "Victory Special" train that carried them over the entire Northern Pacific and Great Northern rail systems, with stops at nearly every village and crossroads in the state. The result was a sweeping victory in the June 25 Republican primary. Frazier carried forty-six of the state's fifty-three counties, and the League succeeded in nominating 17 out of 22 candidates for the state senate and 87 out of 98 for the house. In the fall election the NPL, with a membership near forty thousand, was able to spend $270,000 on the campaign—reviving Frazier's "Victory Special," purchasing additional "Tin Henrys" for organizers and speakers, and spending $40,000 on campaign literature. The Democratic candidate sought to blunt the NPL juggernaut by endorsing the NPL platform but to no avail. In the November 7 election Frazier carried every county in the state, receiving the greatest majority of votes ever given a governor of North Dakota. The League-endorsed candidates for state offices, including the supreme court, also won handily. The League elected 81 of the 113 members of the lower house of the legislature. In the senate, however, where terms were staggered, 24 holdovers from the 1914 election left Republican Stalwarts with a slight majority.

Well aware that most of the Nonpartisan Leaguers in the legislature were political novices, Arthur Townley leased the entire Northwest Hotel in Bismarck for the spring 1917 legislative session. He then arranged nightly meetings of legislators in the hotel's ballroom; these provided instruction in parliamentary procedure, gave inarticulate farmers practice in public speaking, and ensured doctrinal unity. A caucus of the more experienced legislators considered all proposed legislation and determined the League's stance on each bill. League members had pledged themselves to vote in accordance with the majority opinion of the caucus.

The result was a legislative session of extraordinary accomplishments. The only thing the Stalwarts in the senate were able to block was a house-passed revision of the state constitution that specifically allowed the state to own and operate agricultural and manufacturing businesses. Among the laws approved that spring were a state wheat-grading system, a nine-hour workday for women, reduced taxes on farm machinery and improvements, a prohibition on railroads from charging more for a short haul than a long haul, and a tripling of state aid to education. State-owned grain elevators, the centerpiece of the NPL's platform, went down with the defeat of the revised constitution. The senate, however, did approve a small appropriation for a single elevator, but Governor Frazier vetoed it on grounds that it was inadequate. That idea would have to await another election and hoped-for League control of both houses of the legislature.

In the 1916 election the League had declined to nominate

candidates for national office, but the death of one of North Dakota's three congressmen in the spring of 1917 forced it to decide whether to enter the field of national politics. Townley had initially favored focusing on the League's narrow farm-oriented state program, but the League's vote-getting power and legislative success induced him to broaden his vision. Accordingly when Governor Frazier called for a special election for the house seat on July 10, the League nominated the *Leader*'s popular cartoonist, John M. Baer, a Democrat by party affiliation who had been appointed a postmaster in the Red River Valley by the Wilson administration. Baer easily won the election, and Townley decided to expand his organization. By the end of the year the League had a national office in St. Paul and branches in thirteen states (though in truth outside of North Dakota it was a political factor only in Minnesota).

At that juncture Townley and the League encountered difficulties they could not have foreseen and over which they had no control. American entry into World War I in April 1917 stirred a wave of patriotism, abetted by the Wilson administration's "Four Minute Men," and it cast suspicion on anyone who opposed the war. Eugene Debs, the Socialist Party candidate in the election of 1912, was put in jail for opposing the war, and pacifists generally, including many of the NPL's organizers, fell under suspicion. The Bolshevik Revolution in Russia in November 1917 raised the specter of Communist subversion and encouraged NPL critics to denounce programs such as a state-owned grain elevator as "Socialist" and "radical." The "Red Scare" of 1919–20, fomented almost single-handedly by Wilson's attorney general, A. Mitchell Palmer, furthered public hostility to any idea or program that could be considered "radical" or "leftist" (a word coined in 1920). The American public's retreat from Progressivism climaxed with the presidential election of Republican Stalwart Warren G. Harding in 1920. In this wartime and postwar intellectual climate both Townley and the Nonpartisan League gradually withered into insignificance.

Political Backfires

Although Governor Peter Norbeck had brought Progressivism to its pinnacle in South Dakota, Norbeck had no use for the Nonpartisan League. In December 1916 NPL organizers in "tin flivvers" entered the state from Minnesota and within three months claimed twenty thousand members in the eastern counties, with headquarters in Sioux Falls. NPL lobbyists appeared in Pierre during the 1917 legislative session and helped promote Norbeck's spate of Progressive legislation. Fearing loss of control of his state to Townley, Norbeck fought the NPL by endorsing much of its farmer-oriented platform while attempting to discredit League leaders by accusing them of radicalism and disloyalty. In the general election of 1918 Norbeck soundly defeated the League candidate for governor, and in the ensuing legislative session he stole more of the NPL's thunder by securing enactment of state hail insurance, a state-owned coal mine, and an appropriation to survey sites for hydroelectric dams. Significantly he cast doubt on the feasibility of state-owned grain elevators or flour mills, and the legislature buried bills to that effect. One feature of Norbeck's Progressivism that had not been on the NPL's agenda was conservation. He helped create Custer State Park in the Black Hills and expanded it into one of the largest in the nation. As a result of Norbeck's adroit political maneuvers and the public's drift toward conservatism, the NPL was not heard from again in South Dakota.

To the north the League also suffered reverses in 1918, some of them self-inflicted. In April 1917 a handful of NPL legislators felt that the secret caucuses organized by Townley and Lemke perverted the democratic spirit in which the League had been founded. They discovered allies among village leaders and large-scale farmers in the prosperous Red River Valley who were alarmed by the state's drift into "socialism." The two groups thus founded the Anti-Socialist Conference, changing the name to the less ideological Independent Voters Association IVA on the eve of the June 1918 Republican primary.

The IVA's initial challenge failed miserably. Frazier was reelected governor in 1918, and the League at last gained control of both houses of the legislature. In its spring 1919 session the legislature created a state-owned Bank of North Dakota to make low-cost loans to farmers and finance state business enterprises. To ensure that the bank had ample capital the law required county governments to deposit their funds in the bank. The legislature also authorized a statewide system of state-owned grain elevators and flour mills, and it enacted such Progressive measures as a workers' compensation law, an eight-hour day and minimum wage for women, and a constitutional amendment authorizing the recall of state officials accused of misfeasance through a popular petition and special recall election.

These gains, however, were the League's last hurrah. In 1919 Townley was convicted by a Minnesota court of conspiring to disrupt the war effort and was sentenced to a year in prison. That same year North Dakota's attorney general, William Langer, broke with Townley, accused him of dictatorial leadership and misuse of League funds, and joined the IVA. In the Republican landslide of 1920 Stalwarts regained control of the legislature, and although the popular

Frazier won one more term as governor by defeating Langer, he was little more than an executive figurehead during the interval. In 1921 the legislature, with studied irony, turned a Progressive achievement against its authors. It initiated a recall election that forced out of office Governor Frazier and other League officials, including several members of the supreme court.

Although the Nonpartisan League was little more than a shadow organization through the 1920s, several of its leaders had lengthy political careers. Lynn Frazier was elected to the U.S. Senate in 1922, only a year after being removed as governor, and served until 1941. William Langer served two terms as governor in the 1930s, was elected to the U.S. Senate in 1940, and served until his death in 1959. William Lemke was elected to the House of Representatives in 1932 and served, with the exception of a single term, until his death in 1950. Gerald P. Nye, who got his start in politics as an League organizer, was elected to the Senate in 1924 and served until 1945. As final testimonials to the League's legacy, the Bank of North Dakota and the state-owned elevator and flour mill, located in Fargo, remain in operation to the present day. The bank in particular continues to prove its value to the state. It serves as a reserve bank for the state's private banks and helps them fund public projects that would otherwise be beyond their means. It offers cheap loans to farmers, small businesses, and students, and it remains profitable. It has today almost $4 billion in assets, and its conservative management avoided the home-mortgage-induced recession of 2008–10. In 2009 it set a record for the sixth straight year with $58 million in profits, and it had other states looking into the feasibility of adopting North Dakota's brand of "socialism."

CHAPTER NINE

Mount Rushmore
Conceived in Prosperity, Born of Depression

utzon Borglum was a sculptor, and he did it the old
fashioned way, chipping pieces out of a block of stone
with hammer and chisel to fashion a face or figure.
But his vision was hardly old-fashioned. He wanted to carve
an entire mountain into faces and figures.

Borglum's father, Jens, converted to Mormonism in Denmark, brought his wife to America in the 1850s, and followed the Mormon wagon trail to Utah. Because Utah was
under pressure from the government for the Mormons' practice of polygamy, the Borglums moved to Idaho, where their
son Gutzon was born in 1867. Trained as a woodcarver, however, Jens Borglum found himself unable to make a living
in Idaho. He returned east with his family, went to medi-
cal school, and set up practice in Fremont, Nebraska, where
Gutzon spent his childhood.

In a private academy in Kansas City Gutzon demonstrated a talent for painting. He later went to New York for further study, married his instructor, and then spent the 1890s
studying painting and sculpting under masters in Paris and

London. Returning to New York, he opened a studio and in 1909 came to public attention with a massive marble bust of Lincoln, which President Theodore Roosevelt displayed in the White House to celebrate the centennial of Lincoln's birth.

In 1915 the United Daughters of the Confederacy (UDC) asked Borglum to carve a memorial to the Confederate army on Stone Mountain in northern Georgia. The bald chunk of granite rose dramatically out of the Georgia plain, and its massive barren cliffs invited a drawing or sculpture of some sort. Borglum agreed and, never short of grand visions, conceived of a bas-relief on the side of the mountain with horse-drawn artillery coming over the crest at the top. Below that he envisioned columns of infantry and cavalry converging on the largest outward bulge, where Borglum would carve a titanic grouping of mounted figures—Robert E. Lee, Jefferson Davis, and Stonewall Jackson.

Although ultimately a disaster, the Stone Mountain venture provided Borglum with valuable experience in massive sculpture, using jackhammers, dynamite, and picks. Not surprisingly, the project was far too large for the financial resources of the UDC, and in 1923, as Borglum was nearing completion of the bust of Lee, the Confederate ladies forced a new contract upon him, limiting the entire sculpture to the central group of leaders along with a few other leaders to be chosen. The UDC then fell to quarreling over its favorite leaders, and Borglum began looking for other projects. In August 1924 he received a letter from Doane Robinson, state historian of South Dakota, who had conceived the idea of a massive heroic sculpture on one of the barren cliffs of the Black Hills, a once prosperous region suffering the exhaustion of its gold mines and in desperate need of tourist revenue. Borglum sent an excited response by telegram the same day and within a month was on a train to South Dakota.

Borglum's trip west brought his dispute with the UDC to

a head. They fired him and began a search for a new sculptor. In revenge Borglum, on his return to Georgia, smashed the models that the jackhammer and pick workers were using to carve the cliff and formally accepted Robinson's offer. The sculptor whom the UDC retained to replace him was so inept that the entire project was abandoned in 1928.[1]

Choosing a Design and a Mountain

Rapid City boosters quite understandably applauded Robinson's idea of a sculptured mountain and suggested it contain local heroes such as Wild Bill Hickok, General Custer, and Calamity Jane. Robinson, however, realized that to attract tourists it had to be a national monument commemorating the republic's founders and saviors. On the train from Pierre to Rapid City, Borglum sketched a two-hundred-foot-tall bust of George Washington majestically framed by surrounding spruce-sided mountains. Upon returning to his home in Connecticut, Borglum expanded the project to two-hundred-foot-high statues of Washington, Lincoln, and Theodore Roosevelt (who had given him his first national publicity), as well as "large bas-reliefs of Custer and others."

Robinson immediately realized that the project would be costly and that he was going to need political help. Congress would have to approve the use of National Forest land for the memorial, and the $10,000 Borglum demanded for preliminary surveys and models would have to come from the state legislature. A likely ally was Senator Peter Norbeck, the former Progressive governor who was vitally interested in the development of state parks and natural scenery. With Norbeck's support the congressional authorization bill passed, and after expressing some concern over Borglum's handling of the Stone Mountain fiasco, the legislature approved the $10,000 appropriation.

Accompanied by Senator Norbeck, Borglum journeyed to the Black Hills in August 1925 and found rooms in a hunting lodge west of Rapid City. Guided by the superintendent of Custer State Park, within three days Borglum found the mountain that would serve his purpose—Mount Rushmore, a little-known peak named after a New York lawyer who had been employed by a tin mining company in the 1880s. Although dwarfed by surrounding peaks, it caught Borglum's eye because it presented a barren wall of granite, about four hundred feet high and five hundred feet wide, large enough for Borglum's grandiose scheme. In addition the wall contained four deep fissures, giving any figures he carved angular depth, as if half-facing one another. Returning to Rapid City, he informed the local newspaper that Mount Rushmore was his choice because he knew of "no piece of granite comparable to it in the United States." He also informed the world that the "Great American Memorial" would cost a million dollars, but that was no problem because "a number of eastern money-kings have already been interested and promises of large donations have been secured." In fact, Borglum had received no promises of any kind, from "money-kings" or any others.

Borglum did, however, have on his side two earthshakers—Senator Norbeck and Doane Robinson. Both found working with the impulsive and unpredictable Borglum a dizzying experience, but both realized what a boon the monument would be to South Dakota. And they also realized that to obtain state or federal funding Borglum would have to come up with a "definite plan" for the monument. Borglum, ever the professional artist, demanded a retainer of $10,000 to design the monument, and the most the boosters of Rapid City could come up with was a few hundred. Thus the project languished for two years.

In the spring of 1927 it became known that President Calvin Coolidge, who had routinely spent his summer vacations in the Adirondack Mountains as a cure for his chronic bronchitis, thought he might instead visit the drier and more bug-free American West. The South Dakota legislature promptly issued an invitation for the president to visit the Black Hills, writing eloquently of its "lofty peaks," "ideal climate," "magnificent forests," and "sparkling streams." When Senator Norbeck hand-delivered the invitation, Coolidge read it and remarked dryly, "Senator, I cannot tell whether this is a chapter from Revelations or Mohammed's idea of the seventh heaven." A secret service agent visited Rapid City in May, found no trace of radicalism or a potential assassin, and the White House announced that the president would arrive in the Black Hills on June 16. The publicity attending the president's vacation in the Black Hills brought donations from South Dakota businessmen and enabled Norbeck and Robinson to form an association and offer a contract to Borglum to create a design.

The decision to make the monument a memorial to U.S. presidents rather than, say, a war memorial or one depicting a classical western scene was reached in a characteristically haphazard way. As early as 1924, Borglum and Robinson had decided on busts of Washington and Lincoln instead of two-hundred-foot-high statues. A year later Borglum decided to add a bust of Jefferson, a natural choice since he had written the nation's Declaration of Independence and in purchasing the Louisiana territory (which included the Black Hills) had more than doubled the size of the nation. Almost immediately after adding Jefferson, Borglum decided on Theodore Roosevelt as a fourth and final portrait. Of all Borglum's choices the last is the only one that generated controversy and continues to raise questions in the minds of viewers today. The feeling, among Robinson and other critics, was that however important Roosevelt as president might have been, he did not fit the theme of nationhood presented by Washington, Jefferson, and Lincoln. Borglum never explained his decision to add Roosevelt, but he doubtless felt an obligation to the man who had given him his first national publicity. Borglum also had an ally in Senator Norbeck, who was an ardent Roosevelt fan and, as South Dakota's leading Progressive, had been instrumental in Roosevelt's carrying the state in the election of 1912.

With the concept complete Borglum submitted plans to the executive committee of the Mount Rushmore Association. The committee accepted the plan and drafted a contract that Borglum signed. The contract estimated the cost at $312,000 and gave Borglum a sculptor's fee of 25 percent ($78,000), bringing the total cost to nearly $400,000. Borglum's fee was to be paid in monthly installments, the amount calculated on the cost of the previous month's work. For a down payment to Borglum the committee extracted gifts of $5,000 from each of the three railroads that served the Black Hills and an additional $10,000 from Rapid City businessmen. This was sufficient for Borglum to make plaster cast models of his figures and build the bunkhouses for workers, platforms, rope-and-pulley lifts, and other infrastructure. The thousands of dollars needed for actual work, however, would have to come from the state legislature. And the legislature understandably balked because no one outside of South Dakota had even heard of the Black Hills. A potential tourist industry had to be created in order to make the monument financially feasible. The announcement of President Coolidge's visit piqued local interest in a tourist attraction; his vacation there in the summer of 1927 gave the Black Hills national publicity.

The White House announcement of the president's plans that spring had been a mixed blessing for South Dakota governor William Bulow. The president, a White House spokesman had announced, would reside in the Game Lodge (where Borglum had been staying) and use the gymnasium of the Rapid City High School as an office for holding news conferences, signing bills, and so on. Bulow realized that part of the thirty-mile road connecting the two locations was an ungraded dirt trail through the woods. Ordered to upgrade the passage to an all-weather road in a month's time, the state road engineer protested that he could not even get it surveyed in that amount of time. "Do it first and survey it later," Bulow replied. "How's the president going to know he's riding on an unsurveyed road?" Somehow it was done. The road, which would become the main traffic artery for the sculpting of Mount Rushmore, was graded, ditched, and paved with gravel by the time the president, his wife, two collies, and a pet raccoon stepped off the train on June 16.

Bulow's next problem was how to keep the president entertained. Sioux leaders offered to make him an honorary chief, and national rodeo champion "Dakota Clyde" offered riding lessons. But these offers, Bulow realized, would not occupy the planned three-week vacation. Trout fishing, Bulow concluded, was the answer. Bulow and his staff did not know whether the president had ever fished, but they were certain he had never gone after trout with a fly rod in a rushing stream. The president was reluctant, but finding little else to do, he agreed to take a stab at it. To ensure his success Bulow had the fish-and-game department place weirs a few hundred yards apart on an accessible stream in the hills. He then found that the fish hatchery at Spearfish in the Black Hills had a lot of elderly breeding trout it wished to part with—fat, lazy fish that had lived all their lives on ground liver and horsemeat. Several thousand of these were dumped in the stream between the weirs, and the next morning the president, still clad in a business suit from an office hour in Rapid City, cast his first fly. Within a few minutes he had five weighty fish and returned to the lodge, according to Grace Coolidge, "as pleased as a boy with his first pair of red-topped boots." The next morning the presidential party had trout for breakfast and invited Governor Bulow, who managed to hide his nausea at the liver-flavored fish. The president's three-week vacation became months, and in midsummer, at the behest of Senator Norbeck, he officially dedicated the monument-to-be at Mount Rushmore.

On August 2, toward the end of the president's stay, the gymnasium of the Rapid City High School became, for a fleeting moment, the political center of the nation. That morning the president summoned the thirty-some reporters who had been tracking him to the gym for an announcement. At noon the president ushered the reporters into his office, and as they filed past his desk, he handed each a typewritten note that said, "I do not choose to run for president in nineteen twenty-eight." Asked if he would comment further, Coolidge replied, "No," put on his coat, and left the building. Enigmatic though the message was—did it mean he *might* run if asked?—it was clear enough to Coolidge's ambitious secretary of commerce, Herbert Hoover, who promptly announced his own candidacy for the Republican nomination. Although the announcement rendered the president a lame duck, the summer's experience in the Black Hills made him an enthusiastic supporter of the Mount Rushmore memorial.

Learning of the president's support, Senator Norbeck planned to seek a congressional appropriation of $500,000, his current estimate of the project's cost. The first step was to clear the appropriation with treasury secretary Andrew

Mellon. Unfortunately it was Borglum rather than Norbeck who visited the secretary, and he asked for only half the sum, assuring the secretary that the other $250,000 could be raised privately, even though the "eastern money-kings" still existed only in his imagination. When he learned of the amount Borglum had asked from Mellon, Norbeck was dumbfounded, for he was certain that with the president's support he could have had the entire sum. Nevertheless, he was stuck with half when the parsimonious Mellon approved the $250,000. William Williamson of Rapid City, one of South Dakota's three congressmen, introduced the appropriation into the house, and Norbeck shepherded it through the Senate. President Coolidge signed it into law on February 25, 1929, only six days before he left office. A local tourist attraction had become a national monument, and Borglum at last had enough money to go to work.

Carving Up a Mountain

Borglum had decided to make one head at a time, delaying the placement of the next one until he could see how it would blend with the previous carving. He then decided to make Washington the monument's dominant figure. He would carve it first and place it on the highest and frontmost dome of the irregular cliff. The next step was a monumental one—that of transferring a plaster model onto the side of a mountain—and his solution revealed his innovative genius. He built his model bust on a scale of one-to-twelve so that one inch on the model equaled one foot on the mountain. From a "center point" at the top of the model's head his assistants could measure precisely the distance to, and proportion of, the features of the face—eyes, nose, chin, cheekbones, ears—and transfer these measurements to the granite cliff.

Borglum then invented a "pointing machine," essentially a protractor with a swinging boom, situated at the top and center of the model's head, to measure the angles of the face. A similar machine on a larger scale, situated at the top of the cliff with a plumb bob at the end of the boom, could mark out the angled features on the face of the cliff. The boom was made of steel, thirty feet long, and a crank-operated cable raised and lowered the plumb bob. Workers suspended on the cliff by sling seats and pulley-driven ropes made the markings and performed the crude work with compressed air drills. To house the air compressors and eight hand-cranked winches for lowering the workers onto the face, Borglum constructed a steel building anchored into stone on top of the mountain. Materials were hauled to the top of the cliff by a steel bucket suspended on a heavy cable trolley. For the sake of safety the workers, who were housed at the base of the mountain, were not carried on the trolley and instead had to walk up a flight of 506 steps, equivalent to climbing daily a forty-story skyscraper.

Since the cliff had been cracked and weathered by eons of wind, water, and frost, most sculptors would have begun by removing all of the surface until they reached sound, reasonably smooth carving stone. Not Borglum. That would have violated his sense of artistic integrity. He felt that sculptured work must "belong to the mountain as a natural part of it." He thus adapted each bust to the contours of the mountain rather than reshaping the cliff to suit his models. After his assistants had located the "rough points" for the outline of Washington's head, he had his drillers "peel off" the broken stone on the surface and produce an "egg-shaped mass" (Borglum's term) three to six feet larger than the final head. This gave him the flexibility to position the head with respect to light and shadow and its relationship to the mountain around it.

18. Workers on Mount Rushmore fashioning Washington's nose and lips with compressed air drills. Photo courtesy of the State Archives of the South Dakota State Historical Society.

Carving the facial features from the solid mass of cleared granite, however, required more power than air hammers and picks could muster. It required dynamite. Operators of the air-driven jackhammers, many of them unemployed miners, became quite expert at drilling holes the exact depth needed to create the beginning of a nose or chin. Explosives experts then inserted dynamite into the series of holes that formed the facial feature and blasted the rock away. Workers with picks then descended on their sling seats to fashion a crude form of the feature, and sanders and chiselers provided the finishing touches. To help these people, who were of course not trained sculptors, Borglum kept in the winch house, or even suspended among the workers, a mask cast of the model of the bust being worked upon. The chisel wielder thus had a ready sample of the detail he was molding and how it fit into the composition as a whole.

The bust of Washington, although not quite finished, was formally dedicated on July 4, 1930, in a ceremony attended by a swarm of newspaper reporters and some two thousand tourists. The *New York Times* put the event on its front page, and news editorials were generally enthusiastic. Borglum's sculpture had become a national attraction.

A Depression Relief Project

Work began on Jefferson's head in June 1931, and Borglum chose that moment to depart with his family for Europe. Borglum had never regarded Mount Rushmore as occupying him full time. He thought of himself as an artist/architect; he left day-to-day implementation to trusted lieutenants. For the first couple of years of the project he commuted from his home in Connecticut, spending his time in the East on a statue of Woodrow Wilson that had been commissioned by the government of Poland.[2] Borglum departed for Poland for the unveiling of the statue, leaving Jefferson in the hands of assistants, and they soon ran into trouble. Borglum, on his return from Europe, would blame them for incompetently blasting away too much stone and ruining Jefferson's head, but he subsequently discovered that the cliff to Washington's right, where Borglum had initially placed Jefferson, was too fractured to sustain a sculpture. The malformed head was abandoned and a new bust of Jefferson on Washington's left was begun in the fall of 1931.

At that juncture the entire project became a victim of the depression that had struck the country with the stock market panic of 1929. As the nation's production declined and unemployment rose, the government plunged into debt and Congress became reluctant to finance artistic endeavors such as presidential busts on a remote mountain. Work ceased through the spring and summer of 1932, and Borglum, who had moved his family to South Dakota, went unpaid.

Once again it was Senator Norbeck who came to the rescue. In the spring of 1932, despite President Hoover's efforts to limit spending and balance the federal budget, the House of Representatives took up a bill to distribute $300 million to the states for "unemployment relief." South Dakota's share of the appropriation was $150,000; however, Norbeck discovered that the relief was so narrowly focused that the governor, even if willing, would not be able to divert any of the money to Mount Rushmore. Undaunted, the senator prodded Rapid City congressman Williamson to slip in an amendment that would give the governor the needed flexibility. Williamson, who regarded Norbeck as "one of the foxiest men in the Senate," did so, and the bill passed Congress without comment on the latitude given South Dakota.

The governor, who heralded from east of the Missouri River, was reluctant to devote a third of the relief money to Mount Rushmore, as Norbeck suggested, but he relented when Norbeck "got rough about it," as he later confided to a friend. Work on Thomas Jefferson resumed in the fall of 1932, and the bust was dedicated two years later. When he was finally convinced that the new placement of Jefferson would work, Borglum ordered the initial disfigured bust blasted away. The result was an artistic bonus, for it left Washington protruding from the cliff in full three-dimensional strength, causing the afternoon sunlight to highlight the dimensional depth of the entire monument.

When Franklin Roosevelt was inaugurated president on March 4, 1933, 25 percent of the nation's work force—16 million men and women—were unemployed. A special session of Congress that spring voted large sums of money to be distributed among the states to provide temporary jobs and alleviate homelessness and hunger. Senator Norbeck might have persuaded the governor to divert some of South Dakota's share to Mount Rushmore, but the distress among the unemployed in the eastern part of the state was acute, and he felt Mount Rushmore needed a more permanent financial base. Accordingly in the summer of 1933 he persuaded President Roosevelt to place Mount Rushmore under the jurisdiction of the National Park Service. That meant an annual appropriation under the Park Service's budget, but the president's order also directed the Mount Rushmore Association—and hence Borglum himself—to account to the Park Service for the expenditure of all federal funds. That directive produced periodic tantrums from the mercurial Borglum, but the work proceeded without further financial crises.

In 1935 work began on the final two figures, Roosevelt and Lincoln. Borglum thought to place Roosevelt in the deepest fissure of the concave cliff, thus emphasizing the three-dimensional depth of the monument. Unfortunately, workers quickly ran into the sort of problems that had ruined the first Jefferson bust. Working in the crevice to the left of the completed Jefferson, drillers peeled away fissured stone only to discover more broken stone beneath. They finally uncovered good stone some 120 feet back from the cliff's original face and only 30 feet from the rear of the mountain and the canyon beyond. That work, however, enlarged the V-shaped crevice and created an ideal spot on the north side for the placement of the fourth figure, the bust of Lincoln, virtually facing the other three.

In that same year President Roosevelt, finding that his temporary relief efforts had failed to dent the nation's seemingly intractable problem of unemployment, created a new, semipermanent relief agency, the Works Progress Administration (WPA). In the next five years WPA workers improved the roads leading to Rapid City and Mount Rushmore, easing the travel for tourists when people once again had money for extended vacations. Another New Deal relief agency, the Civilian Conservation Corps, did the landscaping that turned the monument into a park with a viewing stand and picnic facilities.

In the summer of 1937 Borglum put the finishing touches on the Lincoln bust, giving the eyes and mouth the artist's touch that made them lifelike, and the bust was dedicated on September 17, the 150th anniversary of the signing of the U.S. Constitution. Theodore Roosevelt presented a special problem, for he was the only one of the four who wore glasses. Borglum ingeniously carved a trompe l'oeil, or optical illusion. He created a ridge across the president's nose and another across each of Roosevelt's upper cheeks. It merely suggested a frame and left the rest to the viewer's imagination. The Roosevelt bust, which had presented the most difficult problems of all, was finally dedicated in July 1940.

And not a moment too soon. That spring German armies had overrun Denmark, Norway, Holland, Belgium, and France, and by midsummer Britain was enduring nightly bombing raids—the infamous Blitz. The Roosevelt administration had all but abandoned work-relief projects such

19. Workers on scaffolds on Mount Rushmore putting the finishing touches on the busts of Lincoln and Theodore Roosevelt. Photo courtesy of the State Archives of the South Dakota State Historical Society.

as the Rushmore monument, and the president was calling for an annual production of fifty thousand warplanes.

And it was just in time for Gutzon Borglum as well. He was diagnosed with prostate cancer during the year, and the resultant surgery produced blood clots that eventually migrated to his brain. He died on March 6, 1941. A diminishing work crew cleaned up the rock debris and dismantled the buildings over the course of the summer. At four o'clock on the afternoon of October 31 work ceased altogether, a mere five weeks before the Japanese raided Pearl Harbor and the United States went to war.

CHAPTER TEN

Paths to the Present

A modern observer, distant by eight decades from the Great Depression and armed only with statistics, might well conclude that the farmers of the northern plains barely felt the impact of the stock market crash of 1929 or the ensuing failures of eastern banks and businesses. Dakota farmers, after all, had been suffering economic depression since the early 1920s, when European agriculture had recovered from the war and world commodity prices plummeted. Wartime demand had induced farmers to mechanize their operations, for which they particularly needed to purchase gasoline-powered tractors, and when the price of wheat collapsed in 1922, they found it virtually impossible to repay their debts. Many lost their farms and found themselves paying rent for land they had once owned to a bank or mortgage company. In 1920 one in every four North Dakota farmers was a tenant, many of them sons renting from their fathers; a decade later the figure was one in three, now mostly fathers renting from banks.

In South Dakota the value of farm real estate fell by more than half from 1920 to 1930.

Despite these devastating statistics the modern observer would be mistaken in assuming that times were already so bad in 1929 that the business crash must have been scarcely noticed on the Great Plains. Things could get worse. And they did. Farm commodity prices continued to fall in the early 1930s, and farmers suffered additional stress from drought and grasshopper plagues. Some were so hard hit they could barely feed their families and had no surplus to sell, except perhaps a few eggs from the family henhouse. In South Dakota land prices fell by half again between 1930 and 1935. In the latter year, when the federal government at last undertook a massive program for relief of the unemployed, it found that 40 percent of the population of South Dakota qualified for relief—the largest percentage of any state. In second place was North Dakota.

The New Deal

Just as their fathers and grandfathers had flirted with Populism in the desperate times of the 1890s, Dakota voters turned to Franklin Roosevelt over Herbert Hoover in the presidential election of 1932. In South Dakota Democrats even swept the state offices, including a governor for the first time in twenty years. North Dakota voters adhered to their tradition of returning Republicans to the state offices, but they did elect as governor William Langer, former leader of the radical Nonpartisan League who, though a nominal Republican, would generally support Roosevelt and the New Deal.

In reality it made little difference which party controlled the state governments because both states were too financially distressed (due to the collapse in land values) to take any positive steps toward relieving the Depression. In North

Dakota Governor Langer did manage to declare a moratorium that forbade foreclosures on real property being farmed by the owner, and the legislature held the moratorium in effect until 1943. The main effect of the moratorium, however, was to take banks out of the farm mortgage business and send farmers to federal mortgage agencies created by the New Deal.

Although Roosevelt had made only the vaguest of promises to farmers during the election campaign, the New Deal made agriculture a priority in the avalanche of legislation passed by Congress during the famous "hundred days" (a special session of Congress that met from April to June 1933). In May Congress attempted to meet the basic necessities of both townspeople and farmers by establishing the Federal Emergency Relief Administration (FERA). To receive help a destitute family had to apply at the local relief office. If the office could find work, it provided a job for those able to work. When work was unavailable, the agency gave out cash or food commodities. If an investigator decided that a family's weekly needs amounted to $10 and it had only $6.70 in income, he granted it $3.30 in relief. Though driven by humanitarian ideals, the program's drawback was its similarity to the European "dole," and reliance on such charity humiliated the proud prairie people, whose tradition of self-reliance had been honed by decades of intermittent drought and depression.

The Agricultural Adjustment Act (AAA), also passed in May 1933, sought to raise farm prices by curtailing production. Farmers who agreed to limit their acreage of corn and wheat or the marketing of hogs were to receive benefit payments, the money derived from a special tax on food processors, who in turn were expected to pass it on to consumers. The limitations on hog production necessarily involved the killing of large numbers of the animals, and the slaughtering led to some lurid newspaper accounts, oft-repeated by historians, of hogs in Iowa being slaughtered and dumped into trenches. In the corn-hog complex of eastern South Dakota government officials were more conscientious. Young pigs were converted to fertilizer, and older animals were sent to slaughterhouses in Huron, Sioux Falls, and Yankton. The meat was distributed to the unemployed to avoid glutting markets. Since the wheat crop was already well along by the time the AAA passed, the government made no attempt to limit acreage in that year. Beginning in 1934 wheat farmers who agreed to cut their acreage by 10 or 15 percent received adjustment payments of $0.29 a bushel. The cut in production that year was in fact forced on farmers not by the government but by drought and grasshoppers. While the drop in production was accomplished by fate as much as by choice, the government benefits allowed many a farm family to get through the year. By 1935 the impact of drought- and government-induced scarcity was evident: the price of wheat had jumped from $0.38 to $0.90 a bushel and hogs went from $3.50 to $8.35 per hundredweight.

In addition to rescuing farmers the government also had to provide relief for the unemployed. The towns and cities of the Dakotas suffered as much as the rural areas, caught in a tidal rip of industrial misfortune in the East and destitution in their rural hinterland. The early relief efforts of the New Deal, such as FERA, were short-term handouts to allay hunger pending an expected revival of the economy. Most of its programs required state fiscal contributions and were generally administered by state officials. By 1935, when President Roosevelt realized that a massive, long-term federal relief program was needed, relief was already the biggest business in North Dakota, providing sustenance for nearly half the population of the state.

In that year at the request of the president, Congress appropriated the astounding sum of $5 billion for unemployment relief, and Roosevelt created the Works Progress Administration to administer the program. One-time social worker Harry Hopkins, head of the WPA, believing that government handouts were degrading to people who honestly could not find work, proposed to treat applicants for relief as government employees working for their pay. Because of the variety of skills among the unemployed, or the lack of them, most of the WPA's work projects involved manual labor—improving roads, cleaning up city parks and playgrounds, and building airports for towns and cities (by 1939, 90 percent of all the airports in the country were WPA-built). WPA workers were often derided as "ditchdiggers," but proper drainage was precisely what rural roads needed. By providing drainage ditches, culverts, and gravel surfaces, the WPA gave Dakota farmers, for the first time, year-round access to their market towns.

Another New Deal relief agency of special benefit to the Dakotas was the Civilian Conservation Corps (CCC). Established by Congress during the frenzied "hundred days," the purpose of the CCC was to provide employment for young men aged seventeen to twenty-five—that is, new entrants into the nation's virtually closed workforce. They would be placed in work camps and engage in forest preservation and conservation projects. The organization of the CCC was one of those governmental miracles, a bureaucratic monstrosity that actually worked. The army established and administered the camps, each designed to accommodate about two hundred men. They woke, ate, and slept to bugle calls and learned to stand in formation for roll call. Local relief agencies selected the recruits, and the nature of the work depended on the federal or state agency supervising the project:

Forest Service, Soil Conservation Service, Bureau of Wildlife Management, or Park Service. The CCC maintained sixteen camps in North Dakota and nineteen in South Dakota. In addition to the CCC boys' role in building the park around Mount Rushmore, other noteworthy improvements included the Sand Lake migratory bird refuge near Aberdeen and development of the park on Farm Island at Pierre. In North Dakota, in addition to tree planting (over 1 million) and the restoration of seven thousand acres of range land, the CCC built replicas of Mandan huts on the site of their ancient village along the Missouri River and the lodge and museum at Fort Abraham Lincoln State Park, both major tourist attractions today. Less well known because it has never been fully documented, the CCC in all likelihood provided an instant cadre of potential noncommissioned officers for the army, which had to be built from scratch when President Roosevelt, anticipating American entry into World War II, initiated the nation's first peacetime draft in the fall of 1940.

World War II

Americans and their political leaders had traditionally maintained a "hands-off" attitude toward Europe, reinforced by a mistrust of the Continent's corrupt, papist monarchies. The separation of the Western Hemisphere from the Eastern was first propounded by George Washington and reinforced by the Monroe Doctrine's promise that the United States would not intervene in Europe's wars and, in turn, would regard European intervention in the New World as an "unfriendly act." During World War I Dakota voters, with a heavy German element in both states, were firmly opposed to American entry down to the very moment that war was declared in April 1917. In the 1930s, as war clouds once again loomed over Europe, Dakotans remained adamant against

American involvement. In January 1933 Adolph Hitler was elected chancellor of Germany on a promise of dismantling the humiliating Treaty of Versailles that had ended World War I, and to that end he began an arms buildup. His threats became more menacing a year later, when he prohibited political opposition within Germany and executed the moderates in his own National Socialist Party. In that year Benito Mussolini, Fascist dictator of Italy since 1922, began voicing an ambition to emulate the Roman Empire and make the Mediterranean an "Italian lake." (Italy already had a colony in North Africa, present-day Libya.) Convinced that the bombastic rhetoric emanating from Rome and Berlin represented no threat to the United States, voters in both Dakotas remained opposed to any sort of intervention in Europe, a position becoming known as "isolationist."

In 1934 the U.S. Senate, seeking the reasons for American entry into World War I in the hope of profiting from the mistakes of the past, established a Committee to Investigate the Munitions Industry. Chair of the committee was Gerald P. Nye of North Dakota, former member of the Nonpartisan League and the Senate's most outspoken isolationist. For two years Nye's committee investigated the Wilson administration's relations with American businessmen in the years prior to American entry into the war. They concluded that America had been drawn into the war by clever propaganda and the machinations of bankers and munitions makers who stood to profit from an Allied victory—"merchants of death" in Nye's unforgettable phrase.

Beginning in 1935 with a joint resolution and culminating in 1937 with a formal Neutrality Act, Congress sought to insulate the United States from war of any sort. By the legislation of 1937 the president was obliged to take formal notice of conflict anywhere in the world and impose an embargo on munitions shipments to the belligerents. Nonmilitary goods could be shipped to the warring nations but only on a "cash and carry" basis. Congressional isolationism thus prevented the president from taking any action upon Italy's invasion of Ethiopia in 1935, the outbreak of civil war in Spain in 1936 (in which Germany and Italy had intervened), or Japan's invasion of China in 1937. Even after war broke out in Europe in September 1939, congressmen from both Dakotas continued to resist Roosevelt's efforts to evade the Neutrality Act and give subtle aid to the beleaguered British and Chinese. They even voted against the Lend-Lease Act of March 1941, by which Roosevelt proposed to lend, rather than sell, munitions to Britain and China. As late as August 1941 Senator Nye gave an address in the Chicago Arena on a nationwide radio hookup accusing the president of luring the United States into war. He reminded listeners of the opening of a Russian front (Hitler had invaded the Soviet Union in June) and declared that this was "precisely where the war would have been—always!" if Britain, France, and the United States had not distracted Hitler toward the West.

Despite their historic opposition to foreign wars, the people of both Dakotas and their congressmen rallied to the support of the war after the Japanese bombed Pearl Harbor in December 1941. The civilian population in both states oversubscribed its share of the government's several war bond issues. South Dakota furnished 64,560 men to the armed forces and North Dakota 58,509, about a third of them volunteers rather than draftees. Their soldiers fought and died in all theaters of the war and, statistics suggest, did so with considerable bravery. Of North Dakota's soldiers and sailors 4.14 percent died in the war, compared to the national average of 2.98 percent. The death rate among South Dakota's men was close to the national average.

Mother Nature cooperated with the war effort on the

northern plains. The Dakotas had above-average rainfall in every year of the war and adequate rainfall for a decade afterward. Farmers brought back into production acres that had lain fallow under the New Deal's allotment programs, and farm production increased dramatically even though thousands of workers left the two states to serve in the armed forces or in eastern defense factories. During the 1930s North Dakota's annual wheat crop had never reached 100 million bushels; the crops of the war years regularly topped 150 million bushels—the largest amounts the state has ever produced. The prosperity of the war and postwar years enabled farmers to pay off their debts and in many cases recover farms that had once been lost to banks and government mortgage agencies. In South Dakota farm tenancy, which had reached an all-time high of 53 percent in 1940, dropped to 29 percent by 1954.

Unfortunately the blessings of Mother Nature are almost always mixed. Beneficial as the wartime rains were for farmers, they also raised the specter of devastating floods. The year 1941 was the wettest in the recorded history of the northern plains, and snowmelt in the spring of 1942, combined with above-average rainfall, produced massive flooding in the Missouri River basin. Thus even though the nation's energies were totally committed to maintaining a three-front intercontinental war in Europe, North Africa, and the Pacific, politicians and government administrators began planning the largest construction project the northern plains had ever witnessed—a series of dams to control and utilize the waters of the Mighty Missouri.

Taming the "Mighty Mo"

Ironically the Dakotas suffered relatively little from the disastrous floods of 1942–43. The Missouri River was too shallow for heavy traffic above Sioux City, Iowa, and there was lit-tle population in the upper river floodplain. The greatest damage occurred in the downstream population centers, notably Omaha, Kansas City, and St. Louis, and it was the congressmen from Iowa, Nebraska, and Missouri who spear-headed the move for federal construction of dams on the upper Missouri (i.e., above freight navigation).

Congress already had a model at hand in the Tennessee Valley Authority (TVA). The godfather of the TVA was Pro-gressive Republican George Norris of Nebraska, who since the 1920s had been arguing for government-produced hy-droelectric power to serve as a yardstick to measure the fairness of rates charged by privately owned power plants. Roosevelt, who as governor of New York had noted the dra-matic difference in the cost of electricity in New York and neighboring Ontario (which utilized hydroelectric power from Niagara Falls), made public power a priority in the New Deal's first "hundred days." The TVA was an experiment in a multipurpose agency that would dam the oft-flooded Ten-nessee River and produce cheap hydroelectric power that would attract industry to the region. Among the products of the new industries would be fertilizer, which would help rehabilitate the soils of an entire nine-state region of the Southeast. Unfortunately when this model was applied to the idea of a Missouri Valley Authority, the multiple pur-poses of the TVA created immediate — and almost inevita-ble — bureaucratic infighting.

In 1943 Colonel Lewis Pick of the Army Corps of Engi-neers devised a comprehensive flood control plan for the Missouri, with five dams along the river north of Sioux City and 1,500 miles of levees in the lower basin. The giant stair-well of dams and reservoirs conceived by Pick would pre-vent flooding and also serve as a plumbing system, enabling engineers to flush water downstream at regular intervals to maintain barge transit during times of low water. W. Glenn Sloan, assistant director of the Department of the Interior's Bureau of Reclamation, had another idea. Responding to the devastating droughts of the 1930s, he proposed a collection of smaller dams and reservoirs on tributaries of the Missouri in Montana and the Dakotas that would provide irrigation canals and hydroelectric power to the farmers and ranchers of the northern plains. Although the plan appealed to the farmers of the region, it ran into opposition from the transportation interests from the lower Missouri who feared that the diversion of the water would not leave enough to float their freight barges. Casting a shadow on the bureaucratic wrangling was the possibility that Congress might try to solve the problem with the formation of a new governmental agency, a Missouri Valley Authority modeled on the TVA—a competitor that neither the Corps of Engineers nor the Bureau of Reclamation wanted. As a result, the two bureaus hastily formed an interagency committee that reached a governmental version of a Solomonic solution—it accepted both schemes and simply combined them, labeling its product the Pick-Sloan Plan. Congress incorporated it into the Flood Control Act of December 1944.

The legislation called for the construction of six earthen dams on the main stem of the Missouri and ancillary dams (twenty-one in total) on its tributaries. Four of the major dams would be located in South Dakota, one in North Dakota, and one in Montana. The one farthest up the river, the Fort Peck Dam in Montana, was already in place, having been constructed as an experiment in irrigation in the 1930s. The Garrison Dam in North Dakota, named after a town about seventy miles north of Bismarck, is the fifth-largest earthen dam in the world. Construction began in

1947 and was completed in 1954. More than two miles long and 210 feet high, it impounds Lake Sakajawea, which extends almost to the mouth of the Yellowstone, some twelve miles from the Montana border.

The next dam downriver is the Oahe, located six miles northwest of Pierre and named after a Lakota Sioux Indian mission. Construction of this structure was begun in 1948 and completed in 1962. Second only in size to the Garrison Dam, it impounds the fourth-largest man-made water reservoir in the United States. Lake Oahe extends north for 250 miles to Bismarck, North Dakota. This massive body of water was the centerpiece of the Bureau of Reclamation's irrigation dream. It was expected to provide water for diversion onto the semiarid plateau between the Missouri River and the James. The next dam downriver, the Big Bend near Chamberlain, South Dakota, was the last to be built under the Pick-Sloan Plan, from 1960 to 1966. Its reservoir, Lake Sharp, extends for eighty miles northwest to the outskirts of Pierre.

Below the Big Bend the Fort Randall Dam, located near the site of the 1850s army post, was the first main stem dam undertaken by the Corps of Engineers. The corps began construction in 1946 and completed the edifice ten years later. The dam's reservoir extends a distance of 140 miles to the base of the Big Bend Dam. The final dam envisioned by the Pick-Sloan Plan and the most downstream dam on the Missouri is Gavins Point, located on the Nebraska–South Dakota border just west of Yankton. Constructed during the years 1952–56, Gavins Point is the smallest dam on the river, but its thirty-seven-mile-long reservoir, Lewis and Clark Lake, is the most popular recreation facility of all the Dakota lakes. From Gavins Point downstream to the head of navigation at Sioux City, the Missouri is a federally designated "wild and scenic" river, a shallow, meandering stream full of islands, sandbars, and snags, still looking much the same as when Lewis and Clark paddled it more than one hundred years ago.

Besides the prevention of downriver floods, the main impact of the Pick-Sloan concept has been in the production of hydroelectric power, and the government created a Missouri Valley Authority to distribute it. Despite the New Deal's establishment of a Rural Electrification Administration in the mid-1930s, the extension of power lines into the northern plains proceeded slowly, hampered by vast distances and relatively few consumers. At the end of the war, for example, only about one-fourth of North Dakota farms had electricity or telephones. All five of the Dakota dams on the Missouri were designed to produce electric power, and their turbines and transformers were enlarged steadily over the years, contributing to a power grid that extended across the northern Midwest. By 1980 returns from the sale of electric power had completely reimbursed the government for the cost of building the six Pick-Sloan dams. Power generated in the heart of the Dakotas promoted rural electrification, and cheap rates benefited both farmers and city dwellers. Although George Norris's dream of using public power as a yardstick to judge the fairness of rates charged by privately owned power companies was never implemented in either the TVA or the Missouri Valley Authority, the cost of electric power in the Dakotas has been lower than elsewhere. In 1985 the attorney general of South Dakota publicized a report indicating that federal power supplied 21 percent of the electricity in the state's municipalities and 47 percent of that used on farms. He estimated that the competition presented by federal hydroelectric power reduced the cost of electricity in the state by 30 percent.

The Bureau of Reclamation's irrigation scheme, by contrast,

never materialized. The lands west of the Missouri were too uneven to allow a system of irrigation canals, and much of the soil was not suited to the sort of crops—corn and potatoes, for instance—that might benefit from irrigation. East of the river, the land between the Missouri and the James, which had been the focal point of the Bureau of Reclamation's dreams, presented other problems. The region, which had adequate rainfall on the average of three years out of four, was not arid enough to justify the immense cost of an irrigation system extending over entire counties. In addition, by the time the dams were in place in the mid-1950s, the Eisenhower administration was facing a growing mountain of farm surpluses and attendant storage problems that bordered on the scandalous. President Eisenhower's proposal of a "soil bank," by which farmers would be paid to take lands out of production, was an imaginative solution, but it was utterly inconsistent with the construction of an irrigation system that would increase the West's productive farmland. Bureaucratic momentum, however, did bring some land immediately adjacent to the reservoirs under irrigation. By 1973 some sixteen thousand acres were receiving water from South Dakota's reservoirs, but the impact on the state's agricultural output was negligible.

The big losers in the implementation of the Pick-Sloan Plan were North Dakota's Indians, whose reservations lay partly in the floodplain that would be inundated by construction of the Garrison and Oahe Dams. It is a token of white attitudes toward the Indian, even in the mid-twentieth century, that the impoundment of Indian lands was not a consideration in the original Pick-Sloan Plan. When the time came to build the dams, federal agents simply loaded up the affected Indians and moved them to higher ground. No consideration was given to any property rights or water rights (both of which were guaranteed by treaty) that the Indians might have. Between 1954 and 1962 the government, belatedly recognizing its injustice, reached settlements with the affected Dakota Indians that partially compensated them for the loss of their lands and provided funds for rehabilitation programs. Unfortunately the agreements with individual tribes varied widely in the estimates of the value of their lands and often depended on the sophistication of tribal leaders and the quality of their legal advice. A better approach would have been to establish a special commission composed of individuals more familiar with local land values and more willing to serve the interests of the Indians.

In a second attempt to remedy the injustice the federal government in 1985 created a Garrison Unit Joint Tribal Advisory Committee, which recommended the development of irrigation on the remaining tribal lands, replacement of health care facilities and roads lost because of the water impoundment, and additional financial compensation to the tribes for their lost land. In later years Congress enacted some of these recommendations, providing reimbursement to those still living and the descendants of those who, by Indian legend, "died of a broken heart." The payments ranged from more than $300 million to the Cheyenne River Sioux for the loss of 104,000 acres at the Oahe Dam to $4.8 million to the Santee Sioux for the loss of 593 acres at the Gavins Point Dam. The focus on compensation for the loss of land unfortunately did not address the loss of the tribes' treaty-guaranteed water rights nor any rights they had for the generation of hydroelectric power. Nor did the trust funds established by the government permit any payments to individual families who had been forced to give up their homes and resettle in an unfamiliar and often more hostile environment. Whether the government will see fit to do more remains to be seen.

Toward a Two-Party Political System

In North Dakota the Nonpartisan League, despite its schism of 1919 and the flight of Arthur Townley to Minnesota, continued to nominate and occasionally elect Republican candidates through the 1920s. In the 1928 election, however, all the candidates endorsed by the NPL lost, largely due to factional infighting. Following the election, William Langer, who despite his break with Townley in 1919 had remained a loyal adherent of the NPL, undertook to reorganize the League. He did so on the model of eastern political "machines," creating a hierarchy of precinct "captains" and county chairs who owed their positions—and thus their loyalty—to Langer. Ideologically Langer retained his NPL Progressivism, responding to the Depression with such ideas as a moratorium on farm mortgage foreclosures, a proposal that was certain to win the votes of the state's rural majority. As a result, Langer was elected governor in 1932, while the state was casting its presidential electoral vote for Franklin Roosevelt.

Although they went for Roosevelt, North Dakota voters adhered to tradition and returned Republicans to the state offices and their accustomed majority in the state legislature. Without effective Democratic Party opposition, Governor Langer and his personal political apparatus were now in complete control of North Dakota politics. And seldom has the axiom of the great English liberal Lord Acton proved so valid: "Power corrupts, and absolute power corrupts absolutely!"

With FERA, President Roosevelt had sought to avoid creating a large federal bureaucracy by having state officials administer the federal funds. Governor Langer treated the federal largesse as a bankroll for his personal political organization. The form that applicants for relief filled out, for example, asked them whom they had supported for governor in the last election. To gain approval the form had to be signed by the local Nonpartisan League precinct committeeman. By the end of 1933, when FERA was replaced by the more work-related Civil Works Administration (CWA), federal expenditures under both programs were commonly referred to in North Dakota as "the William Langer Relief Fund." Harry Hopkins, administrator first of FERA and then the CWA (as well as the later WPA), was anxious to keep politics out of the government's relief efforts, but since the day-to-day administration of the programs was in the hands of state officials, there was little he could do. Nevertheless, through the latter half of 1933 and 1934 he collected complaints from FERA and CWA field supervisors accusing Langer of playing politics with federal funds.

By mid-1934 government prosecutors had enough evidence of corruption to obtain an indictment of Langer and several of his aides. In the ensuing trial he was convicted, but the judgment was reversed by the Court of Appeals. A second trial in 1935 ended in a hung jury. In 1936 Langer underwent a third trial and finally won a jury verdict of not guilty. In the meantime, because Langer was alternately eligible and ineligible to hold the office of governor, the state went through four governors in a period of seven months. Disavowed by his own Nonpartisan League in 1936, Langer ran for governor as an Independent. Although his machine had been badly damaged, he could rely upon a combination of name recognition and personal popularity. In a three-way race, he won by a scant 36 percent of the vote, while Roosevelt, in the national election that year, carried every county in the state.

Accusations of corruption continued to shadow Langer

in his second term as governor, particularly in his appointment of political cronies to the Board of Administration of the state agricultural college at Fargo. The board had then politicized the college by dismissing prominent faculty members and administrators of whom it disapproved. Langer weathered this scandal but then made a fatal mistake in deciding to run for the U.S. Senate in 1938 against the popular incumbent, Gerald Nye. All the long-standing charges of corruption were fully aired in the ensuing campaign with two results: Langer lost the election and opposition to him within the Republican Party was emboldened to organize. A further result was the downfall of the Langer machine, though ironically not of Langer himself. He was elected to the U.S. Senate in 1940 and served until his death in 1959. The unbridgeable schism he caused in the Republican ranks in 1938, however, would eventually bring about a two-party political system for North Dakota.

The leaders of the anti-Langer movement within the Republican Party, who until 1943 simply referred to themselves as "Progressives," were farmers and small-city lawyers whose ambitions had been frustrated by the closed Republican political machine. Popular in their localities, they won seats in the legislature against NPL opposition and gradually gained strength. In 1943 they mobilized themselves as the Republican Organizing Committee (ROC) with a full-time executive secretary. As the June 1944 Republican primary approached, the ROC held a state convention and endorsed a full slate of candidates to run against the NPL. In the election the ROC caught the Langer machine napping and swept all the state offices. In the fall election it easily defeated the Democratic candidates, with the exception of former Democratic governor John Moses, who defeated isolationist Gerald Nye in a contest for the U.S. Senate. When

Moses died the following year, Milton R. Young, principal architect of the ROC movement, won the senate seat.

The Republican Organizing Committee dominated North Dakota politics for the next decade. In 1952 the Nonpartisan League, long since divorced from Bill Langer, split into liberal and conservative factions. The "insurgents" adhered to the traditional liberalism of the NPL, favoring farm organizations, labor unions, and the domestic programs of the Truman-led national Democratic Party. The "old guard" was pro-business and anti-labor and supported Eisenhower for president. In 1956 the "insurgents," having won control of the organization, moved the Nonpartisan League into the Democratic Party, while the "old guard" allied itself with the ROC. The turnout in the Democratic primary that year was the largest in history to that date. Although the Republicans won the fall election, largely due to the popularity of President Eisenhower, North Dakota at last had a viable two-party political system.

The evolution of a two-party system in South Dakota was less turbulent. The Democrats had reached a high point in the traditionally Republican state in the election of 1932, when they won the governorship, a majority of the legislature, and the state's two seats in the U.S. House of Representatives. The Republicans regained control four years later, and Democratic ranks grew ever thinner through the war and postwar years. By 1952 only two Democrats were elected to the state House of Representatives, and not a one served in the state senate. Only a year later, however, George S. McGovern became executive secretary, and the party was "born again."

The son of a Methodist minister, graduate of Dakota Wesleyan University, and World War II bomber pilot, McGovern was bred for leadership, but there was nothing in his early life to steer him in the direction of social reform. The change came in 1947, when he enrolled in the graduate program in history at Northwestern University. He became interested in the social and political struggles of the poor, selecting as the topic for his doctoral dissertation the bloody Colorado Coal Strike of 1913–14. His political awakening must have come rather quickly because by 1948 he was actively supporting the candidacy of Democratic rebel Henry Wallace against both Harry Truman and Thomas E. Dewey. Upon earning his PhD, McGovern joined the faculty of Dakota Wesleyan University in Mitchell, South Dakota. His liberal politics survived the conservative academic environment, and in 1953 he resigned from the faculty to become head of the state Democratic Party.

The position was hardly a sought-after plum, for the party had no grassroots organization or source of funds. To cover his salary and traveling expenses McGovern had to establish a fund-raising Century Club whose members pledged a hundred dollars a year. Because the state Republican Party was controlled by the merchants and lawyers of the larger cities and the prosperous farmers of the Sioux and James River Valleys, McGovern saw that his one chance for political success lay among the smaller farmers of the uplands and trans-Missouri region. In his efforts he received unexpected help from the nation's new president, Dwight Eisenhower. The cost-conscious president disliked the New Deal–born farm subsidy programs that resulted in annual surpluses of cotton and feed grains with attendant storage costs. As a result, "Ike" directed his secretary of agriculture, Ezra Taft Benson, to dismantle the subsidy program and give farmers the "freedom to farm."

Farmers in both Dakotas regarded this as a breach of

Eisenhower's campaign promise of maintaining farm prices at 90 percent of parity. McGovern jumped on the issue and accused Eisenhower of being in league with the large food-processing companies and "eastern capital which directs the GOP." In a 1954 address to a North Dakota state Democratic Convention, McGovern cited a poll indicating that 52 percent of American farmers would now vote, if given a chance, for Adlai Stevenson, the 1952 Democratic candidate. He also claimed that opposition to Benson in the northern plains had given rise to a new slogan: "Vote Democratic; the farm you save may be your own." Although Ike again carried South Dakota in 1956, the Democrats made significant gains in the state assembly, and McGovern became the first Democrat in twenty years to win national office, capturing one of the state's two seats in the House of Representatives.

Six years later McGovern was elected to the U.S. Senate, and that set the stage (based on his opposition to the Vietnam War) for the Democratic nomination for the presidency in 1972. In that presidential campaign McGovern developed a theme that remains viable among Democrats even today: by our "excessive outlays for military overkill," he reminded youthful audiences, we have "neglected our central cities" and such national infrastructure as schools and transportation. The nation needs, he said, "to employ more of our people in such enterprises as the building of a modern rail and mass-transit system." Although McGovern lost the presidential election that year and lost his Senate seat in the Reagan landslide of 1980, the foundation he built was strong enough to sustain a two-party system in South Dakota for the remainder of the century. Among his protégés was Tom Daschle, Senate majority leader at the turn of the century and a strong voice in the national Democratic Party.

Wounded Knee Revisited, 1973

From 1887 to 1934 the policy of the federal government was to remake American Indians into independent farmers by giving each family a parcel of a reservation. The policy failed in large part because most of the reservations had been placed on barren land too arid for normal agriculture and because the parcels allotted were too small for ranching. In 1934 Congress changed direction and passed the Indian Reorganization Act, which restored the integrity of the reservations and gave the Indians a voice in their governance by authorizing the election of a tribal council. The federal Bureau of Indian Affairs (BIA), however, retained ultimate authority, and the result was a colonial system in which the "colonists" had authority only over local affairs, such as law and order and civil justice. The continued subordination to Washington DC inevitably led to tribal indifference and occasional resistance. Compounding the problem, Congress, in a misguided gesture toward democracy, placed a term of two years on the tribal council members, thus requiring biennial elections. Because tribal politics usually involved family factions and charismatic leaders, council elections often resulted in a political turnover, with a new leader filling executive and judicial offices with friends and family members. As a result, there was little collective memory or policy continuity. (By contrast, the U.S. Constitution strives for continuity by setting the terms for representatives at two years, the president at four, and the senators at six, with one-third being up for election every two years.)

Endemic poverty made the tangled political system appear even more inept than it was. On the Pine Ridge Reservation of the Oglala Sioux in the southwestern corner of South Dakota, site of the martyred memory of the 1890 Wound Knee massacre, unemployment in 1970 exceeded 50 percent, and the federal government, through the BIA and various poverty programs, provided more than half the jobs available. Unable to farm the arid land, many Oglala men moved their families off the reservation to work as migrant farm laborers. Paid a minimum wage, they returned to the reservation in the fall (in time to send their children to school), penniless and on the dole. The tribal council, which was responsible for education, as well as other social services, had a barren tax base and staggered from one financial crisis to another.

The lethal blend of poverty and dysfunctional politics reached critical mass in February 1972, when a fifty-one-year-old Oglala man, Raymond Yellow Thunder, was beaten to death in the Nebraska border town of Gordon. A string of border towns lay along the southern edge of the Pine Ridge Reservation, supplying groceries, hardware, and liquor not available on the reservation. Although largely dependent on the reservation for customers, the townspeople were white, ill-educated, and racially biased. On February 20, 1972, a group of young men decided to assault an Indian just for fun and kidnapped the hapless Yellow Thunder. The Indian was severely beaten, struggled to his truck, sprawled across the front seat, and died of head injuries. The relatives of Yellow Thunder appealed to Nebraska authorities, the BIA, and the Oglala Tribal Council, getting only meager results. Nebraska authorities arrested five people, but all went free on bond and most left the state. Desperate for help, Yellow Thunder's sisters appealed to a nephew who happened to be a member of the American Indian Movement (AIM).

AIM was formed in 1968 at a meeting of Indian residents of Minneapolis–St. Paul. Its inspiration was the Civil Rights Movement, then reaching a violent climax with riots in northern cities. The leaders of AIM — only one of whom, Russell

Means, was an Oglala—adopted the confrontational tactics of the most radical civil rights organizations and developed an ideology that stressed the unity among all Native peoples and the need for resistance to white oppression. The Yellow Thunder affair was an opportunity for them to gain publicity for their youthful movement and expand its membership beyond the cities. They held a meeting in the town hall of the village of Pine Ridge, followed by a press conference, and a series of protest marches in Gordon, Nebraska. The display of Native American pride and fearless activism galvanized the people of Pine Ridge, and hundreds joined the American Indian Movement.

Significantly most of those who joined AIM were full-blooded Dakota who favored the preservation of traditional Indian culture and values. One of the major fault lines within the Oglala and other Dakota subdivisions was between full-blooded and mixed-blood individuals, the former usually traditionalists and the latter regarding themselves as "progressives" who wanted to integrate with white society and adopt modern technology. (A similar division in white society has pitted traditionalists against liberals on the issue of Darwinian evolution.) The "progressives" usually controlled the Oglala Tribal Council, and they retained control in the spring election of 1972. Elected chair of the council that year was Dick Wilson, who though of mixed blood ($^5/_{16}$ by his own count) actively courted the full-blooded vote in the election.

Following through with this moderate stance, Wilson initially approved and cooperated with the tactics of the AIM leaders. In the course of the summer, however, he reversed himself, probably because he saw his political opponents, all of whom were full-bloods, joining the AIM organization. In the fall, using AIM funds, Wilson formed a personal militia with the announced object of preserving law and order on the reservation, thus perverting his original attempt to bridge the gap between traditionalists and "progressives" into a power grab. Critics labeled this militia the "Goon Squad," and members accepted it as a matter of pride, making the "Goon" into an acronym, "Guardians of the Oglala Nation." The activities of the GOON Squad, which included arbitrary arrests and harassment, led to a political alliance of full-bloods and the American Indian Movement. The Oglala's need for an ally against Chairman Wilson meshed nicely with AIM's need to shed its image of urban activists and generate appeal among reservation Indians. The result of this alliance was an attempt to impeach Wilson in early 1973. The temporary chair of the council for the impeachment trial proved to be an ally of Wilson's, causing the opponents of Wilson to walk out of the session, and Wilson survived impeachment.

In the meantime, on the eve of the trial, Wilson had sought to strengthen his position by appealing for help from the federal government. He claimed, falsely, that AIM leaders, who were staying in Rapid City, were planning to attack Pine Ridge and turn his impeachment trial into a bloody coup. The U.S. Marshals Service, conditioned to overreact by the violence of the Civil Rights Movement, sent sixty-five marshals into Pine Ridge on February 11. The FBI, which saw Communists behind every radical movement in those years, began investigating the background of AIM leaders, just as it had done with Martin Luther King and other civil rights leaders a decade earlier. The presence of the U.S. marshals further emboldened the GOON Squad, which began assaulting the lawyers who had led the impeachment hearing. At that point the women—often a force in traditional Indian culture—took charge of the opposition. Ellen

Moves Camp explained, "We decided that we did need the American Indian Movement in here because our men were scared, they hung in the back.... This way we knew we had the backing, and we would have more strength to do what we wanted to do against the BIA and Dick Wilson. All the people wanted it."

With the approval of all seven of the traditional chiefs, AIM leaders were invited down from Rapid City to attend a February 27 meeting of more than three hundred anti-Wilson protesters at Calico Hall in Pine Ridge. While the meeting assembled, Dennis Banks, a Minnesota Ojibwa, and Russell Means met privately with the traditional chiefs. They decided that any confrontation in Pine Ridge would be suicidal, loaded as the town was with U.S. marshals, FBI agents, and the GOON Squad militia. They decided instead to publicize their grievances by seizing the tiny hamlet of Wounded Knee, which had grown up on the edge of the Indian cemetery to serve the needs of the occasional tourist who had a vague memory of having read in history class about the 1890 massacre. It was a brilliant stroke because the site had recently been brought to national attention by the publication of Dee Brown's best-seller *Bury My Heart at Wounded Knee*.

While the traditional leaders mobilized the crowd at Calico Hall into a caravan of fifty vehicles, Banks and Means sent experienced AIM activists ahead to secure the town and procure arms and ammunition from the town's hardware store. Taken by surprise and initially confused by the sudden departure of the Calico Hall protesters, the U.S. marshals and FBI agents quickly recovered and surrounded the town of Wounded Knee. The South Dakota National Guard supplied them with automatic weapons and helicopters.

Thus began the seventy-one-day siege of Wounded Knee,

which earned national headlines as journalists swarmed into Rapid City and Pine Ridge. Neither side was willing to risk an all-out attack and the bloodshed that would ensue. What violence there was came from snipers armed with rifles, who claimed the lives of two AIM leaders and left one U.S. marshal severely wounded and paralyzed for life. When the protesters laid down their arms after protracted negotiations with BIA agents on May 8, 1973, they could hardly claim a victory. The American public by then had virtually lost interest, distracted by the unfolding Watergate scandal, and more than two hundred protesters were arrested. Dick Wilson had used the crisis to consolidate his power, forcing out of office any tribal executives who had opposed him and rigging the tribal election to ensure he retained office the following year. The result was a three-year "reign of terror" on Pine Ridge as the GOON Squad worked its will while the BIA turned its back. More than seventy of Wilson's opponents died violently in those years, by gunshot wounds, beatings, and unexplained car accidents. Although Wilson was finally turned out of office in a fair election in 1976, conditions on the reservation failed to improve. By 1990 unemployment on the reservation still stood at around 50 percent, and half of those who were employed worked for federal agencies or poverty programs.

In 1988 Congress passed an Indian Gaming Regulatory Act, which permitted the development of gambling casinos on tribal lands under federal regulation. By 2000 eight casinos had been built on South Dakota reservations, and more were on the way. The Prairie Wind Casino on Pine Ridge opened in 1994, and its economic impact was among the most significant of all the reservation casinos. For the remainder of the decade employment grew at the rate of 6.6 percent a year, more than double that of South Dakota as a whole. Gambling, nevertheless, is but a single industry, and sustained economic growth will depend on the development of new ventures and opportunities.

What's Next?

In 1987, looking toward North Dakota's statehood centennial, historians conducted a survey of members of the Fiftieth Legislative Assembly. They asked legislators to identify the most critical issues confronting the state in the next hundred years and what social changes could be expected that would have an impact on public policy. Interestingly not one respondent listed ethical behavior on the part of elected or appointed officials as a concern. More transparent government and a competitive two-party system had clearly, in the minds of state legislators, freed the state of machine politics and manipulation by outside corporate interests.

Surprisingly no one in the 1987 legislature emphasized the problem of depopulation. North Dakota's population peaked at 680,000 in 1930, and by 2005 it had declined to fewer than 640,000. South Dakota has gone through a similar decline. Those who did not leave the Dakotas completely moved into the cities. As a result, farm market towns have declined, and rural churches and schools are closing. And it is the younger, healthier families that are moving. Some rural school districts have no children enrolled under the age of five. As in pioneer days, rural isolation has become once again a problem. Some farm families find themselves thirty miles from a school, fifty to seventy miles from a doctor. Again as in pioneer days, communal efforts often staffed by women have come to fill the void. Many communities have a volunteer ambulance service, and volunteer nurses care for the ill or the victims of farm accidents until the ambulances arrive. Whether depopulation and its social effects can be cured is uncertain; to date the legislature of neither state seems to have addressed it seriously.

There is, on the other hand, a positive side to rural depopulation. In the counties west of the Missouri River, where depopulation has been most severe, the average size of farms has increased dramatically. By the 1990s the average number of farms was only a third of the 1930s number; average farm size had quadrupled to more than three thousand acres. This means that the labor of each farmer is more efficient and thus more productive. Education and experience have also changed the crops being planted. Corn has virtually disappeared from the west river lands, and fewer than a third of farms still grow wheat. They've turned instead to hay and forage crops, such as milo and sorghum, to provide food for greater herds of cattle. They have thus become less vulnerable to short-term drought—another plus. As in early America the low ratio between population and the resources of the land appears to have enhanced the value of labor. In mid-2010, while the nation as a whole was battling high unemployment due to the recession, North Dakota's jobless figure was 3.6 percent, the lowest of any state. South Dakota was the next lowest.

A theme that did run through the responses of 1987 North Dakota legislators was concern over the state's dependence on federal agricultural subsidies and the need for economic diversification. The latter goal had been a subject of political discourse in both the Dakotas since statehood and even before.

One source of diversity that was latent and not highly regarded in 1987 is oil. Two miles below the surface of western North Dakota is a gigantic oil field. It is in a formation called the Bakken shale, and by some estimates it contains more oil than the Arctic National Wildlife Refuge in Alaska.

The first well in the area was drilled in 1951, but the infant industry went through a lengthy boom-and-bust period following fluctuations in the world demand for oil. The problem is that shale oil is expensive to extract, and wells are profitable only when the price of oil is high. New technology and the rising world demand for oil since the late 1990s promise stability for North Dakota oil production.

In order to extract the oil a well must be dug two miles down to reach the layer of oil shale, which is only about ten to twenty feet thick. The technology involves a steerable drill bit, which at a depth of two miles can be turned horizontally. The bit then bores through the shale layer for another mile. The oil seeps slowly out of the shale into this lined hole and is pumped to the surface. Because oil prices are expected to remain high for the foreseeable future due to demand in countries such as China and India, oil companies have been flocking to North Dakota. In 2006 state officials estimated that they would approve permits for five hundred new wells in that year alone. Industry officials estimate that each oil rig directly and indirectly generates about 120 jobs. The oil industry in the state expected to need twelve thousand new workers by 2010. If the boom continues, it will certainly slow, if not reverse, the trend toward rural depopulation that has been going on since the 1930s.

Another new industry of some promise is bison ranching. Ecologists had been arguing for some years that overgrazing from cattle ranching on the semiarid high plains was destroying the ecosystem. For a time they recommended a return to a pre-settlement ecology by reintroducing bison and developing an economy based on buffalo hunting and eco-tourism. That fanciful dream acquired some substance with the farm crisis of the mid-1980s, when the price of beef, along with other farm staples, plummeted. Farmers in Wisconsin and Minnesota began experimenting with exotic animals, such as elk and llamas, in an effort to find a niche market for their product. An alternative for western grassland ranchers was bison. This realization coincided with growing numbers of the animals in state and national parks and game reserves. Park officials were running out of space for the increasing herds and looking for buyers. They have since developed an annual sale of surplus animals, the number depending on the health of the herd, which, in turn, is largely dependent on annual rainfall.

Bison ranching seems particularly well adapted to the Indian reservations. For cultural and historical reasons several of the reservations had kept small herds of bison for many years, but they began a concerted effort to increase tribal herds in the early 1990s. The Inter-Tribal Bison Cooperative was founded in 1992, and in its first six years it doubled the number of tribal buffalo programs and increased the number of animals on reservations from about 2,800 to around 8,000. The herds have continued to grow. At present, for example, the Cheyenne River Sioux Reservation in South Dakota possesses a herd of about 3,500 animals. For the Indians bison represent traditional culture and revered virtues, such as individual responsibility and generosity. Not surprisingly buffalo ranching has also been subject to the conflict between "traditionalists" and "progressives" on some reservations. "Traditionalists" want the buffalo to roam free on the reservation, with the herd culled occasionally through hunting, while "progressives" would prefer to place mature animals in feeding pens where they can be fattened with corn for a widened public market.

Growing public concern for proper diet in the last twenty years has provided a promising demand for buffalo meat. Trend-setting consumers and restaurants on both the East and West Coasts, preoccupied with lipid fats and high omega-3s, have found in grass-fed buffalo a meat they could love. As a result, American consumption of buffalo meat is at an all-time high, though it is still miniscule in volume compared with beef, pork, or chicken. In January 2011 Theo Weening, the global meat coordinator for the Whole Foods Market chain, stated, "For the last two years, [buffalo meat has] been one of the fastest-growing categories in our meat department." Although some buffalo ranchers fear a supply glut, the price of buffalo meat has continued to climb. In early 2011 the federal Department of Agriculture found that the price of an average buffalo steak had gone up 28 percent in the past year. At a meat market in Denver, for example, the price for a New York strip buffalo steak was $24.98 a pound, ten dollars more than that of premium beef for the same cut. All this bodes well for high plains ranchers, whether white or Indian.

From the standpoint of the end of the first decade of the twenty-first century, however, one wonders if there remains a need for diversity in the sense often expressed earlier—that is, attracting manufacturing and commercial enterprises. Both states are now nearly as diverse agriculturally as California. In the arid high plains, for example, which were once devoted almost exclusively to cattle ranching and wheat, the casual traveler today often encounters fields of sunflowers and soybeans. There is currently a worldwide food and fuel shortage, and the scarcity is likely to continue so long as world population and wealth continue to increase. Food prices have risen dramatically and with them the value of Dakota farmland. Agricultural prosperity will, in turn, benefit the Dakotas' towns and cities, as William Jennings Bryan predicted a century ago. Barring natural disasters, such as might be brought on by global climate change, the prospect for the Dakotas seems robust indeed.

NOTES

2. Lords of the Northern Plains

1. Linguists have found that the languages of American Indian tribes fall into groups that have ancient origins (much like the language groups of Europe—Romance, Germanic, Slavic, etc.). All of the tribes of the Northeastern Woodlands, for instance, fell within one of two groups, Algonquian or Iroquoian. Most tribes of the upper Mississippi Valley—Dakota, Winnebago, Iowa—spoke a Siouan language. Tribes of the central and southern plains—Pawnee, Kiowa, Comanche—were members of the Caddoan language group. The tribes inhabiting the Dakotas had origins in one of these three language groups.

2. The plains tribes generally placed their dead on scaffolds, where the bones were cleaned by birds. The Cheyennes took down the cleaned bones for burial, while the Dakotas and Crows apparently left them on the scaffolds.

3. Explorers and Fur Traders

1. Despite the trans-Pacific voyages of Ferdinand Magellan and Sir Francis Drake in the seventeenth century, the French persisted in the belief that the ocean was somehow divided between a "South Sea" (first viewed and named by Balboa when he crossed the Isthmus of Panama in 1513) and a "Western Sea" that somehow lay between North America and Asia. The search for a "River of the West" was, in some ways, a variant on the earlier hunt for a Northwest Passage.

2. The French livre was roughly equivalent to the Spanish dollar, the standard silver coin of both Spanish America and the English colonies. Also known as a "piece of eight," it was mint-marked for cutting into eighths or quarters ("two bits") in making change.

3. French fur traders were soon to make a distinction between *mangeurs de lard* (pork eaters), mere canoe paddlers who stopped at a halfway point (Mackinac Island or Grand Portage) and returned to Montreal the same summer, and *hivernants*, who lived year-round in the woods trading with the Indians, bringing their pelts to a rendezvous (such as Grand Portage) in midsummer. The *hivernants*, usually the more experienced woodsmen, viewed with condescension the "pork eaters," who had a varied diet while paddling and spent the winter in warm homes; the *hivernants* wintered in snow-blanketed huts and gnawed on pemmican, a mixture of dried venison and wild berries.

4. The bay enclosed by the peninsula is known today as Northwest Angle Inlet. When the American-Canadian boundary was drawn in 1842, the surveyors gave the United States (Minnesota) a share of the lake by drawing the line northwest from the mouth of the Rainy River to Vérendrye's peninsula and thence southwest to the 49th parallel, which is the boundary west to the Pacific.

5. A span was the distance from the tip of the thumb to the tip of the little finger when a person's hand is spread.

6. Vérendrye's tablet was uncovered in 1913 on the grounds of the city high school of Pierre, South Dakota.

4. Ventures under the American Flag

1. Clark was correct. Modern geologists call this sort of formation a *roche moutonée*, a knob of bedrock hard enough to resist the shaping force of the glacier. The round stones noted by Clark were deposited by the glacier, whose terminal moraine was along the river to the south.

2. Among the "blanket legends," sometimes credited by writers eager to blame whites for the Indians' troubles, is that the U.S. Army deliberately spread small pox among the Indians with infected blankets. Such a tale is patently false, with respect to this epidemic at least, as there was no military presence on the upper Missouri in the 1830s.

5. From "Desert" to Gold Mine

1. Since Pope a few weeks earlier had been humiliated by Lee and Stonewall Jackson at the Second Battle of Bull Run, wags speculated that giving him command of the "Great American Desert" was punishment enough.

2. For the genesis and implementation of the concept of Indian reservations, see chapter 7.

3. In jail awaiting his hanging, McCall told Hickok's brother, who had come west from Illinois for the trial, that he had been paid by Hickok's enemies to commit the murder. This seems unlikely since Hickok had not been involved in a gunfight for five years and had been in Deadwood for only three weeks when he was killed.

8. Political Prairie Fires

1. Many states used printed ballots, one for each political party, often designated by color. By selecting one of the ballots to be dropped in the box, the voter publicly revealed his affiliation, thus potentially subjecting himself to intimidation.

2. *The Spoilers* was made into a 1942 movie starring John Wayne and Randolph Scott.

9. Mount Rushmore

1. The United Daughters of the Confederacy revived the idea of a Stone Mountain sculpture in the 1960s and commissioned an enormous bas-relief of three Confederate leaders on horseback—Jefferson Davis, Robert E. Lee, and "Stonewall" Jackson. It was dedicated in 1970.

2. President Wilson and the American delegation at the Paris Peace Conference in 1919 had been largely instrumental in creating Poland and other national republics in Eastern Europe out of the old German and Austrian empires.

SELECTED READING

The Dakotas are well served by excellent histories: Elwyn B. Robinson, *History of North Dakota* (Lincoln: University of Nebraska Press, 1966; with a new preface and postscript, 1995), and Herbert S. Schell, *History of South Dakota* (Pierre: South Dakota State Historical Society Press, 1961, 2004). For the physical environment and its history one might consult James Richard Smith, *Geography of the Northern Plains and Other Essays* (Sioux Falls: Augustana College Press, 1990), and Sven G. Froiland, *Natural History of the Black Hills and Badlands* (Sioux Falls: Augustana College Press, 1990).

The prehistoric peoples of the northern plains have received a good deal of attention from recent scholars: Larry J. Zimmerman, *Peoples of Prehistoric South Dakota* (Lincoln: University of Nebraska Press, 1985); Stanley A. Ahler et al., *People of the Willows: Prehistory and Early History of the Hidatsa Indians* (Grand Forks: University of North Dakota Press, 1991); Karl H. Schlesier, *The Wolves of Heaven: Cheyenne Shamanism, Ceremonies, and Prehistoric Origins* (Norman: University of Oklahoma Press, 1987); and J. D. Speth, *Bison Kills and Bone Counts: Decision Making by Ancient Hunters* (Chicago: University of Chicago Press, 1983). There is also an extensive literature on the Indian tribes that the first white explorers encountered. Among the more interesting are John H. Moore, *The Cheyenne Nation* (Lincoln: University of Nebraska Press, 1987); Roy W. Meyer, *Village Indians of the Upper Missouri* (Lincoln: University of Nebraska Press, 1977); and George E. Hyde, *Red Cloud's Folk: A History of the Oglala Sioux Indians* (Norman: University of Oklahoma Press, 1937). On the much debated issue of when horses arrived on the Great Plains, see Frank Gilbert Roe, *The Indian and the Horse* (Norman: University of Oklahoma Press, 1955).

Nellis M. Crouse, *La Verendrye, Fur Trader and Explorer* (Ithaca NY: Cornell University Press, 1956), is a judicious biography of the first European to visit the northern plains. G. Hubert Smith, *The Explorations of the La Verendryes in the Northern Plains, 1738–43* (Lincoln: University of Nebraska Press, 1980), includes the journals kept by the La Vérendrye brothers in their travels and has valuable editorial insights. David Thompson, *Travels in Western North America, 1784–1812*, edited by Victor C. Hopwood (Toronto: Macmillan, 1971), contains excerpts from Thompson's voluminous journals with a biographical sketch of the intrepid adventure-seeker. The army's exploration of the northern plains, beginning with Lewis and Clark, is recounted by William H. Goetzmann, *Army Exploration in the American West, 1803–1863* (New Haven: Yale University Press, 1979). Also recommended is Edmund C. Bray and Martha Coleman Bray, trans. and eds., *Joseph Nicollet on the Plains and Prairies* (St. Paul: Minnesota Historical Society Press, 1976). David J. Wishart, *The Fur Trade of the American West, 1807–1840* (Lincoln: University of Nebraska Press, 1979), described by the author as "a geographical synthesis," is marred by numerous factual errors. Better sources on the subject are R. E. Oglesby, *Manuel Lisa and the Opening of the Missouri Fur Trade* (Norman: University of Oklahoma Press, 1963), and John E. Sunder, *The Fur Trade on the Upper Missouri* (Norman: University of Oklahoma Press, 1965). In *Homeland to Hinterland: The Changing Worlds of the Red River Metis in the Nineteenth Century* (Toronto: University of Toronto Press, 1996) Gerhard J. Ens examines the culture of the Red River Metis and their impact on the buffalo skin trade. On trade and travel generally, see William E. Lass, *A History of Steamboating on the Upper Missouri River* (Lincoln: University of Nebraska Press, 1962).

Oscar William Coursey, *Pioneering in Dakota* (Mitchell: Educator Supply, 1937), and Everett Dick, *The Sod-House Frontier, 1854–1890* (New York: D. Appleton-Century, 1937), treat the beginnings of white settlement on the northern plains. William C. Sherman, ed., *Plains Folk: North Dakota's Ethnic History* (Fargo: North Dakota Institute for Regional Studies, 1988), is a nice exploration of the immigrant population. Two finely detailed but rather dry studies of pre-statehood politics are Herbert S. Schell, *Dakota Territory during the Eighteen-Sixties* (Vermillion: Governmental Research Bureau, University of South Dakota,

1954), and Howard Roberts Lamar, *Dakota Territory, 1861–1889: A Study of Frontier Politics* (New Haven: Yale University Press, 1956).

Post–Civil War economic development is treated in Edward Everett Dale, *The Range Cattle Industry: Ranching on the Great Plains from 1865 to 1925* (Norman: University of Oklahoma Press, 1936, 1960); Hiram M. Drache, *The Day of the Bonanza: A History of Bonanza Farming in the Red River Valley of the North* (Fargo: North Dakota Institute for Regional Studies, 1964); Thomas D. Isern, *Bull Threshers and Bindlestiffs: Harvesting and Threshing on the North American Plains* (Lawrence: University Press of Kansas, 1990); Robert E. Riegel, *The Story of the Western Railroads* (New York: Macmillan, 1926); and Bill Yenne, *The Great Northern Empire Builder* (St. Paul: MBI, 2005). The wonderful story of the Black Hills gold rush of 1875–76 and its semimythical heroes is told by Watson Parker, *Deadwood: The Golden Years* (Lincoln: University of Nebraska Press, 1981); Joseph G. Rosa, *Wild Bill Hickok: The Man and His Myth* (Lawrence: University Press of Kansas, 1996); and James D. McLaird, *Calamity Jane: The Woman and the Legend* (Norman: University of Oklahoma Press, 2005).

Robert M. Utley, *The Indian Frontier, 1846–1890* (Albuquerque: University of New Mexico Press, 2003), focuses on the army's treatment of Indians in the late nineteenth century. Jeffrey Ostler, *The Plains Sioux and U.S. Colonialism from Lewis and Clark to Wounded Knee* (New York: Cambridge University Press, 2004), covers relations between the U.S. government and the Dakota nation over the course of the century. Especially poignant for the events leading to Wounded Knee is Robert M. Utley's *The Last Days of the Sioux Nation* (New Haven: Yale University Press, 1963, 2004). Paula M. Nelson, *After the West Was Won: Homesteaders and Town Builders in Western South Dakota, 1900–1917* (Iowa City: University of Iowa Press, 1986), explores the drama of attempting to farm the desolate country taken from the Indians. Also of value is Barbara Handy-Marchello, *Women of the Northern Plains: Gender and Settlement on the Homestead Frontier, 1870–1930* (St. Paul: Minnesota Historical Society Press, 2005).

North and South Dakota reacted quite differently to the Populist and Progressive reform movements at the turn of the twentieth century. For North Dakota the story is well told by Robert L. Morlan, *Political Prairie Fire: The Non-Partisan League, 1915–1922* (St. Paul: Minnesota Historical Society Press, 1985), and Edward C. Blackorby, *Prairie*

Rebel: The Public Life of William Lemke (Lincoln: University of Nebraska Press, 1963). South Dakota's experience with political reform is treated by R. Alton Lee, *Principle over Party: The Farmers' Alliance and Populism in South Dakota, 1880–1900* (Pierre: South Dakota State Historical Society Press, 2011), and Gilbert C. Fite, *Peter Norbeck: Prairie Statesman* (Columbia: University of Missouri Press, 1948). The opposition of Dakota congressmen to American entry into World War I is recounted in H. C. Peterson and Gilbert C. Fite, *Opponents of War, 1917–1918* (Madison: University of Wisconsin Press, 1957). Rex Alan Smith, *The Carving of Mount Rushmore* (New York: Abbeville Press, 1985), is a delightful account of the most important event of the 1920s. A highly recommended tour guide of South Dakota that focuses on the Black Hills is John E. Miller, *Looking for History on Highway 14* (Ames: Iowa State University Press, 1993).

A good account of the impact of the Depression is D. Jerome Tweton and Daniel F. Rylance, *The Years of Despair: North Dakota in the Depression* (Grand Forks ND: Oxcart Press, 1973). A more recent account, of undoubted value to North Dakota historians but the equivalent of a sleeping pill to the general reader, is David B. Danbom, *Going It Alone: Fargo Grapples with the Great Depression* (St. Paul: Minnesota Historical Society Press, 2005). Paula M. Nelson provides an excellent treatment of the Depression in South Dakota in *The Prairie Winnows Its Own: The West River Country of South Dakota in the Years of Depression and Dust* (Iowa City: University of Iowa Press, 1996).

Wayne S. Cole, *Senator Gerald P. Nye and American Foreign Relations* (Minneapolis: University of Minnesota Press, 1962), examines the isolationist feelings of the 1930s. Thomas W. Howard, ed., *The North Dakota Political Tradition* (Ames: Iowa State University Press, 1981), contains excellent essays on William Langer: "William Langer and the Art of Personal Politics," by Glenn H. Smith, and (on Langer's opposition) "Fred G. Aandahl and the ROC Movement," by Daniel F. Rylance. The best assessment of South Dakota politics in the second half of the twentieth century is Robert P. Watson, ed., *George McGovern: A Political Life, a Political Legacy* (Pierre: South Dakota State Historical Society Press, 2004). The best study of the 1973 siege of Pine Ridge is Akim D. Reinhardt, *Ruling Pine Ridge: Oglala Lakota Politics from the IRA to Wounded Knee* (Lubbock: Texas Tech University Press, 2007). The effort of the federal government in the late twentieth century to compensate the various Dakota tribes for their losses due to the construction of the Missouri River dams is treated in Michael L. Lawson, *Damned Indians Revisited: The Continuing History of the Pick-Sloan Plan and the Missouri River Sioux* (Pierre: South Dakota State Historical Society Press, 2009).

Richard E. Wood discusses the problem of rural depopulation on the plains in *Survival of Rural America: Small Victories and Bitter Harvests* (Lawrence: University Press of Kansas, 2008). Although the work focuses on rural Kansas, the problems that Wood describes would seem equally applicable to the Dakotas. Another book that treats the Midwest generally but applies well to the Dakotas is Dennis S. Nordin and Roy V. Scott, *From Prairie Farmer to Entrepreneur: The Transformation of Midwestern Agriculture* (Bloomington: Indiana University Press, 2005). On the subject of buffalo ranching, see Sebastian Felix Braun, *Buffalo, Inc.: American Indians and Economic Development* (Norman: University of Oklahoma Press, 2008).

INDEX

Hickok, James Butler, 122–28, 205
Hickok, "Wild Bill." *See* Hickok, James Butler
Hidatsa Indians: culture of, 17; economy of, 25; and fur trade, 82; houses of, 21–22; small pox among, 35, 97; warfare of, 24
Hill, George, 115
Hill, James J., 136–37, 145
Homestake Mine, 130–31
Homestead Act (1862), 107–8, 172
Hoover, Herbert, 210
Hopewell Culture, 12–13, 15
Hopkins, Harry, 225
horses, 31–33, 34–35
Hotchkiss guns, 169, 171
Hudson Bay, 37–38, 57
Hudson Bay Company, 89, 91, 100
Hunkpapa Sioux Indians, 158, 167
hydroelectric power, 233

immigrants: Black Sea German, 139; 190; Danish, 139; Finnish, 139; German, 135, 137; Norwegian, 138; Scandinavian, 135, 137–39, 190; Swedish, 138–39
Independent Voters Association, 200
Indian Gaming Regulatory Act, 247
Indian policy, evolution of, 158, 160–63
Indian Reorganization Act (1934), 242
Indian reservations, concept of, 155
Indian Rights Association, 158–59
intermarriage, 99
irrigation, 233–34
isolationism, 28

James River, 105
James River Valley, 16
Jayne, William, 109–10, 112, 115
Jefferson, Thomas, 64–65, 160, 207, 214–16
Jemeraye, Christophe de la, 42–44

keelboats, 66

King, Martin Luther, 245
Kiowa Indians, 18, 53
Kyle, James H., 180, 182

La Follette, Robert M., 186–89
Lake Agassiz, 4
Lake Oahe, 232
Lake of the Woods, 4, 39, 42, 56, 58
Lake Sakajawea, 232
Lake Sharp, 232
Lake Winnipeg, 4, 39–40, 57, 91
Lamarque, Charles Nolan, 45
Langer, William, 196, 201, 222–23, 236–38
Laramie WY, 128
Lead SD, 130–31
Leavenworth, Henry, 88–89
Lemke, William, 196, 200–201
Lend-Lease Act, 228
Lewis, Meriwether, 81. *See also* Lewis and Clark
Lewis and Clark, 65–75, 77, 78
Lewis and Clark Lake, 232
Lincoln, Abraham, 104, 107–9, 115, 205, 207, 216–17
Lisa, Manuel, 78–81, 83–84, 91
Little Crow (Mdewakanton), 113
"Little Ice Age," 15
Little Missouri River, 82, 119, 146
Livingston, Robert R., 64
longhorn cattle, 143–44
Loucks, Henry, 182
Louisiana, division of, 56
Louisiana Purchase, 63–65

Mackenzie, Alexander, 58, 185–86, 190–92
Mandan Indians: culture of, 17, 20–21, 46–47, 72–74; diet of, 23, 61; entertainment of, 61; and fur trade, 90, 93–94; horses of, 60–61; houses of, 21–22, 48, 59–61; and Lewis and Clark, 72–75; pottery of, 22–23; sexual attitudes of, 61–62; small pox among, 35; villages of, 21, 47–48, 51–52; warfare of, 49

Maximilian, Alexander Philip, 92, 94, 101
May, George, 128
McCall, Jack, 128–29
McCoy, Joseph G., 143–44
McGovern, George, 239–41
"McKenzie Ring," 186
McKinley, William, 191
McLaughlin, James, 167–68
Means, Russell, 243–44, 245
Mellette, Arthur C., 151
Mellon, Andrew, 210–11
Metis, 99–102, 107
Middle Border, 155
middle Missouri Valley culture, 13–14, 17
Miles, Nelson A., 166–67, 169, 171
Miniconjou Sioux Indians, 158, 168–72
Minneapolis, 178
Minnesota, statehood of, 104–5
Minnesota River, 4, 30
Missouri Fur Company, 81–82, 86
Missouri River, 49–50, 56, 66, 156, 229–33
Missouri Valley Authority, 230–31
Mitchell SD, 240
Monroe, James, 64
Monroe Doctrine, 226
Montana Territory, 118
Montreal canoes, 41
Moody, Gideon C., 150
Mormonism, 203
Moses, John, 238–39
"mountain men," 86–87
"Mountain of Spirits," 67
Mount Moriah, 128
Mount Rushmore, 204–8, 210–19
Moves Camp, Ellen, 245–46

National Park Service, 216
Nelson River, 57
Neutrality Act (1937), 227–28
New Deal, 222–26
Newman, John, 75

New Ulm MN, 113
Nichols, George Ward, 123
Nonpartisan Leader, 195
Nonpartisan League, 153, 191; decline and fall of, 198–200; founding of, 194; legislative achievements of, 197–98; lingering influence of, 236–37; and 1916 election, 195; recruitment tactics of, 194–95; in South Dakota, 199; and World War I, 198–99
Norbeck, Peter, 189, 199, 205–8, 210–11, 215
Norris, George, 191, 230, 233
North Dakota: admission of, to Union, 152; constitution of, 152–53, 177; and farm foreclosures, 223; oil boom in, 249–50; statehood movement in, 150–51
North Dakota State Agricultural College, 238
Northern Pacific Railroad, 116–17, 119, 133–36, 196
Northwest Angle Inlet, 254n4
Northwest Company, 57–59
Nuttall & Mann's Number 10 Saloon, 126
Nye, Gerald P., 201, 227–28, 238

Oglala Sioux Indians, 30, 35, 158, 244
Ojibwa Indians, 18, 30
Okipa ceremony, 20
Oneota Culture, 15, 17–18, 20, 23
Oregon Trail, 87, 89, 103

Paleo-Indians, 11–16
Panic of 1873, 119
Pawnee Indians, 18, 54–55
Peace of Paris (1763), 56
Peace of Utrecht (1713), 38
Peffer, William A., 181
Pembina, 62, 100–102, 107
pemmican, 102
Peoples' Party, 152–53, 177, 179, 180–84

Other Works by Norman K. Risjord

Shining Big Sea Water: The Story of Lake Superior (2008)
Wisconsin: The Story of the Badger State (2nd ed., 2007)
A Popular History of Minnesota (2005)